D1204538

Better Homes and Gardens®

CHRISTMAS COOKING FROM THE HEART™

Fresh and Simple

Meredith® Books
Des Moines, Iowa

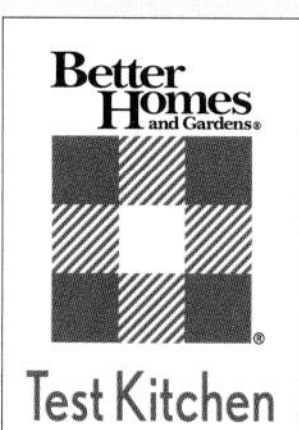

Our seal assures you that every recipe in *Christmas Cooking from the Heart*™ has been tested in the Better Homes and Gardens® Test Kitchen. This means that each recipe is practical and reliable, and meets our high standards of taste appeal. We guarantee your satisfaction with this book for as long as you own it.

All of us at Meredith® Books are dedicated to providing you with information and ideas to enhance your home. We welcome your comments and suggestions. Write to us at: Meredith Books Editorial Department, 1716 Locust St., Des Moines, IA 50309-3023. *Christmas Cooking from the Heart* is available by mail. To order editions from past years, call 800/627-5490.

Cover Photography:
Front cover: Marshmallow Pops (page 121), Triple Chocolate-Pistachio Layer Cake (page 94), Candy Cane Cookie Drops (page 120), Fabulous Five-Minute Fudge (page 118), Key Lime Spritz Cookies (page 105), and Lime Shortbread Trees (page 109)
Back cover: Key Lime Spritz Cookies (page 105)

Better Homes and Gardens®

CHRISTMAS COOKING FROM THE HEART™

Contributing Editor: Lois White
Contributing Designer: Angie Haupert Hoogensen
Editorial Assistant: Diane Mason
Book Production Manager: Mark Weaver
Contributing Copy Editor: Carol DeMasters
Contributing Proofreaders: Judy Friedman, Susan J. Kling, Staci Scheurenbrand
Contributing Photographers: Jason Donnelly, Scott Little, Blaine Moats
Contributing Prop Stylist: Lori Hellander
Contributing Recipe Development: Juliana Hale
Contributing Food Stylists: Nicole Faber-Peterson, Greg Luna, Dianna Nolin
Test Kitchen Director: Lynn Blanchard
Test Kitchen Product Supervisor: Jill Moberly
Test Kitchen Culinary Specialists: Marilyn Cornelius, Juliana Hale, Maryellyn Krantz, Colleen Weeden, Lori Wilson
Test Kitchen Nutrition Specialists: Elizabeth Burt, R.D., L.D.; Laura Marzen, R.D., L.D.

Meredith® Books
Executive Editor: Jennifer Darling
Managing Editor: Kathleen Armentrout
Brand Manager: Gina Rickert
Group Editor: Jan Miller
Design Director: Shawn Roorda
Copy Chief: Doug Kouma
Senior Copy Editors: Kevin Cox, Jennifer Speer Ramundt, Elizabeth Keest Sedrel
Assistant Copy Editor: Metta Cederdahl
Proofreader: Joleen Ross

Executive Director, Sales: Ken Zagor
Director, Operations: George A. Susral
Business Director: Janice Croat

Vice President and General Manager, SIP: Jeff Myers

***Better Homes and Gardens®* Magazine**
Editor in Chief: Gayle Goodson Butler
Deputy Editor, Food and Entertaining: Nancy Wall Hopkins

Meredith Publishing Group
President: Jack Griffin
President, Better Homes and Gardens®: Andy Sareyan
Vice President, Corporate Solutions: Michael Brownstein
Vice President, Manufacturing: Bruce Heston
Vice President, Consumer Marketing: David Ball
Director, Creative Services: Grover Kirkman
Consumer Product Marketing Director: Steve Swanson
Consumer Product Marketing Manager: Wendy Merical
Business Manager: Todd Voss

Meredith Corporation
Chairman of the Board: William T. Kerr
President and Chief Executive Officer: Stephen M. Lacy

In Memoriam: E.T. Meredith III (1933–2003)

ISSN: 1540-5478 ISBN: 978-0-696-24227-4

table of contents

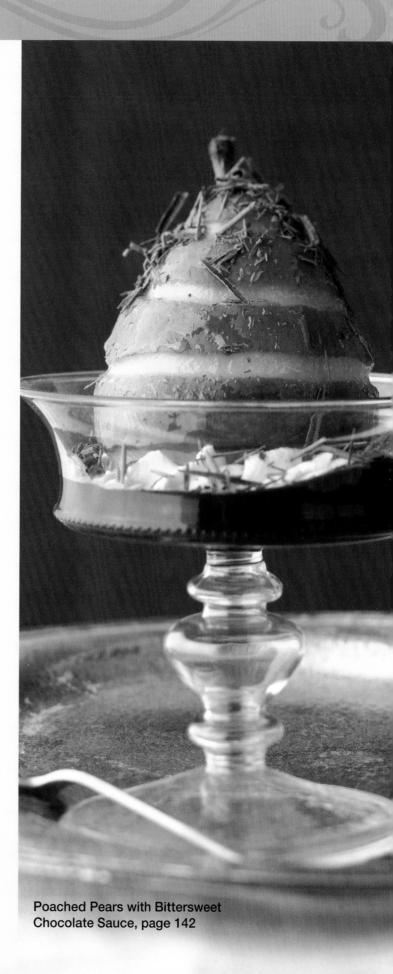

Poached Pears with Bittersweet Chocolate Sauce, page 142

season's eatings

There's so much to love about the holidays—the abundance of food that draws cooks back into the kitchen to prepare favorite dishes for hungry friends and family. Whether you are cooking as a host or taking food as a guest, take advantage of these great recipes, menus, and do-ahead hints to make this your best holiday ever. Every year the culinary experts in the Better Homes and Gardens® Test Kitchen challenge themselves to create new spins on tried-and-true classics. Let these recipes inspire a feast of the season's most flavorful appetizers, entrées, desserts, and edible gifts. Because food is such a memorable part of the holiday festivities from Thanksgiving to New Year's Day, you will find, in addition to the recipes, dozens of tips to help you plan, prepare, and organize for the busy days ahead. Take time to shop and cook in advance so you will be on your way to hosting a memorable celebration—and enjoying it, too. Happy holidays!

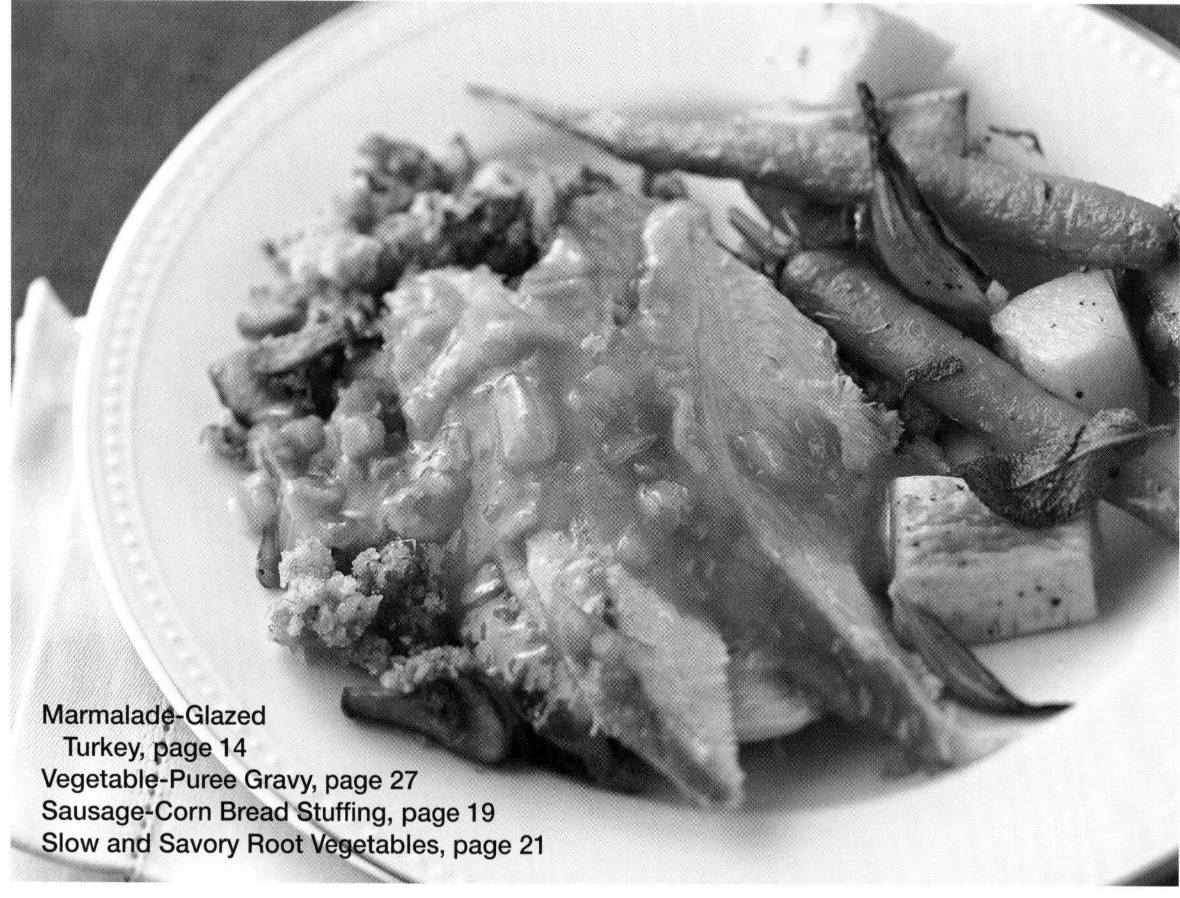

Marmalade-Glazed Turkey, page 14
Vegetable-Puree Gravy, page 27
Sausage-Corn Bread Stuffing, page 19
Slow and Savory Root Vegetables, page 21

Chocolate-Hazelnut
Tart, page 88

Spiced Cranberry
Tea, page 46

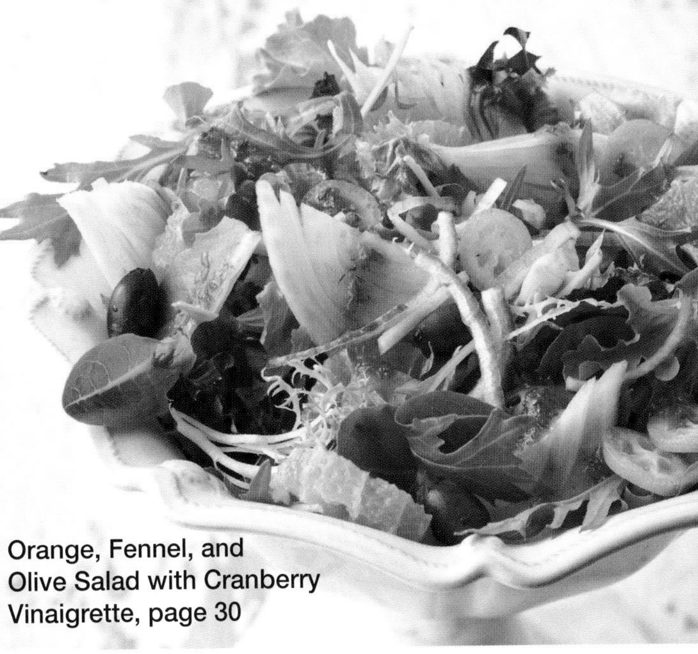

Orange, Fennel, and
Olive Salad with Cranberry
Vinaigrette, page 30

feasts of joy

From the grand bird that graces the holiday table to regal roasts and a cornucopia of sides, these tasty recipes and timesaving tips guarantee success, whether it's your first time hosting or your twentieth. If you're invited to a potluck gathering, take one of the make-ahead portable sides.

Marmalade-Glazed Turkey, page 14

Rib Roast with Dried Fruits

Rib Roast with Dried Fruits

This orange- and Dijon mustard-flavored rib roast—sometimes labeled as standing rib roast or beef prime rib—is served with a medley of oven-roasted fruits.

Prep: 40 minutes **Roast:** 1¾ hours
Oven: 325°F **Makes:** 12 servings

- **1 6-pound beef rib roast**
- **1 tablespoon anise seeds, lightly crushed**
- **3 tablespoons olive oil**
- **3 tablespoons Dijon-style mustard**
- **3 cloves garlic, minced**
- **3 cups dried figs, apricots and/or pears**
- **12 red boiling onions, peeled and halved**
- **2⅓ cups orange juice**
- **3 fresh pears, cored and cut into wedges**
- **1 tablespoon all-purpose flour**
- **Fresh rosemary sprigs**

1. Preheat oven to 325°F. Trim fat from roast. Combine anise seeds, olive oil, 2 tablespoons of the mustard, the garlic, ¾ teaspoon *salt,* and ¼ teaspoon *ground black pepper.* Spread 2 tablespoons of the mixture over roast; set remaining mustard mixture aside. Place roast on a rack in a shallow roasting pan.

2. Roast, uncovered, for 1¾ to 2¼ hours for medium-rare doneness (135°F) or 2¼ to 2¾ hours for medium doneness (150°F).

3. Meanwhile, in a large bowl combine dried fruit, onions, ⅓ cup of the orange juice, and reserved mustard mixture. Toss to coat. Fold a 36×18-inch piece of heavy duty foil in half to make an 18-inch square. Place fruit mixture in center of foil. Bring two sides of foil together and make a double fold. Double fold each end, leaving room for steam to build. Add foil packet to the oven rack beside roast for last 1 hour of roasting time. Place pear wedges in roasting pan beside roast the last 30 minutes of roasting; stir pears once halfway through roasting.

4. Place roast on serving platter. Spoon pears onto platter with roast. Cover; let stand for 15 minutes. Remove foil packet from oven; set aside. Drain all but 1 tablespoon fat from the roasting pan. Whisk flour into reserved fat in the roasting pan. Whisk together 2 remaining cups orange juice and remaining mustard. Add orange juice mixture to roasting pan. Place over two burners on stove. Heat over medium-high heat, scraping up any brown bits from bottom of pan. Whisk until thickened and bubbly. Whisk for 1 to 2 minutes or until desired consistency. Strain, if desired. Serve with beef and fruit mixture. Garnish with fresh rosemary.

Per serving: 397 cal., 15 g total fat (5 g sat. fat), 75 mg chol., 312 mg sodium, 38 g carbo., 5 g fiber, 28 g pro.

Pork with Cherry and Wild Rice Stuffing

Prep: 1 hour **Roast:** 1¾ hours **Stand:** 15 minutes
Oven: 325°F **Makes:** 8 to 10 servings

- **⅓ cup wild rice**
- **2 teaspoons snipped fresh rosemary or ½ teaspoon dried rosemary, crushed**
- **¾ cup coarsely chopped dried cherries**
- **1 3-pound boneless pork top loin roast (single loin)**
- **6 ounces bulk pork sausage**
- **½ cup chopped onion**
- **1 tablespoon snipped fresh parsley**
- **1 teaspoon snipped fresh thyme or ¼ teaspoon dried thyme, crushed**
- **Snipped fresh thyme**
- **2 tablespoons all-purpose flour**

1. Rinse wild rice well; drain. In a saucepan combine wild rice, 1¼ cups *water,* rosemary, and ½ teaspoon *salt.* Bring to boiling; reduce heat. Cover and simmer for 40 to 45 minutes or until rice is tender. Remove from heat. Stir in dried cherries. Set aside.

2. Trim fat from pork. Butterfly the meat by making a lengthwise cut down the center of the meat, cutting to within ½ inch of the other side. Spread open. Place knife in the V of the first cut. Cut horizontally to the cut surface and away from the first cut to within ½ inch of the other side of the meat. Repeat on opposite side of the V. Spread these sections open. Cover the roast with plastic wrap. Working from center (thicker part) to edges, pound with flat side of a meat mallet until meat is ½ to ¾ inch thick. Make sure the meat is a uniform thickness. Remove plastic wrap. Set meat aside.

3. For filling, in a large skillet cook sausage and onion until sausage is browned and onion is tender. Drain fat. Stir in the parsley, 1 teaspoon thyme, and ¼ teaspoon *ground black pepper.* If necessary, drain the cooked rice mixture to remove liquid. Stir cooked rice mixture into sausage mixture.

4. Preheat oven to 325°F. Spread the filling over the surface of the butterflied roast. Roll loin into a spiral from a short side. Tie meat with 100%-cotton heavy kitchen string. (Wrap several strands of string crosswise around the meat and tie securely.) Place on a rack in a shallow roasting pan. Sprinkle with snipped fresh thyme, *salt,* and *ground black pepper.* Insert an ovenproof meat thermometer in center of roast. Roast, uncovered, for 1¾ to 2¼ hours or until thermometer registers 155°F, covering ends of meat after 45 minutes to keep rice moist. Transfer meat to serving platter. Cover loosely with foil; let stand 15 minutes before carving. (The temperature of the roast after standing should be 160°F.)

5. For gravy, add 1 cup *water* to roasting pan; scrape up browned bits. In saucepan whisk together ⅓ cup *cold water* and the flour. Whisk in pan juices. Cook and stir over medium heat until thickened and bubbly. Cook and stir 1 minute. Season to taste with *salt* and *black pepper.*

6. Remove string from pork roast; discard. Slice roast; serve with pan gravy.

Advance Preparation: Prepare the wild rice and sausage mixture and butterfly the roast the day before. Cover and chill separately up to 24 hours. Stuff the pork and roast as directed.

Per serving: 364 cal., 13 g total fat (4 g sat. fat), 122 mg chol., 406 mg sodium, 17 g carbo., 1 g fiber, 43 g pro.

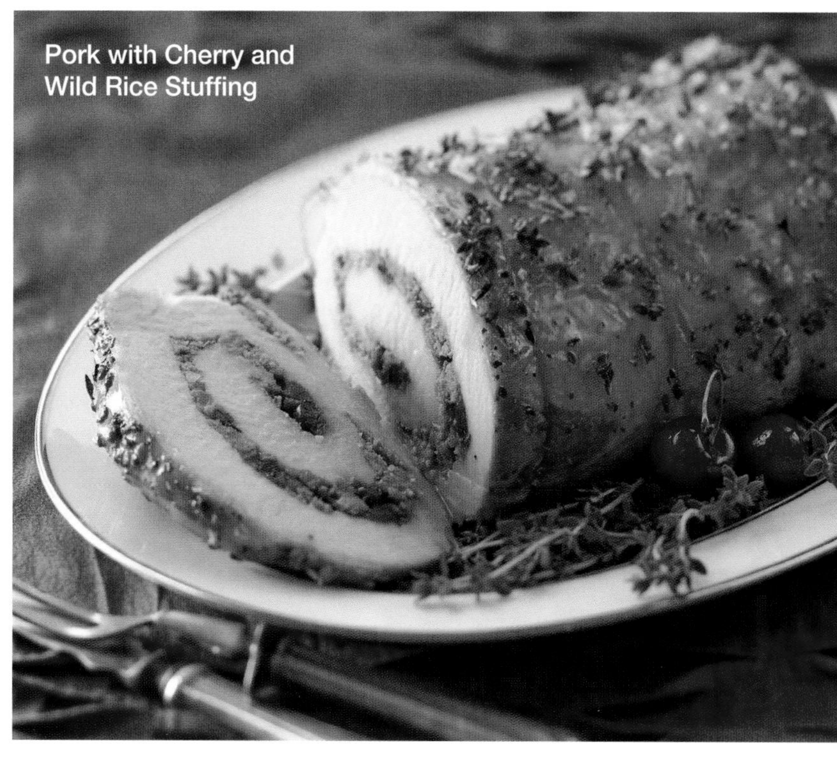
Pork with Cherry and Wild Rice Stuffing

Fennel and Lime-Crusted Beef Tenderloin

Make this ahead and chill for several hours before serving. Fennel is a bulb vegetable with a licorice taste and a texture like celery.

Prep: 30 minutes **Roast:** 45 minutes
Stand: 10 minutes **Chill:** 4½ to 24 hours
Oven: 425°F **Makes:** 12 servings

- **½ cup lime-infused olive oil**
- **¼ cup fennel seeds**
- **¼ cup snipped fresh tarragon**
- **¼ cup finely shredded lime peel (5 or 6 limes)**
- **1 3-pound center-cut beef tenderloin**
- **1 pound peeled onions (such as cipollini, pearl, and/or cut-up yellow onions)**
- **3 cups sliced fennel**
- **½ cup dry red wine**
- **1 pound fresh green beans, trimmed**

Fennel and Lime-Crusted Beef Tenderloin

1. Combine 6 tablespoons of the oil, fennel seeds, tarragon, lime peel, 2 teaspoons *ground black pepper,* and ½ teaspoon *salt.* Coat tenderloin with the seed mixture. Place meat on a nonreactive tray; cover loosely with foil. Chill for at least 30 minutes or up to 1 hour.

2. Preheat oven to 425°F. Place meat on a roasting rack in an ungreased 3-quart rectangular baking pan. Return any coating left on tray to meat. Insert an ovenproof meat thermometer into the thickest portion of meat. In a medium bowl toss together onions and 1 tablespoon of the remaining oil. Place onions on half of the pan or dish alongside meat. Roast, uncovered, for 30 minutes.

3. Meanwhile, toss together fennel and remaining oil. Stir onions and add fennel to other half of pan or dish alongside meat. Roast, uncovered, for 15 to 20 minutes or until thermometer registers 135°F for medium-rare doneness.

4. Transfer meat to a cutting board; cover with foil. Let stand for 10 to 15 minutes. The temperature of the meat after standing should be 145°F for medium-rare doneness. Wrap meat in plastic wrap and chill until ready to serve. Transfer onions and fennel to separate bowls. Cover and chill until ready to serve.

5. For sauce, pour pan drippings into a small saucepan, scraping and adding the crusty browned bits. Add red wine; cook until bubbly, stirring constantly to dissolve browned bits. Transfer sauce to bowl. Cover; refrigerate until serving.

6. To serve, cook green beans in a small amount of boiling salted water about 5 minutes or until crisp-tender. Drain. Rinse with cold water until chilled; drain again. Toss green beans with the sauce. Arrange on serving platter. Thinly slice tenderloin and arrange on top of beans. Serve with roasted onions and fennel.

Advance Preparation: Prepare and roast meat, onions, and fennel as directed. Prepare sauce and cook green beans as directed. Cover and chill separately for 4½ to 24 hours. Serve as directed.

Per serving: 288 cal., 17 g total fat (4 g sat. fat), 57 mg chol., 165 mg sodium, 7 g carbo., 8 g fiber, 25 g pro.

Orange-Glazed Ham

Orange-Glazed Ham

Cook a large ham to provide plenty of meat for your holiday meal, plus extra for later.

Prep: 15 minutes **Roast:** 1½ hours
Oven: 325°F **Makes:** 16 to 20 servings

- **1 5- to 6-pound cooked ham (rump half or shank portion)**
- **24 whole cloves (optional)**
- **1 recipe Orange Glaze or Chutney Glaze**
- **Fresh bay leaves, cranberries, orange slices and/or fresh rosemary sprigs**

1. Preheat oven to 325°F. Score ham by making diagonal cuts in a diamond pattern. If desired, stud ham with cloves. Place ham on a rack in a shallow roasting pan. Insert an ovenproof meat thermometer in center of ham so thermometer does not touch bone. Bake, uncovered, for 1½ to 2¼ hours or until thermometer registers 140°F. Brush ham with some of the desired glaze during the last 20 minutes of baking. Serve with remaining glaze. Garnish with bay leaves, cranberries, orange slices, and/or fresh rosemary sprigs.

Orange Glaze: In a medium saucepan combine 2 teaspoons finely shredded orange peel, 1 cup orange juice, ½ cup packed brown sugar, 4 teaspoons cornstarch, and 1½ teaspoons dry mustard. Cook and stir over medium heat until thickened and bubbly. Cook and stir for 2 minutes. Makes 1¼ cups glaze.

Chutney Glaze: In a food processor bowl or blender container, combine one 9-ounce jar mango chutney, ¼ cup maple syrup, and 2 teaspoons stone-ground mustard. Cover and process or blend until smooth. Makes about 1¼ cups glaze.

Advance Preparation: Prepare desired glaze; cover and chill up to 1 week. Reheat glaze before brushing on ham.

Per serving with orange or chutney glaze: 166 cal., 5 g total fat (2 g sat. fat), 47 mg chol., 1,078 mg sodium, 10 g carbo., 0 g fiber, 19 g pro.

Fruit-Stuffed Pork Tenderloins with Mustard-Cranberry Sauce

Fruit-Stuffed Pork Tenderloins with Mustard-Cranberry Sauce

Cranberries, apricots, and rice create a moist, flavorful stuffing for pork tenderloin. A cream-based mustard and cranberry sauce makes this dish exceptionally delicious.

Prep: 45 minutes **Roast:** 50 minutes
Stand: 5 minutes **Oven:** 375°F **Makes:** 8 servings

- **2 stalks celery, sliced**
- **1 medium onion, finely chopped**
- **1 clove garlic, minced**
- **¼ cup butter**
- **2 cups cooked brown rice**
- **¼ cup dried cranberries**
- **¼ cup snipped dried apricots**
- **1 teaspoon finely shredded orange peel**
- **½ teaspoon dried thyme, crushed**
- **½ teaspoon salt**
- **⅛ teaspoon ground black pepper**
- **¼ cup apple juice (optional)**
- **2 1-pound pork tenderloins**
- **Salt**
- **Ground black pepper**
- **1 recipe Mustard-Cranberry Sauce**

1. Preheat oven to 375°F. In a medium saucepan cook celery, onion, and garlic in hot butter over medium heat until tender, about 4 minutes. Remove from heat. Stir in rice, cranberries, apricots, orange peel, thyme, ½ teaspoon salt, and ⅛ teaspoon pepper. Stir in apple juice to moisten, if needed. Set stuffing aside.

2. Trim any fat from pork. Use a sharp knife to make a lengthwise cut down the center of each pork tenderloin, cutting to, but not through, the other side of the meat. Repeat by making two cuts on either side of the first cut. Place each tenderloin between two pieces of plastic wrap. Pound lightly with the flat side of a meat mallet to make a 12×8-inch rectangle, working from the center out to the corners. Season pork with salt and pepper.

3. Spoon half of the stuffing over one of the tenderloins to within 1 inch of the edges. Roll tenderloin into a spiral, beginning with a short side. Tie meat with 100%-cotton heavy kitchen string. Place seam side down on a rack in a shallow roasting pan. Repeat with remaining tenderloin and remaining stuffing, placing second tenderloin next to the first on the rack.

4. Roast, uncovered, for 50 to 60 minutes or until an instant-read thermometer inserted in the stuffing registers 165°F. Loosely cover with aluminum foil and let stand for 5 minutes.

5. Meanwhile, prepare Mustard-Cranberry Sauce. Cut tenderloins into slices. Serve with sauce.

Mustard-Cranberry Sauce: In a small saucepan cook 1 clove garlic, minced, in 2 tablespoons hot butter over medium heat for 1 minute. Stir in 2 tablespoons all-purpose flour and 1 tablespoon Dijon-style mustard until combined. Stir in 1¼ cups chicken broth. Cook and stir until thickened and bubbly. Cook and stir 1 minute. Stir in ¼ cup half-and-half or light cream and ¼ cup dried cranberries; heat through. Makes 1⅔ cups.

Advance Preparation: Prepare tenderloins through Step 3. Cover and chill up to 8 hours. Let stand at room temperature 15 minutes before roasting as directed in Step 4.

Per serving: 317 cal., 13 g total fat (7 g sat. fat), 98 mg chol., 550 mg sodium, 24 g carbo., 2 g fiber, 26 g pro.

Herbed Turkey Breast with Wild Mushroom Gravy

Dried cherries and sage tucked under the skin of a turkey breast give each serving a hint of sweetness and a fabulous herb flavor.

Prep: 20 minutes **Roast:** 1½ hours
Stand: 15 minutes **Oven:** 325°F
Makes: 6 to 8 servings

½ cup dried cherries
2 tablespoons olive oil
1½ teaspoons snipped fresh sage
1 4½- to 5-pound whole turkey breast (bone-in)
1 lemon, quartered
1 medium onion, quartered
½ cup dried porcini, oyster, shiitake, and/or chanterelle mushrooms
1 cup boiling water
¼ cup all-purpose flour
Chicken broth
2 tablespoons dry sherry
Salt
Freshly ground black pepper

1. Preheat oven to 325°F. In a blender or food processor, combine dried cherries, 1 tablespoon of the olive oil, and sage. Cover and blend or process just until cherries are finely chopped.

2. Slip your fingers between the skin and meat of the turkey breast to loosen the turkey skin. Lift the skin and, using a spatula, carefully spread the cherry mixture directly over the turkey breast meat. Place the turkey breast on a rack in a shallow roasting pan. Place the lemon and onion quarters underneath the turkey breast. Insert an ovenproof meat thermometer into the thickest part of the turkey breast, making sure bulb does not touch bone. Brush with remaining 1 tablespoon oil.

3. Roast, uncovered, for 1½ to 2¼ hours or until thermometer registers 170°F, covering with foil for the last 45 minutes of roasting to prevent overbrowning. Let stand, covered, for 15 minutes before carving.

4. Meanwhile, place dried mushrooms in a small bowl. Pour the boiling water over mushrooms to cover. Let stand for 10 minutes. Drain mushrooms, reserving liquid. Strain mushroom-soaking liquid through a fine-mesh sieve lined with 100%-cotton cheesecloth, paper towels, or a coffee filter; reserve strained liquid. Rinse and drain mushrooms again.

5. Pour pan drippings from turkey into a large measuring cup. Skim and reserve fat from drippings. Pour ¼ cup of the fat (if necessary, add butter) into a medium saucepan. Stir in flour. Add enough of the strained mushroom liquid and chicken broth to remaining drippings in the measuring cup to equal 2 cups liquid. Add broth mixture all at once to flour mixture. Cook and stir over medium heat until thickened and bubbly. Stir in soaked mushrooms and dry sherry. Cook and stir for 1 minute. Season to taste with salt and freshly ground pepper.

Per serving: 293 cal., 13 g total fat (3 g sat. fat), 99 mg chol., 198 mg sodium, 7 g carbo., 0 g fiber, 35 g pro.

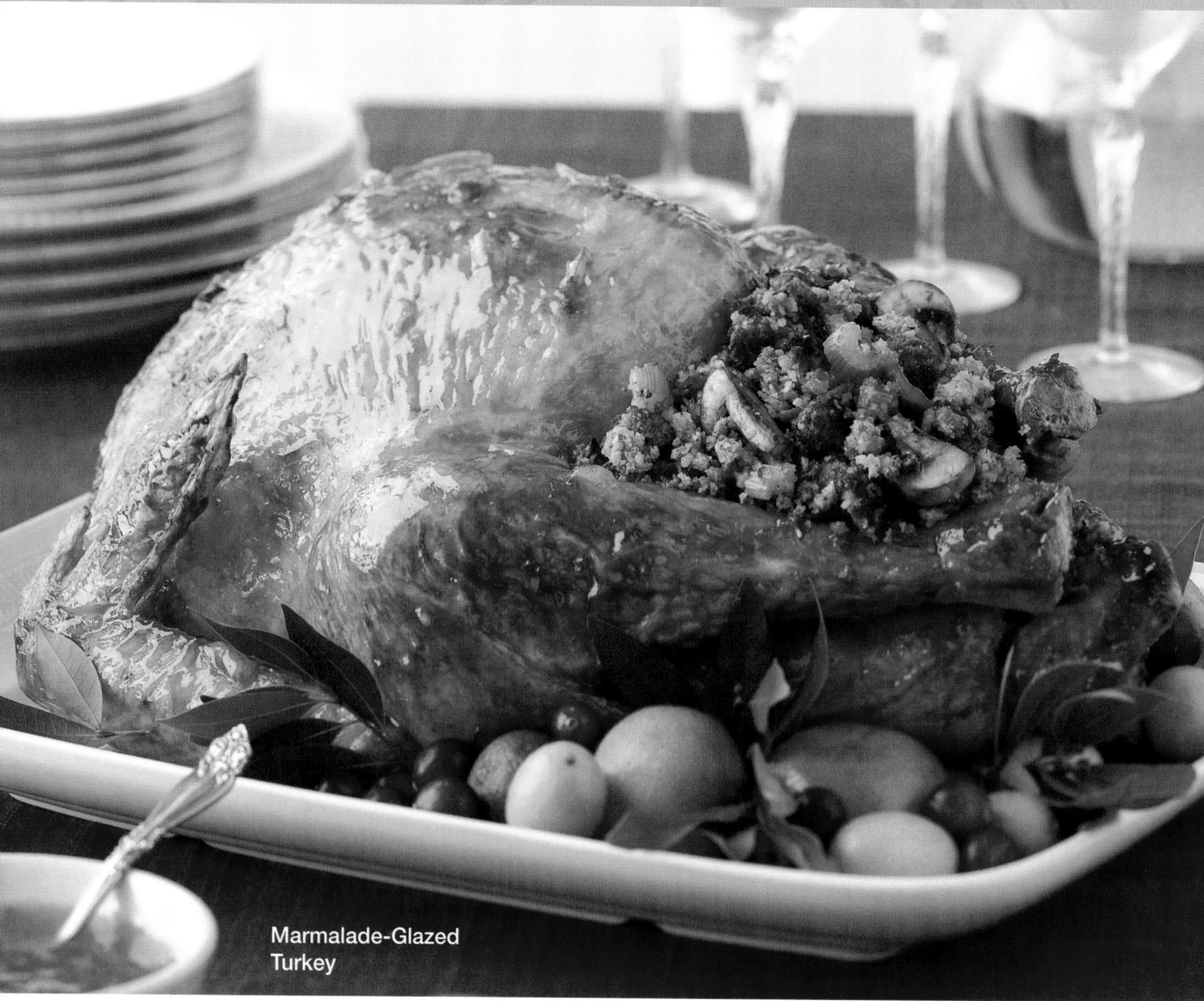
Marmalade-Glazed Turkey

Marmalade-Glazed Turkey

Guests are sure to devour the tasty sausage and cornbread stuffing that bakes with the bird. If space is tight in the oven for the casserole, bake the stuffing when the turkey comes out. Increase the temperature to 375°F and allow 30 to 40 minutes to heat through.

Prep: 1¼ hours **Roast:** 4¼ hours
Stand: 20 minutes **Oven:** 325°F **Makes:** 16 servings

- **1 16-pound frozen turkey**
- **1 recipe Sausage-Corn Bread Stuffing, recipe on page 19**
- **Fresh bay leaves, fresh cranberries, key limes, kumquats, clementines and/or tangerines (optional)**
- **1 cup orange marmalade**
- **¼ cup honey**
- **1 tablespoon lemon juice**
- **1 tablespoon Dijon-style mustard**

1. Thaw turkey in refrigerator, allowing 24 hours for every 5 pounds.

2. Prepare Sausage-Corn Bread Stuffing; set aside.

3. Preheat oven to 325°F. Remove neck and giblets from turkey. Rinse turkey inside and out; drain and pat dry with paper towels. Spoon some of the stuffing into the neck cavity. Pull the neck skin over stuffing; fasten to back with a skewer. Loosely spoon stuffing into body cavity (no more than ¾ cup per pound of turkey). (Place any remaining stuffing in a 3-quart casserole; cover and chill. Bake stuffing alongside turkey for 45 minutes or until heated through.) Tuck drumstick ends under the band of skin across the tail or tie the drumsticks securely to the tail. Twist wing tips under back, if desired.

4. Place turkey, breast side up, on a rack in a shallow roasting pan. Insert an ovenproof meat thermometer into the center of an inside thigh muscle without the thermometer touching bone. Cover turkey loosely with foil.

5. Roast turkey for 3¾ hours. Cut string or band of skin between drumsticks so thighs will cook evenly. Uncover; roast 30 to 45 minutes or until thermometer registers 180°F to 185°F and stuffing registers at least 165°F.

6. Remove the turkey from the oven. Cover and let stand for 20 minutes before carving. Transfer to serving platter. If desired, place bay leaves, fresh cranberries, key limes, kumquats, clementines and tangerines around turkey to garnish.

7. For marmalade glaze, in a small saucepan combine marmalade, honey, lemon juice, and mustard. Cook and stir until heated through. Spoon one-third of the mixture over the turkey and pass remaining sauce.

Advance Preparation: Prepare marmalade glaze as directed. Cover and chill up to 24 hours. Reheat before serving.

Per serving: 860 cal., 32 g total fat (11 g sat. fat), 339 mg chol., 1,262 mg sodium, 51 g carbo., 3 g fiber, 87 g pro.

Fresh Oyster Stew

A touch of tarragon updates this classic holiday stew.

Start to Finish: 35 minutes **Makes:** 6 main-dish servings or 10 appetizer servings

- **4 cups shucked oysters (2 pints)**
- **⅔ cup sliced leeks (2 medium)**
- **2 tablespoons butter**
- **2 tablespoons all-purpose flour**
- **½ teaspoon salt**
- **¼ teaspoon dried tarragon, crushed**
- **2½ cups half-and-half, light cream, or whole milk**
- **Sliced leeks (optional)**

1. Drain oysters, reserving liquid. Strain liquid. Add enough water to strained liquid to measure 2 cups. Set aside. Rinse the oysters thoroughly to remove any sand or shell.

2. In a large saucepan cook the ⅔ cup leeks in hot butter over medium heat about 4 minutes until tender, stirring occasionally. Stir in flour, salt, and tarragon. Slowly stir in half-and-half. Cook and stir until slightly thickened and bubbly. Cook and stir for 1 minute. Keep warm.

3. In a medium saucepan combine reserved oyster liquid and oysters. Bring just to simmering over medium heat; reduce heat. Cook, covered, for 1 to 2 minutes or until oysters curl around the edges. Skim and discard fat from surface of cooking liquid. Stir oyster mixture into cream mixture. Heat through. If desired, garnish with additional sliced leeks. Serve immediately.

Per serving: 170 cal., 12 g total fat (7 g sat. fat), 77 mg chol., 358 mg sodium, 8 g carbo., 0 g fiber, 8 g pro.

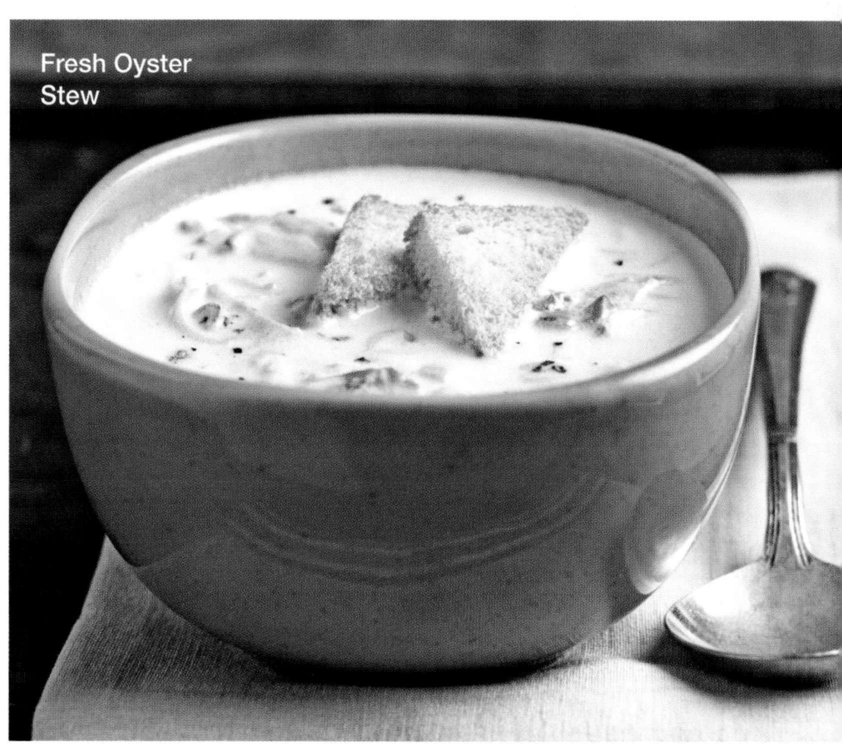
Fresh Oyster Stew

Curry Pumpkin Soup

Just the right amount of curry powder and pumpkin pie spice complements canned pumpkin puree for an easy, flavorful soup.

Prep: 20 minutes **Cook:** 30 minutes
Makes: 8 appetizer servings

- **1 recipe Orange-Cranberry Topper**
- **2 tablespoons butter**
- **1 cup chopped onion (2 medium)**
- **½ cup chopped carrot (1 medium)**
- **½ cup chopped celery (1 stalk)**
- **1 teaspoon curry powder**
- **1 teaspoon pumpkin pie spice**
- **2 15-ounce cans pumpkin puree**
- **2 14-ounce cans reduced-sodium chicken broth**
- **1 cup half-and-half or light cream**

1. Prepare Orange-Cranberry Topper.

2. In a 4-quart kettle melt butter over medium heat. Add onions, carrot, and celery. Cook, 10 minutes, stirring occasionally, until soft. Add curry powder and pumpkin pie spice. Cook and stir 1 minute. Add pumpkin, broth, and ⅔ cup *water.* Increase heat to medium-high; bring to boiling. Reduce heat to medium-low. Simmer, covered, 15 minutes. Remove from heat; cool slightly.

Curry Pumpkin Soup

3. In food processor or blender add one-third of the pumpkin mixture at a time, cover, and process or blend until smooth. Return all mixture to kettle.

4. Stir half-and-half, ½ teaspoon *salt,* and ¼ teaspoon *ground black pepper* into pumpkin mixture and heat through. Sprinkle each serving with Orange-Cranberry Topper.

Orange-Cranberry Topper: In a small bowl combine ½ cup dried cranberries, 1 tablespoon finely shredded orange peel, and 2 tablespoons snipped fresh Italian (flat-leaf) parsley.

Advance Preparation: Prepare recipe as directed through Step 3. Cover and chill up to 3 days or freeze up to 3 months. To serve, thaw, reheat, and proceed with Step 4.

Per serving (1 cup): 145 cal., 7 g total fat (4 g sat. fat), 19 mg chol., 433 mg sodium, 20 g carbo., 4 g fiber, 4 g pro.

Wild Rice Mushroom Bisque

Dry sherry brings out the rich mushroom flavor in this soup that makes an impressive first course for an elegant dinner party.

Prep: 25 minutes **Cook:** 55 minutes **Cool:** 5 minutes
Makes: 12 appetizer or side-dish servings

- **1 cup wild rice**
- **1 pound shiitake or cremini mushrooms**
- **3 medium leeks, sliced (1 cup)**
- **1 tablespoon butter**
- **2 tablespoons dry sherry (optional)**
- **1 32-ounce box chicken broth**
- **2 large russet potatoes, peeled and chopped (12 ounces)**
- **1 cup half-and-half or light cream**
- **1 medium carrot, shredded**
- **1 teaspoon snipped fresh thyme or ¼ teaspoon dried thyme crushed**

1. Rinse wild rice well. In a small saucepan combine wild rice and 2 cups *water.* Bring to boiling. Reduce heat and simmer, covered, 40 minutes or until most of the water is absorbed. Drain, if necessary.

2. Meanwhile, remove stems from shiitake mushrooms. Slice mushrooms. In a 4-quart kettle cook mushrooms and leeks in hot butter until tender. If desired, remove kettle from heat. Carefully add sherry. Return to heat and cook and stir, uncovered, until all of the sherry evaporates. Remove half of the mushroom mixture from the kettle; set aside.

3. Add chicken broth and potatoes to kettle. Bring to boiling. Reduce heat and simmer, covered, for 10 minutes or until potatoes are tender. Remove from heat; cool slightly.

4. Place one-third of the soup mixture in a food processor or blender. Cover and process or blend until almost smooth. Repeat with remaining soup mixture. Return all the soup mixture to the kettle. Stir in wild rice, reserved mushrooms, half-and-half, carrot, thyme, and ¼ teaspoon each *salt* and *ground black pepper*. Return to boiling, reduce heat and simmer, uncovered, 5 minutes or until heated through and carrot is tender.

Advance Preparation: Prepare bisque as directed. Cover and chill up to 24 hours. Reheat, thinning to desired consistency with additional chicken broth.

Per serving: 145 cal., 4 g total fat (2 g sat. fat), 11 mg chol., 379 mg sodium, 25 g carbo., 3 g fiber, 4 g pro.

Apricot-Pecan Stuffing

Take advantage of the low, moist heat of a slow cooker to make a flavor-rich stuffing. Transfer the stuffing to an attractive dish for serving.

Prep: 25 minutes **Cook:** Low 3½ to 4 hours
Oven: 300°F **Makes:** 12 servings

- **12 cups dry whole wheat or white bread cubes (18 to 20 bread slices)**
- **1 cup trimmed, sliced leek (3 medium)**
- **1 cup chopped onion (1 large)**
- **6 tablespoons butter**
- **2 medium apples, peeled if desired, cored, and chopped (2 cups)**
- **1 cup chopped pecans**
- **¾ cup snipped dried apricots**
- **1 teaspoon dried thyme, crushed**

Apricot-Pecan Stuffing

- **½ teaspoon ground nutmeg**
- **1 14-ounce can chicken broth**
- **Nonstick cooking spray**

1. Preheat oven to 300°F. Spread bread cubes in a 15½×10½×2-inch baking pan. Bake, uncovered, for 10 to 15 minutes or until cubes are dry, stirring twice; cool. (Cubes will continue to dry and crisp.)

2. In a large skillet cook leek and onion in hot butter over medium heat for 5 minutes or until tender, stirring frequently. Stir in apples, pecans, apricots, thyme, nutmeg, ½ teaspoon *salt,* and ⅛ teaspoon *ground black pepper.* Cook for 3 minutes, stirring occasionally.

3. In a very large bowl combine apple mixture and bread cubes. Drizzle broth over bread mixture to moisten, tossing gently. Lightly coat a 5- to 6-quart slow cooker with cooking spray. Transfer bread mixture to prepared cooker.

4. Cover and cook on low-heat setting (do not use high-heat setting) for 3½ to 4 hours. Transfer to a serving dish.

Advance Preparation: Prepare toasted bread cubes as directed in Step 1. Store in an airtight container up to 2 days.

Per serving: 348 cal., 17 g total fat (5 g sat. fat), 16 mg chol., 512 mg sodium, 47 g carbo., 6 g fiber, 7 g pro.

Apple, Bacon, and Onion Stuffing Muffins

Apple, Bacon, and Onion Stuffing Muffins

Bake this savory stuffing in convenient individual servings using a standard muffin pan.

Prep: 45 minutes **Bake:** 20 minutes
Cool: 10 minutes **Oven:** 375°F **Makes:** 12 servings

- **9 cups bread cubes (12 slices bread)**
- **Nonstick cooking spray**
- **9 slices bacon**
- **2 tablespoons butter**
- **1½ cups coarsely chopped red onions**
- **3 stalks celery, chopped**
- **1 teaspoon dried sage, crushed**
- **1 teaspoon dried thyme, crushed**
- **2 large Granny Smith apples, peeled (if desired), cored, and coarsely chopped (about 3 cups)**
- **1 tablespoon minced garlic (6 cloves)**
- **¼ teaspoon ground black pepper**
- **1 cup chicken broth**
- **Small fresh sage leaves (optional)**

1. Preheat oven to 300°F. Spread bread cubes in a 15½×10½×2-inch baking pan. Bake, uncovered, for 10 to 15 minutes or until cubes dry, stirring twice; cool. (Cubes will continue to dry and crisp as they cool.) Or let bread cubes stand, loosely covered, at room temperature for 8 to 12 hours.

2. Preheat oven to 375°F. Lightly coat twelve 2½-inch muffin cups with cooking spray; set aside.

3. In an extra large skillet, cook bacon over medium heat until crisp. Drain on paper towels; crumble bacon. Drain fat, reserving 2 tablespoons drippings in skillet.

4. Add butter to skillet. Add onions, celery, sage, and thyme; cook over medium heat for 7 to 10 minutes or until vegetables are tender, stirring occasionally. Add apples and garlic; cook and stir for 2 to 4 minutes or until apple softens. Transfer to an extra large bowl.

5. Add bread cubes, crumbled bacon, and pepper to vegetable mixture; toss gently to combine. Add broth and toss until moistened.

6. Spoon about ⅔ cup stuffing into each prepared muffin cup; press to pack tightly. If desired, top each cup with a fresh sage leaf. Bake, uncovered, for 20 to 25 minutes or until stuffing is hot and tops are light brown. Cool about 10 minutes. Carefully remove from pans; serve warm.

Advance Preparation: Prepare stuffing as directed. Remove stuffing servings from muffin cups and transfer to large covered container; cover and chill up to 24 hours. To reheat, transfer stuffing servings to a 3-quart rectangular baking pan; cover with foil. Bake in a 400°F oven for 15 to 20 minutes or until heated through.

Per serving: 138 cal., 5 g total fat (2 g sat. fat), 12 mg chol., 411 mg sodium, 18 g carbo., 2 g fiber, 5 g pro.

Sausage-Corn Bread Stuffing

Spoon stuffing loosely into the Marmalade-Glazed Turkey recipe on page 14. The stuffing needs room to expand in order to reach a safe temperature of 165°F by the time the bird is done.

Prep: 45 minutes **Bake:** 40 minutes
Oven: 325°F **Makes:** 16 cups (16 to 18 servings)

- **1 pound bulk Italian, pork, or turkey sausage**
- **3 cups chopped mushrooms (8 ounces)**
- **1½ cups chopped celery**
- **1 cup chopped onion**
- **4 ounces finely chopped prosciutto (optional)**
- **½ cup butter or margarine**
- **⅓ cup snipped fresh Italian (flat-leaf) parsley or curly parsley**
- **1 teaspoon snipped fresh thyme or ¼ teaspoon dried thyme, crushed**
- **1 teaspoon snipped fresh rosemary or ¼ teaspoon dried rosemary, crushed**
- **1 teaspoon pepper**
- **2 eggs, lightly beaten**
- **6 cups cornbread stuffing mix**
- **6 cups herb-seasoned bread stuffing mix**
- **1½ cups chicken broth**

1. In a large skillet cook sausage until brown. Drain fat. Set sausage aside. In the same skillet cook mushrooms, celery, onion, and prosciutto, if desired, in hot butter until tender but not brown. Stir in parsley, thyme, rosemary, and pepper; set mixture aside.

2. In an extra-large mixing bowl combine eggs and vegetable mixture. Add cornbread stuffing mix and herb-seasoned bread stuffing mix; toss until all ingredients are well-coated. Add the cooked sausage. Add broth and enough *water* to moisten as desired, tossing lightly to mix.

3. Use stuffing to stuff Marmalade-Glazed Turkey on page 14. Place remaining stuffing in a casserole. Bake, covered, in a 325°F oven for 40 to 45 minutes or until heated through.

Per serving: 337 cal., 18 g total fat (7 g sat. fat), 63 mg chol., 1,032 mg sodium, 33 g carbo., 3 g fiber, 11 g pro.

Rosemary Roasted Vegetables

Green beans and Brussels sprouts are a delectable veggie combo when roasted with aromatic rosemary and smoky bacon.

Prep: 30 minutes **Roast:** 20 minutes
Oven: 425°F **Makes:** 12 servings

- **1 pound fresh Brussels sprouts**
- **12 ounces fresh whole green beans**
- **1 bunch green onions, trimmed and chopped**
- **12 fresh rosemary sprigs**
- **8 slices pancetta or bacon, partially cooked, drained, and chopped**
- **2 tablespoons olive oil**
- **Salt**
- **Freshly ground black pepper**
- **1 lemon, halved**

1. Preheat oven to 425°F. Wash Brussels sprouts and green beans; drain. Halve any large Brussels sprouts. In a covered large saucepan, cook Brussels sprouts in a small amount of lightly salted boiling water for 3 minutes; add green beans and cook for 5 minutes. Drain.

2. Transfer Brussels sprouts and green beans to an ungreased 3-quart rectangular baking pan. Add green onions and rosemary sprigs; toss to combine. Top with pancetta. Drizzle vegetable mixture with oil. Sprinkle with salt and pepper.

3. Roast, uncovered, about 20 minutes or until vegetables are crisp-tender and pancetta is crisp. Transfer to a serving platter. Squeeze juice from lemon over vegetables.

Advance Preparation: Cook green beans and Brussels sprouts in boiling water as directed. Cover and chill up to 24 hours. Continue as directed.

Per serving: 143 cal., 10 g total fat (4 g sat. fat), 10 mg chol., 275 mg sodium, 6 g carbo., 3 g fiber, 4 g pro.

Caramelized Acorn Squash

This recipe for brown sugar-glazed squash can be easily doubled for a large gathering. Be sure to use two baking dishes.

Prep: 20 minutes **Bake:** 50 minutes
Cool: 20 minutes **Oven:** 350°F **Makes:** 6 servings

- **2 1- to 1½-pound acorn squash**
- **¼ cup butter**
- **¼ cup packed brown sugar**
- **¼ cup apple cider**
- **½ teaspoon ground cinnamon**
- **¼ teaspoon salt**
- **¼ teaspoon freshly ground nutmeg**

1. Preheat oven to 350°F. Line a shallow baking pan with parchment paper or aluminum foil. Cut each squash in half; discard and remove seeds and fibrous material. Place halves, cut side down, in the prepared baking pan. Bake, uncovered, for 40 to 45 minutes, or until the squash is tender. Let stand until cool enough to handle; cut into 1-inch slices.

2. Arrange squash slices in a 2-quart rectangular baking dish, overlapping as necessary.

3. In a large skillet heat butter, brown sugar, cider, cinnamon, salt, and nutmeg to boiling, stirring to dissolve sugar. Reduce heat and boil gently, uncovered, for 5 minutes or until syrupy. Drizzle glaze over squash. Bake, uncovered, about 10 minutes or until heated through. Spoon glaze over squash before serving.

Advance Preparation: Prepare squash as directed through Step 2. Cover and chill overnight. Let the squash come to room temperature, then proceed as directed.

Per serving: 154 cal., 8 g total fat (5 g sat. fat), 20 mg chol., 160 mg sodium, 22 g carbo., 2 g fiber, 1 g pro.

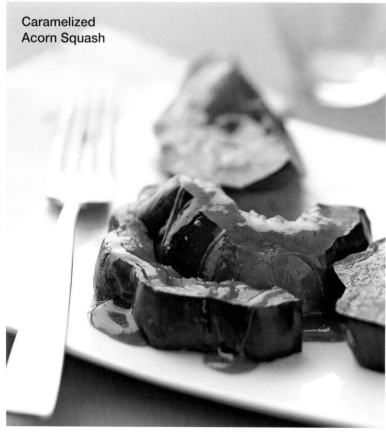

Caramelized Acorn Squash

Mashed Potatoes with Caramelized Onions

The super juicy varieties of onions, such as Vidalia, Walla Walla, or Maui, will add an extra hint of sweetness to the potatoes.

Start to Finish: 40 minutes **Makes:** 12 servings

- **3 pounds russet (baking) potatoes, peeled and quartered**
- **2 tablespoons olive oil**
- **2 large onions, peeled and cut into thin wedges (about 2 cups)**
- **¼ cup butter or margarine, softened**
- **2 tablespoons snipped fresh sage or 1 teaspoon dried sage, crushed**
- **½ to ¾ cup half-and-half, light cream, or milk**
- **1 ounce aged white cheddar cheese, shaved into thin shards with a vegetable peeler**

1. In a large saucepan cook potatoes and ½ teaspoon *salt,* covered, in enough boiling water to cover for 20 to 25 minutes or until tender; drain.

2. Meanwhile, in a large skillet heat oil. Stir in the onion wedges. Cook, uncovered, over medium heat for about 20 minutes or until onions are tender, stirring frequently. (If necessary, reduce heat to medium-low to prevent too much browning before onions are tender.) Increase heat to medium-high and cook about 5 minutes or until onions are golden brown, stirring frequently.

3. Use a potato masher to mash drained potatoes. Add butter, sage, ½ teaspoon *salt,* and ¼ teaspoon *freshly ground black pepper.* Gradually mash in enough half-and-half to make mixture light and fluffy.

4. Mound potatoes in a serving dish. Top with onions and cheese shards; serve immediately.

Advance Preparation: Prepare mashed potatoes as directed and keep warm up to 2 hours in a slow cooker on low-heat setting.

Per serving: 187 cal., 10 g total fat (5 g sat. fat), 21 mg chol., 309 mg sodium, 20 g carbo., 3 g fiber, 4 g pro.

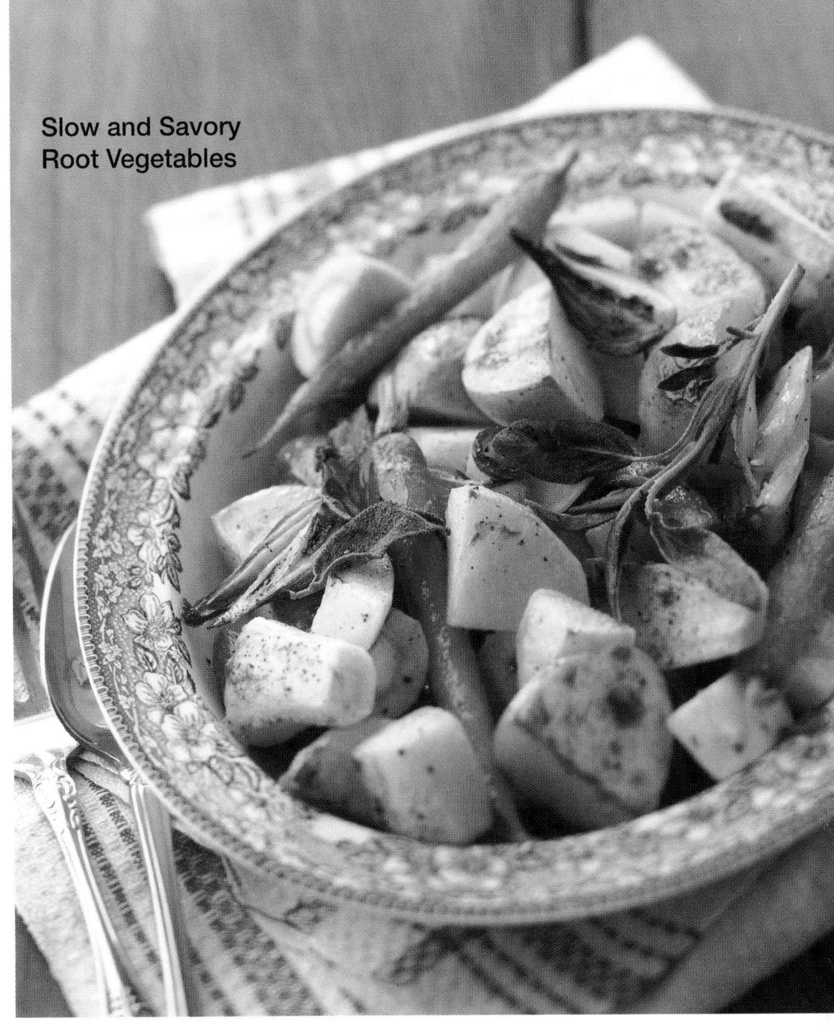
Slow and Savory Root Vegetables

Slow and Savory Root Vegetables

A hint of honey brings out the natural sweetness of these roasted vegetables.

Prep: 25 minutes **Roast:** 35 minutes
Oven: 425°F **Makes:** 4 servings

- **2 medium parsnips, peeled, halved lengthwise, and cut into 1-inch pieces**
- **2 medium turnips, peeled and cut into 1-inch pieces, or 1 medium rutabaga, peeled and cut into 1-inch pieces**
- **2 small Yukon gold potatoes, peeled and cut into quarters, or 1 medium sweet potato, peeled and cut into 1-inch pieces**
- **4 baby carrots with tops, trimmed**
- **1 small red onion, cut into 1-inch wedges**
- **4 fresh sage sprigs**
- **4 fresh sage leaves, slivered**
- **2 tablespoons olive oil**
- **¾ teaspoon salt**
- **¼ teaspoon freshly ground black pepper**
- **2 tablespoons honey**
- **Fresh sage (optional)**

1. Grease a 3-quart rectangular baking pan. Preheat oven to 425°F. In prepared pan combine parsnips, turnips, potatoes, carrots, onion, sage sprigs and the slivered sage. In a small bowl combine oil, salt, and pepper; drizzle over vegetables in pan. Toss lightly to coat.

2. Roast, uncovered, for 30 to 35 minutes or until vegetables are lightly browned and tender, stirring occasionally. Drizzle honey over vegetables. Stir gently to coat. Roast for 5 minutes. To serve, garnish with sage.

Per serving: 209 cal., 7 g total fat (1 g sat. fat), 0 mg chol., 506 mg sodium, 36 g carbo., 5 g fiber, 3 g pro.

Maple-Glazed Sweet Potatoes and Apples

Maple-Glazed Sweet Potatoes and Apples

Syrup, cider, and butter make an easy glaze for a dish that complements roast turkey or ham.

Prep: 25 minutes **Bake:** 75 minutes **Oven:** 350°F
Makes: 10 servings

- **⅓ cup butter**
- **¼ cup maple or maple-flavor syrup**
- **¼ cup apple cider or juice**
- **3 pounds sweet potatoes, peeled and cut into 1½- to 2-inch chunks (8 cups)**
- **1¾ pounds tart red and/or green apples (such as Macintosh, Granny Smith, or Rome Beauty), cored and cut into eighths (4½ cups)**
- **1 cup pecan halves, toasted**

1. Preheat oven to 350°F. In a medium saucepan combine butter, syrup, and cider; heat to boiling, stirring occasionally. Boil gently, uncovered, for 1 minute. Remove from heat; set aside. Place potatoes in a 3-quart rectangular baking dish. Pour butter mixture over potatoes; stir to coat. Cover and bake for 45 minutes.

2. Uncover dish; add apples and stir to coat evenly. Bake, uncovered, about 30 minutes or until sweet potatoes are tender, stirring once halfway through baking. Sprinkle with pecans before serving.

Per serving: 278 cal., 14 g total fat (5 g sat. fat), 16 mg chol., 99 mg sodium, 38 g carbo., 6 g fiber, 3 g pro.

Baked Butternut Squash

A spiced molasses and brown sugar sauce is a delicious and simple way to jazz up the milder-flavored winter squashes such as butternut and acorn.

Prep: 20 minutes **Bake:** 55 minutes **Oven:** 350°F
Makes: 6 side-dish servings

- **3 small butternut squash (about 1 pound each)**
- **1 tablespoon olive oil**
- **½ teaspoon salt**
- **¼ cup packed brown sugar**
- **2 tablespoons butter, melted**
- **2 tablespoons molasses**
- **1 teaspoon finely shredded orange peel**
- **½ teaspoon ground cinnamon**
- **¼ teaspoon ground cloves**

1. Preheat oven to 350°F. Halve squash lengthwise and remove and discard seeds and pulp. Brush inside of squash halves with oil and sprinkle with salt. Place squash halves, cut side down, in a large roasting pan. Bake, covered, for 40 minutes.

2. In a small bowl combine brown sugar, butter, molasses, shredded orange peel, cinnamon, and cloves. Turn squash halves cut side up. Spoon spice mixture into squash halves. Return to oven.

3. Bake, uncovered, 15 to 20 minutes or until squash is tender.

Per serving: 211 cal., 6 g total fat (3 g sat. fat), 10 mg chol., 235 mg sodium, 41 g carbo., 5 g fiber, 2 g pro.

Butternut Squash Risotto with Sage

Repeatedly adding liquid slowly to arborio rice and cooking and stirring until the liquid absorbs is a traditional Italian technique that produces a creamy rice consistency.

Start to Finish: 50 minutes **Makes:** 8 servings

- **¾ cup finely chopped onion**
- **2 tablespoons olive oil**
- **2 cups uncooked arborio rice**
- **¾ cup dry white wine or dry vermouth**
- **1 pound butternut squash, seeded, peeled, and chopped**
- **5 to 6 cups chicken broth**
- **⅓ cup grated Parmesan cheese**
- **1 tablespoon snipped fresh sage**
- **¼ teaspoon salt**
- **⅛ teaspoon ground black pepper**
- **3 tablespoons butter (optional)**
- **¼ cup small fresh sage leaves (optional)**

1. In a large saucepan cook onion in hot oil over medium heat until tender. Add rice; cook and stir for 1 to 2 minutes or just until rice starts to brown. Carefully add wine. Cook and stir until wine is absorbed. Stir in squash.

2. Meanwhile, in a medium saucepan bring 6 cups broth to boiling; reduce heat and simmer. Slowly add 1 cup of the broth to rice mixture, stirring constantly. Continue to cook and stir over medium heat until liquid is absorbed. Add enough of the remaining broth, ½ cup at a time, cooking and stirring just until rice is tender. (This should take about 25 minutes total). Stir in cheese, the snipped sage, salt, and pepper.

3. Transfer risotto to a serving bowl. If desired, in a small skillet melt butter over medium heat and add the small sage leaves; cook until crisp, stirring occasionally. Spoon sage mixture over risotto.

Per serving: 213 cal., 5 g total fat (1 g sat. fat), 5 mg chol., 786 mg sodium, 35 g carbo., 1 g fiber, 5 g pro.

Mashed Yukon Gold Potatoes with Chives

Prep: 35 minutes **Cook:** 20 minutes
Makes: 8 to 10 servings

- **5 pounds Yukon gold potatoes**
- **1¼ cups half-and-half, light cream, or milk**
- **¼ cup butter**
- **¼ cup snipped fresh chives**

1. Peel and quarter potatoes. In a large kettle cook potatoes in enough lightly salted boiling water to cover about 20 minutes or until tender. Meanwhile, in a small saucepan combine half-and-half and butter; heat just until butter melts. Cover and keep warm.

2. Drain potatoes, reserving ⅓ cup cooking water. Return potatoes to kettle; mash potatoes, gradually adding half-and-half mixture until smooth. If necessary, add reserved potato water until potatoes are desired consistency. Season to taste with *salt* and *pepper*. Just before serving, stir in chives.

Advance Preparation: Prepare mashed potatoes as directed and keep warm up to 2 hours in a slow cooker on low-heat setting.

Per serving: 325 cal., 10 g total fat (6 g sat. fat), 29 mg chol., 67 mg sodium, 54 g carbo., 5 g fiber, 6 g pro.

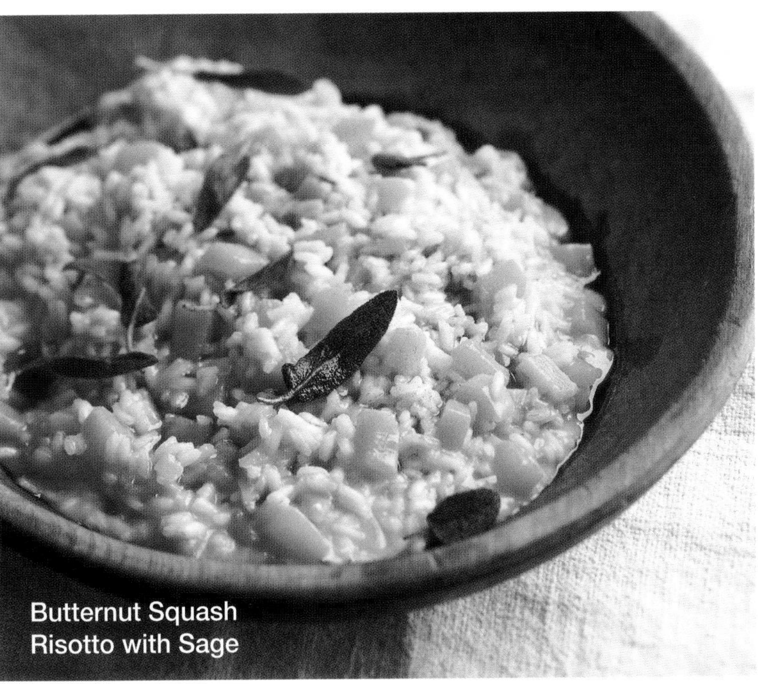

Butternut Squash Risotto with Sage

Green Beans with Almonds

Prep: 35 minutes **Cook:** 8 minutes **Makes:** 8 servings

1½ pounds haricot verts or thin green beans, trimmed
¾ cup whole almonds, coarsely chopped
3 tablespoons olive oil
2 cloves garlic, minced
½ cups coarsely chopped parsley
1 tablespoon finely shredded lemon peel
Finely shredded lemon peel (optional)

1. In a kettle cook beans in boiling, lightly salted water for 8 minutes or just until tender. Drain and return to pan.

2. Meanwhile, in a large skillet cook almonds in hot oil over medium heat for 3 minutes, stirring frequently. Add garlic; cook for 1 minute. Add almond mixture, parsley, and 1 tablespoon lemon peel to beans. Toss to coat. Transfer mixture to a serving bowl. Season to taste with *salt* and *ground black pepper.* If desired, top beans with additional lemon peel.

Green Beans with Almonds

Advance Preparation: Cook green beans one day ahead. Drain beans and plunge into a bowl of ice water; drain and pat dry. Chill beans in resealable plastic bag. To serve, let beans stand at room temperature for 30 minutes. Place beans in a 2-quart casserole. Microwave, covered, on 100% power (high) for 3 to 4 minutes, stirring once. Continue with Step 2.

Per serving: 124 cal., 9 g total fat (1 g sat. fat), 0 mg chol., 80 mg sodium, 9 g carbo., 4 g fiber, 4 g pro.

Potatoes au Gratin with Mustard and Cheddar

Round out a traditional holiday menu of roasted ham, beef, or lamb with creamy crumb-topped potatoes served directly from the baking dish.

Prep: 30 minutes **Bake:** 35 minutes **Cook:** 10 minutes **Stand:** 10 minutes **Oven:** 350°F **Makes:** 10 servings

3 pounds baking potatoes, thinly sliced (9 cups)
8 ounces white cheddar cheese, shredded (2 cups)
¼ cup all-purpose flour
1¼ cups chicken broth
1 cup whipping cream
3 tablespoons Dijon-style mustard
¾ teaspoon salt
¾ teaspoon ground black pepper
¾ teaspoon dried thyme, crushed
1 cup soft bread crumbs
1 tablespoon butter or margarine, melted

1. Preheat oven to 350°F. In a 4-quart kettle cook potato slices in enough boiling water to cover for 10 minutes or just until tender. Drain; set aside.

2. Meanwhile, in a bowl toss together cheese and flour; set aside. In another bowl whisk together broth, whipping cream, mustard, salt, pepper, and thyme; set aside. In a small bowl combine bread crumbs and butter; set aside.

3. In a 3-quart rectangular baking dish layer half of the potatoes and half of the cheese mixture; repeat layers. Pour broth mixture over potatoes. Sprinkle with bread crumb mixture.

4. Bake, uncovered, for 35 minutes or until potatoes are tender and sauce is bubbly. Let stand for 10 to 15 minutes before serving.

Per serving: 316 cal., 18 g total fat (11 g sat. fat), 60 mg chol., 590 mg sodium, 29 g carbo., 3 g fiber, 10 g pro.

Glazed Carrots with Pistachios

Toasted pistachios bring out an enticing nutty flavor that complements the carrots.

Start to Finish: 30 minutes **Oven:** 350°F
Makes: 12 servings

- **3 pounds small carrots with tops**
- **½ cup pistachio nuts**
- **½ cup butter**
- **⅓ cup packed brown sugar**
- **1½ teaspoons snipped fresh thyme**

1. Preheat oven to 350°F. Trim carrots; leave about ½ inch of the tops. In a 12-inch skillet, combine 3 cups *water* and ¼ teaspoon *salt*. Bring to boiling. Add carrots. Return to boiling; reduce heat. Cover and simmer for 10 to 12 minutes or until carrots are tender. Drain carrots in a colander; set aside.

2. Meanwhile, place pistachios in a single layer in a shallow baking pan. Bake for 8 to 10 minutes or until lightly toasted, stirring once. Set aside.

3. In the same skillet melt butter over medium heat. Add brown sugar and thyme, stirring until brown sugar melts. Add drained carrots. Bring just to boiling; reduce heat. Cook, uncovered, over medium-low heat about 10 minutes or just until carrots are well glazed, stirring occasionally.

4. Transfer carrots to a serving bowl or platter. Sprinkle with toasted pistachios.

Advance Preparation: Cook carrots as directed; cool. Cover and chill up to 24 hours. Toast the pistachios. Place in a resealable plastic bag; store at room temperature. Continue with Step 3 to glaze carrots. Serve as directed.

Per serving: 163 cal., 10 g total fat (5 g sat. fat), 20 mg chol., 196 mg sodium, 17 g carbo., 3 g fiber, 2 g pro.

Glazed Carrots with Pistachios

Lemon-Pepper Baby Broccoli

Find preserved lemon in large supermarkets or specialty food stores in the condiment section, or substitute a mixture of 2 teaspoons finely shredded lemon peel, 1 teaspoon olive oil, and ½ teaspoon coarse salt.

Start to Finish: 30 minutes **Makes:** 8 servings

- **1 cup reduced-sodium chicken broth**
- **2 slices preserved lemon**
- **1 tablespoon snipped fresh dillweed**
- **⅛ teaspoon crushed red pepper**
- **⅛ teaspoon ground black pepper**
- **1 pound baby broccoli or broccoli rabe**
- **2 tablespoons butter**
- **Fresh lemon halves or slices (optional)**

1. In a large skillet combine chicken broth, preserved lemon, dillweed, crushed red pepper, and black pepper. Bring to boiling; reduce heat. Cover and simmer for 15 minutes.

2. Add broccoli and butter to skillet. Cover and cook over medium heat for 6 to 8 minutes or until broccoli is tender. If desired, drain. Transfer broccoli mixture to a serving bowl. If desired, garnish with fresh lemon halves.

Per serving: 47 cal., 3 g total fat (2 g sat. fat), 8 mg chol., 489 mg sodium, 4 g carbo., 2 g fiber, 2 g pro.

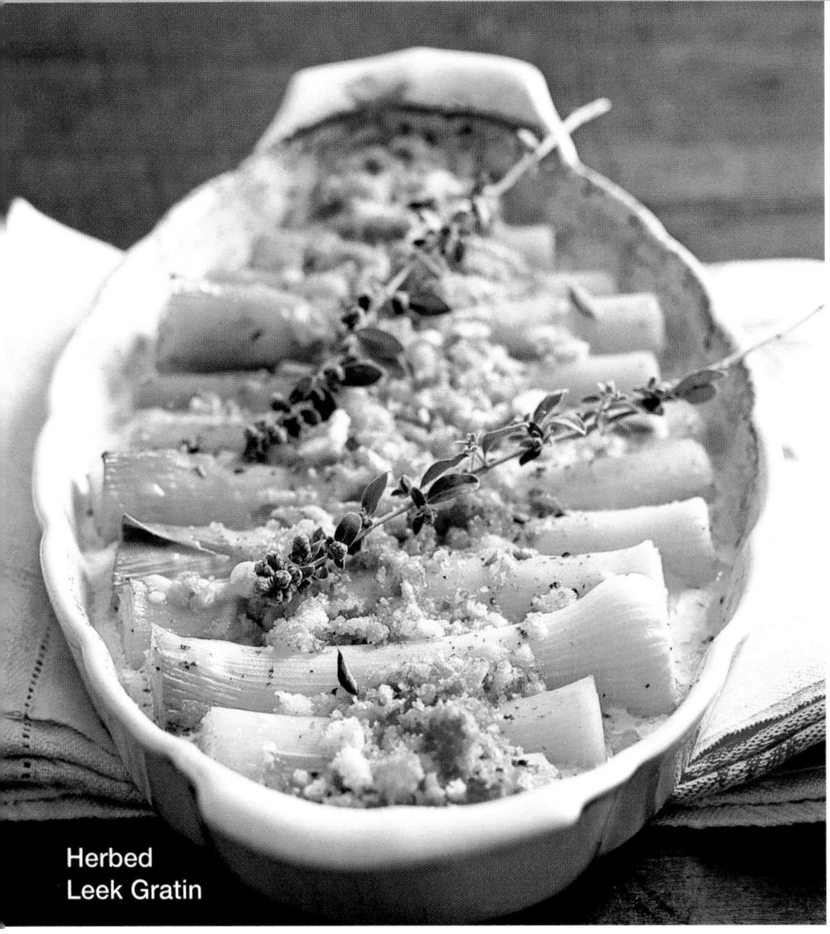
Herbed Leek Gratin

Herbed Leek Gratin

Leeks are the gentle giant cousins of green onions. Line an au gratin dish with leeks; then add a creamy marjoram sauce and cheese-crumb topping.

Prep: 20 minutes **Bake:** 35 minutes **Oven:** 375°F
Makes: 6 servings

- **3 pounds slender leeks**
- **½ cup whipping cream**
- **½ cup chicken broth**
- **2 tablespoons snipped fresh marjoram or 1½ teaspoons dried marjoram, crushed**
- **½ teaspoon salt**
- **½ teaspoon freshly ground black pepper**
- **1½ cups soft French or Italian bread crumbs**
- **3 tablespoons grated Parmesan cheese**
- **3 tablespoons butter, melted**
- **Fresh marjoram sprigs (optional)**

1. Preheat oven to 375°F. Trim roots off leeks, leaving pieces 4 to 5 inches long with white and pale green parts. Cut leeks in half lengthwise. Rinse leeks thoroughly under cold running water; pat dry with paper towels. Arrange leeks, cut side down, in a greased 2-quart au gratin dish or rectangular baking dish, overlapping leeks as necessary to fit. (Face leeks the same direction).

2. In a small bowl combine whipping cream and chicken broth; pour over leeks. Sprinkle with half of the snipped or dried marjoram, salt, and pepper. Cover tightly with foil and bake for 20 minutes.

3. Meanwhile, in a small bowl combine bread crumbs, Parmesan cheese, and remaining snipped or dried marjoram. Drizzle with melted butter; toss to coat. Sprinkle leeks with bread crumb mixture. Bake, uncovered, for 15 to 20 minutes or until leeks are tender and crumbs are golden brown. If desired, garnish with fresh marjoram sprigs.

Per serving: 224 cal., 15 g total fat (9 g sat. fat), 45 mg chol., 457 mg sodium, 21 g carbo., 2 g fiber, 4 g pro.

Peas and Celery

This quick-and-easy vegetable medley adds a light, garden-fresh note to any holiday meal.

Start to Finish: 20 minutes **Makes:** 8 servings

- **½ cup coarsely chopped red onion (1 medium)**
- **1 tablespoon olive oil**
- **½ cup sliced celery (1 stalk)**
- **2 10-ounce packages frozen peas**
- **¼ cup chopped celery leaves (optional)**
- **½ teaspoon salt**
- **¼ teaspoon ground black pepper**

1. In a large skillet cook red onion in hot oil over medium heat about 3 minutes or until soft. Stir in celery; cook about 2 minutes or just until tender. Increase heat to medium-high; add peas. Cook, covered, for 5 to 7 minutes or until peas are heated through. Remove skillet from heat; stir in celery leaves (if desired), salt, and pepper.

Per serving: 75 cal., 2 g total fat (0 g sat. fat), 0 mg chol., 236 mg sodium, 11 g carbo., 3 g fiber, 4 g pro.

Vegetable-Puree Gravy

Scrape the crusty browned bits of turkey from the roasting pan and use some of the pan drippings to make this rich-tasting gravy.

Prep: 30 minutes **Cook:** 1½ hours **Cool:** 1 hour
Makes: 14 servings

- **3 bay leaves**
- **3 sprigs fresh thyme**
- **2 large sprigs fresh parsley**
- **Giblets, neck, and wing tips of turkey (but not the liver)**
- **4½ cups water**
- **2 large carrots, cut into chunks**
- **2 large stalks celery, cut into chunks**
- **1 large onion, coarsely chopped**
- **½ cup dry white wine**
- **1 tablespoon cornstarch**
- **¼ teaspoon salt**
- **¼ teaspoon freshly ground black pepper**

1. For bouquet garni, place bay leaves, thyme, and parsley in the center of a double-thick, 8-inch square of 100%-cotton cheesecloth. Bring the corners of the cheesecloth together and tie with clean kitchen string.

2. For vegetable stock, while turkey is roasting, in a large saucepan combine bouquet garni, giblets, neck, wing tips, water, carrot, celery, and onion. Bring to boiling; reduce heat. Simmer, uncovered, for 1½ hours. Cool for 1 hour.

3. Remove and discard bouquet garni, giblets, neck, and wing tips. Use a slotted spoon to transfer vegetables to a blender or food processor; add cooking liquid from saucepan. Cover and blend or process until nearly smooth (yield should be about 2¾ cups).

4. While the roasted turkey is standing after being removed from the oven, prepare the gravy. Pour roasting pan drippings into a measuring cup. Skim and reserve fat from drippings; return 3 tablespoons of the fat to hot roasting pan. Add vegetable stock, stirring with a large wooden spoon or spatula to scrape up the browned bits from roasting pan.

5. In a small bowl combine wine and cornstarch. Add wine mixture all at once to vegetable stock. Cook and stir over medium heat until slightly thickened and bubbly. Cook and stir for 2 minutes. Sprinkle with salt and pepper.

Advance Preparation: Prepare pureed vegetable stock as directed. Transfer to an airtight container and chill up to 24 hours. While the roasted turkey is standing after being removed from the oven, prepare gravy.

Per serving: 44 cal., 3 g total fat (1 g sat. fat), 3 mg chol., 53 mg sodium, 3 g carbo., 1 g fiber, 0 g pro.

Vegetable-Puree Gravy

Creamy Brussels Sprouts

For a green bean side dish, substitute 2 pounds of trimmed green beans for the Brussels sprouts, and reduce the baking time to 15 to 18 minutes.

Prep: 30 minutes **Bake:** 20 minutes
Oven: 350°F **Makes:** 8 to 10 servings

- Nonstick cooking spray
- 1 medium onion, quartered and thinly sliced
- 3 cloves garlic, minced
- 3 tablespoons butter
- 2 pounds Brussels sprouts, trimmed and halved
- 1 teaspoon snipped fresh thyme or ¼ teaspoon dried thyme, crushed
- ¾ cup reduced-sodium chicken broth
- ¾ cup whipping cream
- ¼ teaspoon ground nutmeg
- ½ cup finely shredded Parmesan cheese or Pecorino Romano cheese

1. Preheat oven to 350°F. Lightly coat a 1½-quart oval gratin baking dish or baking dish with nonstick cooking spray.

2. In a 12-inch skillet cook onion and garlic in butter over medium heat for 3 minutes or until soft. Stir in Brussels sprouts and thyme. Cook for 4 minutes or until onion begins to brown. Add broth. Bring to boiling. Cook, stirring occasionally, for 3 to 4 minutes or until broth nearly evaporates. Add whipping cream and nutmeg. Cook for 4 minutes or until mixture begins to thicken. Transfer to prepared baking dish. Stir in half of the cheese, ¼ teaspoon *salt,* and ⅛ teaspoon *ground black pepper.* Sprinkle with remaining cheese.

3. Bake, uncovered, 20 to 25 minutes or until Brussels sprouts are tender.

Per serving: 193 cal., 14 g total fat (9 g sat. fat), 46 mg chol., 279 mg sodium, 13 g carbo., 5 g fiber, 7 g pro.

Creamy Brussels Sprouts

Broccoli Rabe with Currants and Pine Nuts

Slightly bitter, crisp-tender broccoli rabe tastes superb when tossed with a sweet balsamic dressing. If you can't find broccoli rabe, use broccoli flowerets or broccolini.

Start to Finish: 20 minutes **Makes:** 8 servings

- ½ cup balsamic vinegar
- 2 pounds broccoli rabe, stems trimmed
- 4 cloves garlic, chopped
- 4 teaspoons olive oil
- 3 tablespoons currants or golden raisins
- 2 tablespoons pine nuts, toasted
- 2 ounces Parmigiano-Reggiano cheese, shaved

1. In a medium saucepan bring vinegar to boiling; boil steadily about 10 minutes or until thickened and reduced to about 1 tablespoon. Watch carefully so it does not become too thick.

2. Meanwhile, bring a large pot of water to boiling. Add broccoli rabe; cook for 30 seconds. Drain and immerse broccoli rabe in ice water to cool quickly. Drain well; pat dry with paper towels.

3. In a very large skillet cook garlic in hot oil over medium heat just until tender. Add broccoli rabe and currants. Cook 2 to 3 minutes or until crisp-tender, tossing occasionally. Toss with balsamic vinegar and pine nuts. Divide among 8 serving plates. Top with shaved cheese.

Per serving: 110 cal., 6 g total fat (2 g sat. fat), 5 mg chol., 145 mg sodium, 10 g carbo., 3 g fiber, 6 g pro.

Pear and Blue Cheese Salad

If you plan to serve this salad as part of a buffet meal, add only about ¼ cup of the dressing; serve the remaining dressing on the side.

Start to Finish: 25 minutes **Makes:** 8 to 10 servings

- **1 recipe Holiday Dijon Vinaigrette or ¾ cup bottled vinaigrette**
- **2 tablespoons butter**
- **1 cup pecan halves**
- **1 tablespoon sugar**
- **⅛ teaspoon salt**
- **16 cups torn curly endive, romaine lettuce, or spinach**
- **3 ripe pears, cored and thinly sliced**
- **1 cup crumbled blue cheese (4 ounces)**

1. Prepare Holiday Dijon Vinaigrette. In a large skillet melt butter over medium heat. Add pecan halves. Cook for 4 to 5 minutes or until pecans are lightly toasted, stirring frequently. Sprinkle sugar and salt over pecans; cook and stir for 1 minute. Transfer pecans to a medium bowl; cool.

2. In a 6- to 8-quart salad bowl combine greens, pears, blue cheese, and half of pecans. Pour Holiday Dijon Vinaigrette over salad. Toss gently to coat. Divide mixture among salad plates. Sprinkle with remaining pecans.

Holiday Dijon Vinaigrette: In a screw-top jar combine 5 tablespoons extra virgin olive oil, 3 tablespoons finely chopped onion, 2 tablespoons white wine vinegar, 1 tablespoon Dijon-style mustard, ½ teaspoon salt, and ¼ teaspoon ground black pepper. Cover and shake well. Makes ⅔ cup.

Advance Preparation: Prepare pecans as directed; store in airtight container at room temperature up to 24 hours. Prepare vinaigrette as directed; cover and chill up to 1 week. Shake before using.

Per serving: 265 cal., 21 g total fat (6 g sat. fat), 16 mg chol., 390 mg sodium, 17 g carbo., 7 g fiber, 6 g pro.

Pear and Blue Cheese Salad

Winter Fruit Salad with Balsamic Vinaigrette

Prep: 25 minutes **Chill:** 30 minutes
Makes: 12 servings

- **1 recipe Balsamic Vinaigrette**
- **3 medium pink grapefruit**
- **3 medium oranges**
- **1½ cups red and/or green seedless grapes**
- **3 tablespoons pomegranate seeds (optional)**
- **1 head red-tip or green leaf lettuce, torn**

1. Prepare Balsamic Vinaigrette. Chill for at least 30 minutes.

2. Peel grapefruit and oranges. Section fruit; place in bowl. Add grapes and, if desired, pomegranate seeds. To serve, toss fruit with dressing. Line a bowl with torn lettuce and top with fruit mixture.

Balsamic Vinaigrette: In a screw-top jar combine ⅓ cup vegetable oil, ⅓ cup orange juice, ¼ cup balsamic vinegar, 4 teaspoons honey, and ¼ teaspoon cracked black pepper. Shake before using. Makes 1 cup.

Advance Preparation: Prepare dressing as directed; cover and chill up to 3 days. Store prepared fruit mixture, covered, in refrigerator up to 4 hours.

Per serving: 140 cal., 7 g total fat (1 g sat. fat), 0 mg chol., 5 mg sodium, 21 g carbo., 2 g fiber, 1 g pro.

Orange, Fennel, and Olive Salad with Cranberry Vinaigrette

When choosing fennel, look for firm, cream-colored bulbs with some of the stems and leaves attached.

Start to Finish: 25 minutes **Makes:** 10 to 12 servings

- **1 small fennel bulb, thinly sliced (4 ounces)**
- **6 cups torn mixed greens**
- **4 medium navel oranges, peeled and sliced; 6 tangerines, peeled and sliced; and/or 8 kumquats, sliced**
- **1 medium red onion, thinly sliced and separated into rings (½ cup)**
- **½ cup pitted kalamata olives**
- **1 recipe Cranberry Vinaigrette**

1. Place sliced fennel in a medium bowl and pour enough boiling water over fennel to cover. Let stand for 5 minutes; drain. Place greens in a large salad bowl. Arrange fennel, orange slices, onion, and olives on top of the greens. Drizzle Cranberry Vinaigrette over salad. Toss lightly before serving.

Cranberry Vinaigrette: In a medium saucepan combine 1 cup cranberry juice cocktail, ½ cup dry red wine, and ¼ cup dried cranberries; bring to a boil. Reduce heat and simmer, uncovered, for 15 minutes or until mixture is reduced to ⅓ cup;

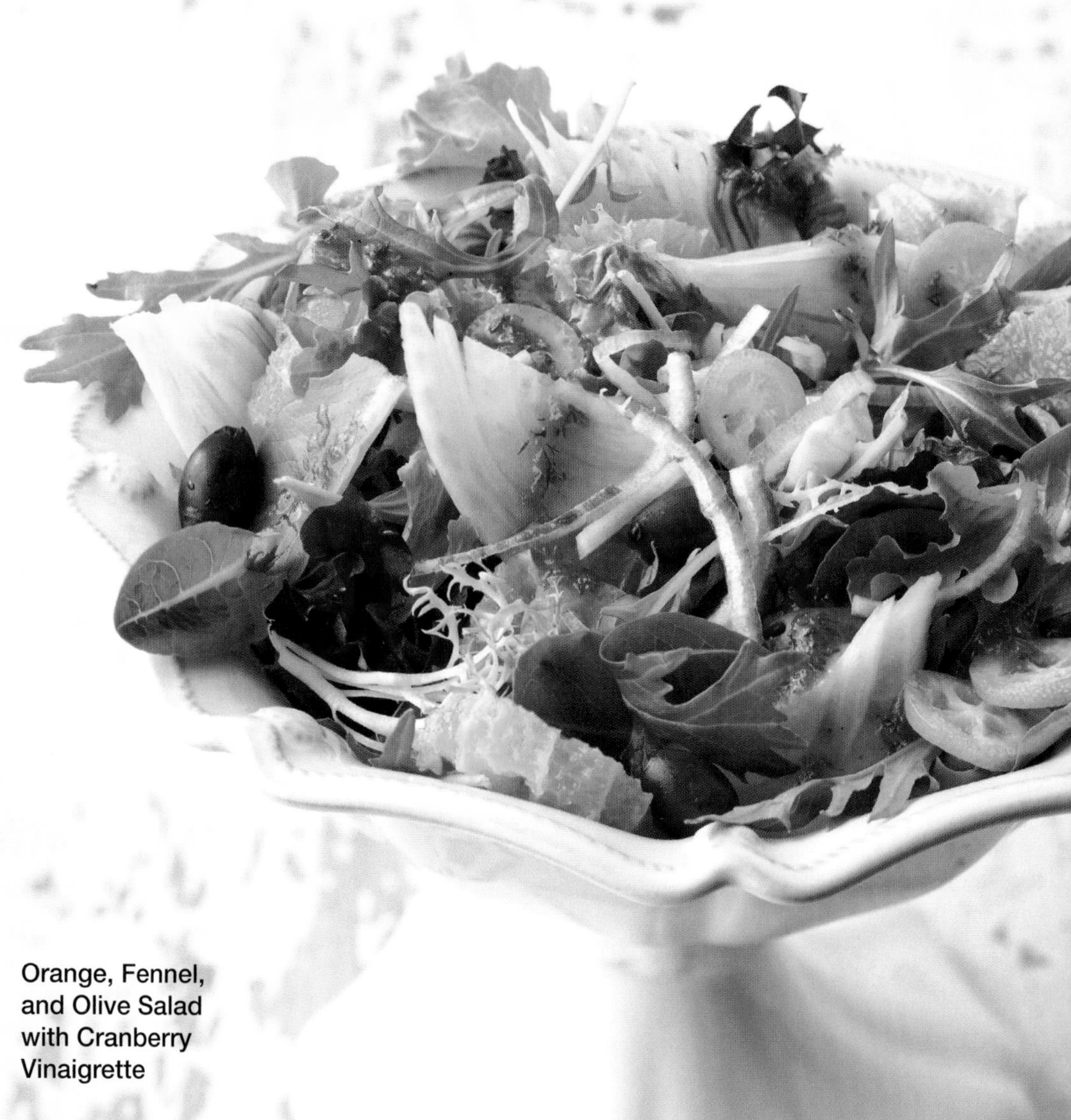

Orange, Fennel, and Olive Salad with Cranberry Vinaigrette

cool slightly. Meanwhile, in a small saucepan cook 2 tablespoons finely chopped shallots in 1 tablespoon hot olive oil until tender but not brown. In a food processor or blender, combine cranberry mixture, shallots, 1 tablespoon olive oil, 2 tablespoons orange juice, 1 tablespoon red wine vinegar, 1 tablespoon honey, 1 teaspoon snipped fresh dillweed, and salt and pepper to taste. Cover; process or blend until smooth. Makes about ½ cup.

Advance Preparation: Prepare Cranberry Vinaigrette as directed. Cover and chill up to 3 days. Stir before using.

Per serving: 116 cal., 4 g total fat (0 g sat. fat), 0 mg chol., 147 mg sodium, 18 g carbo., 3 g fiber, 1 g pro.

Festive Apple Slaw

Red cabbage and green apples reverse the colors of the usual salad pairing. A light, tangy vinaigrette keeps both crisp and appealing.

Prep: 25 minutes **Chill:** 1 hour **Makes:** 8 servings

- **1 recipe Apple Cider Vinaigrette**
- **3 cups thinly sliced tart green apples, such as Newtown Pippin or Granny Smith, and/or sweet red apple, such as Red Delicious or McIntosh**
- **1 cup shredded red cabbage**
- **½ cup seedless green or red grapes, halved**
- **⅓ cup chopped celery**
- **¼ cup slivered almonds, toasted**

1. Prepare Apple Cider Vinaigrette. Cover and chill until ready to serve.

2. In a large bowl combine apples, red cabbage, grapes, and celery. Shake vinaigrette well. Pour vinaigrette over apple mixture; toss gently to coat. Cover and chill slaw for 1 hour.

3. Before serving, sprinkle apple mixture with almonds; toss gently to combine.

Apple Cider Vinaigrette: In a screw-top jar combine ¼ cup cider vinegar, 3 tablespoons vegetable oil, and 2 tablespoons honey. Cover and shake well. Makes about ½ cup.

Advance Preparation: Prepare vinaigrette as directed. Cover and chill up to 1 week. Shake well before adding to slaw.

Per serving: 161 cal., 10 g total fat (1 g sat. fat), 0 mg chol., 6 mg sodium, 19 g carbo., 3 g fiber, 2 g pro.

Cranberry Orange Relish

Spice-infused cranberries, oranges, and raisins in a splash of orange liqueur make a most unusual and refreshing seasonal relish.

Prep: 25 minutes **Cook:** 15 minutes
Makes: about 4 cups or 16 servings

- **12 whole cloves**
- **6 whole allspice**
- **1 cinnamon stick, broken**
- **3 cups cranberries**
- **2 cups peeled and sectioned oranges (3 to 4 oranges)**
- **1 cup cranberry-apple drink**
- **½ cup chopped onion**
- **½ cup golden raisins**
- **2 tablespoons granulated sugar**
- **2 tablespoons orange liqueur (optional)**
- **1 teaspoon salt**

1. Place cloves, allspice, and cinnamon in the center of a double thick 6-inch square of 100%-cotton cheesecloth. Bring up corners and tie with clean 100%-cotton kitchen string.

2. In a large saucepan combine cranberries; oranges; cranberry-apple drink; onion; raisins; sugar; orange liqueur, if desired; and salt. Add spice bag. Bring to boiling; reduce heat. Simmer, uncovered, for 15 minutes or until slightly thickened. Remove and discard spice bag before serving. Serve warm or cover and chill.

Advance Preparation: Prepare relish as directed. Cool; cover and chill up to 1 week.

Per serving: 54 cal., 0 g total fat, 0 mg chol., 147 mg sodium, 14 g carbo., 2 g fiber, 0 g pro.

Cranberry-Pear Chutney

Cranberry-Pear Chutney

Cranberry relish is a Thanksgiving necessity. This version gets crunch from Asian pears and a glossy texture from peach preserves.

Prep: 25 minutes **Cook:** 30 minutes **Cool:** 1 hour **Chill:** 4 hours **Makes:** about 4 cups or 16 servings

- **1 12-ounce package fresh cranberries (3 cups)**
- **1½ cups chopped Asian pears or chopped, peeled jicama**
- **1½ cups finely chopped onion**
- **1 cup peach preserves**
- **⅓ cup packed brown sugar**
- **¼ cup balsamic vinegar**
- **1 teaspoon dry mustard**
- **1 teaspoon finely shredded lemon peel**
- **½ teaspoon crushed red pepper**

1. In a large saucepan combine cranberries, pears, onion, preserves, brown sugar, vinegar, mustard, lemon peel, and red pepper. Bring to boiling; reduce heat. Simmer, covered, for 30 minutes, stirring occasionally. Remove from heat.

2. Transfer chutney to a heatproof glass bowl. Let cool to room temperature. Serve warm or cover and chill.

Advance Preparation: Prepare relish as directed. Cool; cover and chill for 4 hours or up to 5 days.

Per serving: 108 cal., 0 g total fat, 0 mg chol., 10 mg sodium, 27 g carbo., 2 g fiber, 0 g pro.

Cashew Crunch Salad

Add the salad dressing just before tossing and serving so the greens stay crisp.

Start to Finish: 20 minutes **Makes:** 6 servings

- **1 10-ounce package mixed salad greens (8 to 9 cups)**
- **1 medium Granny Smith apple, cored and thinly sliced**
- **⅓ cup dried cranberries or snipped dried apricots**
- **⅓ cup dry roasted cashews**
- **1 medium shallot, thinly sliced**
- **1 clove garlic, minced**
- **2 tablespoons olive oil**
- **1 teaspoon honey**
- **½ teaspoon Dijon-style mustard**
- **⅛ teaspoon salt**
- **⅛ teaspoon ground black pepper**
- **2 tablespoons balsamic vinegar**

1. In a serving bowl toss together mixed greens, apple, cranberries, and cashews.

2. In a medium skillet cook shallot and garlic in hot olive oil over medium heat about 3 minutes or until tender. Remove from heat. Whisk in honey, mustard, salt, and pepper until combined. Stir in vinegar. Add dressing to the salad; toss to coat. Serve immediately.

Advance Preparation: Prepare vinaigrette as directed. Cover and chill up to 1 week. Reheat dressing before serving.

Per serving: 136 cal., 8 g total fat (1 g sat. fat), 0 mg chol., 70 mg sodium, 15 g carbo., 2 g fiber, 2 g pro.

Orange-Ginger Gelatin Salad

Crystallized ginger and ginger ale give this make-ahead salad a double dose of lively flavor.

Prep: 15 minutes **Chill:** 4 to 24 hours
Makes: 15 servings

- **2 6-ounce packages orange-flavor gelatin**
- **2 cups water**
- **3 tablespoons finely chopped crystallized ginger**
- **4 cups ginger ale, chilled**
- **2 medium apples, cored and chopped**
- **1 11-ounce can mandarin oranges, drained**
- **¾ cup chopped pecans, toasted**
- **½ cup shredded carrot**
- **1 8-ounce carton dairy sour cream**
- **⅓ cup sugar**
- **1 teaspoon vanilla**

1. In a large saucepan combine gelatin, water, and crystallized ginger; heat and stir until gelatin dissolves. Remove from heat. Carefully stir in ginger ale, stopping occasionally to let foam subside if necessary. Transfer to a very large bowl. Cover and chill for 1 to 1½ hours or until partially set (the consistency of unbeaten egg whites). Fold in apples, mandarin oranges, pecans, and carrot.

2. Pour into a 3-quart rectangular baking dish. Cover and chill for at least 3 hours or up to 24 hours or until firm. In a small bowl combine sour cream, sugar, and vanilla. Cover and chill until serving time.

3. To serve, cut gelatin mixture into squares. Top servings with sour cream mixture.

Per serving: 233 cal., 8 g total fat (3 g sat. fat), 7 mg chol., 51 mg sodium, 38 g carbo., 1 g fiber, 3 g pro.

Strawberry Pretzel Salad

Crunchy pretzels are the surprise ingredient in this crowd-pleasing gelatin salad. It's the perfect dish for a holiday potluck.

Prep: 20 minutes **Bake:** 10 minutes
Chill: 4 to 24 hours **Oven:** 350°F
Makes: 24 servings

- **3 cups finely crushed pretzels**
- **½ cup sugar**
- **¾ cup butter or margarine, melted**
- **1 8-ounce package cream cheese, softened**
- **1 cup sugar**
- **1 8-ounce container frozen whipped dessert topping, thawed**
- **2 10-ounce packages frozen strawberries in syrup, thawed**
- **2 3-ounce packages strawberry-flavor gelatin**
- **2 cups boiling water**

1. Preheat oven to 350°F. For crust, in a medium bowl combine crushed pretzels and the ½ cup sugar. Add melted butter; stir well to combine. Press pretzel mixture into an ungreased 3-quart rectangular baking dish. Bake for 10 minutes. Cool in dish on a wire rack.

2. In a large bowl combine cream cheese and the 1 cup sugar; beat with an electric mixer on medium speed until well mixed. Slowly beat in the dessert topping. Spread over cooled crust.

3. In another large bowl combine strawberries and gelatin. Stir in the boiling water. Stir about 2 minutes or until gelatin dissolves. Carefully pour gelatin mixture over the cream cheese layer. Cover and chill at least 4 hours or up to 24 hours or until set.

Advance Preparation: Prepare as directed. Cover and chill at least 4 hours or up to 24 hours.

Per serving: 252 cal., 11 g total fat (8 g sat. fat), 26 mg chol., 240 mg sodium, 35 g carbo., 1 g fiber, 3 g pro.

party bites and sips

Eat, drink, and be merry! Hosting a yuletide cocktail party is stress-free with this collection of fabulous make-ahead appetizers and drinks. For an open house, serve a series of small bites with some store-bought additions such as assorted cheeses and crackers as well as pickled and fresh vegetables.

Bruschetta with Tomato and Arugula, page 36

Brie and Artichoke Dip

Brie and Artichoke Dip

Flecks of roasted red sweet peppers give this rich cheesy dip a touch of color.

Start to Finish: 25 minutes **Makes:** 3 cups

- **2 tablespoons butter**
- **2 tablespoons all-purpose flour**
- **1 tablespoon dry mustard**
- **1 cup milk**
- **3 4½-ounce rounds Brie cheese, rinds removed and cut into 1-inch cubes**
- **1 6-ounce jar marinated artichoke hearts, well drained and chopped**
- **¼ cup chopped roasted red sweet peppers**
- **Belgian endive leaves, toasted baguette slices, red sweet pepper strips, and/or artichoke leaves**

1. In a medium saucepan melt butter over medium heat. Stir in flour and mustard. Stir in milk; whisk until smooth. Cook and stir over medium heat until mixture is thickened and bubbly. Gradually add Brie, whisking until smooth. Stir in artichoke hearts and roasted peppers. Heat through.

2. Transfer mixture to a serving bowl. Serve with endive leaves, baguette slices, red pepper strips, and/or artichoke leaves.

Per ¼ cup dip: 153 cal., 12 g total fat (7 g sat. fat), 39 mg chol., 267 mg sodium, 4 g carbo., 0 g fiber, 8 g pro.

Bruschetta with Tomato and Arugula

This Italian-inspired appetizer—toasted bread with a tomato-relish topper—is perfect for party buffets. *Pictured on page 35.*

Prep: 25 minutes **Bake:** 7 minutes **Stand:** 1 hour
Oven: 425°F **Makes:** about 24 servings

- **2 medium tomatoes, seeded and chopped (1½ cups)**
- **½ cup chopped arugula leaves**
- **1 small onion, finely chopped**
- **¼ cup snipped fresh basil**
- **1 clove garlic, minced**
- **1 tablespoon olive oil**
- **1 tablespoon balsamic vinegar**
- **1 8-ounce loaf baguette-style French bread**
- **2 to 3 tablespoons olive oil**

1. Preheat oven to 425°F. In a medium bowl stir together tomatoes, arugula, onion, basil, garlic, 1 tablespoon olive oil, balsamic vinegar, and ¼ teaspoon each *salt* and *ground black pepper*. Let stand at room temperature for 1 hour.

2. Slice bread diagonally into ½-inch slices. Lightly brush both sides with the 2 to 3 tablespoons olive oil. Place on a baking sheet. Bake for 5 to 7 minutes or until crisp and light brown, turning once. Cool on a wire rack.

3. To serve, top toasted bread slices with tomato mixture. Serve immediately.

Advance Preparation: Toast bread slices as directed in Step 2. Place in an airtight container; cover. Store at room temperature up to 24 hours.

Per serving: 46 cal., 2 g total fat (0 g sat. fat), 0 mg chol., 87 mg sodium, 6 g carbo., 0 g fiber, 1 g pro.

Sloppy Joe Meatballs

Ingredients that make the sloppy joe sandwich so good taste equally delicious in a sauce for meatballs.

Prep: 35 minutes **Bake:** 12 minutes
Cook: 5 minutes **Oven:** 350°F **Makes:** 21 servings

- **1 egg, beaten**
- **¼ cup fine dry bread crumbs**
- **1 medium onion, finely chopped (½ cup)**
- **¼ teaspoon dried oregano, crushed**
- **¼ teaspoon salt**
- **1 pound lean ground beef**
- **½ cup chopped green sweet pepper**
- **1 tablespoon vegetable oil**
- **1 15-ounce can tomato sauce**
- **2 tablespoons packed brown sugar**
- **1 tablespoon prepared mustard**
- **1 teaspoon chili powder**
- **¼ teaspoon ground black pepper**
- **¼ teaspoon garlic salt**
- **Dash bottled hot pepper sauce (optional)**

1. Preheat oven to 350°F. In a large bowl combine egg, bread crumbs, ¼ cup of the onion, oregano, and salt. Add ground beef and mix well. Shape into 42 meatballs about ¾ inch in diameter. Arrange in a single layer on a 15×10×1-inch baking pan. Bake for 12 to 15 minutes or until no pink remains. Drain well.

2. Meanwhile, in a large saucepan cook remaining ¼ cup onion and sweet pepper in hot oil until tender. Stir in tomato sauce, brown sugar, mustard, chili powder, black pepper, garlic salt, and, if desired, hot pepper sauce. Bring mixture to boiling; reduce heat. Simmer, uncovered, for 5 minutes. Serve immediately.

Advance Preparation: Prepare meatballs and sauce as directed. Carefully place baked and drained meatballs in sauce; cool slightly. Place in shallow freezer containers; cover. Freeze up to 1 month. To serve, thaw meatball mixture in refrigerator overnight. Place in a large saucepan. Cook over medium-low heat about 10 minutes or until heated through, stirring occasionally. Serve meatballs and sauce in a fondue pot or slow cooker. Or to reheat in a slow cooker, heat thawed meatballs and sauce, covered, on high-heat setting for 2 to 2½ hours.

Per 2-meatball serving: 78 cal., 5 g total fat (2 g sat. fat), 26 mg chol., 187 mg sodium, 4 g carbo., 1 g fiber, 5 g pro.

Sloppy Joe Meatballs

Herb and Cheese Mini Quiches

Accented with just the right hint of tarragon and adorned with a garnish of roasted red sweet pepper and snipped chives, these quiches make a colorful extravaganza in any appetizer offering.

Prep: 1 hour **Bake:** 25 minutes **Oven:** 325°F
Makes: 48 mini quiches

- **1 cup butter, softened**
- **2 3-ounce packages cream cheese, softened**
- **2 cups all-purpose flour**
- **¼ cup shredded Asiago cheese (1 ounce)**
- **2 eggs, beaten**
- **½ cup half-and-half, light cream, or milk**
- **¼ cup finely shredded Gouda or Havarti cheese**
- **2 tablespoons pine nuts, toasted and coarsely chopped**
- **1 tablespoon snipped fresh tarragon or 2 teaspoons dried tarragon, crushed**
- **1 tablespoon snipped fresh chives**
- **⅛ teaspoon cracked black pepper**
- **Roasted red sweet pepper, finely chopped**
- **Snipped fresh chives**

1. Preheat oven to 325°F. For pastry, in a large mixing bowl, beat butter and cream cheese with an electric mixer on medium to high speed for 30 seconds. Beat in flour and Asiago cheese until a soft dough forms. Press 1 rounded teaspoon of the pastry evenly onto the bottom and up the sides of each of 48 ungreased 1¾-inch muffin cups.

2. For filling, in a medium bowl stir together eggs, half-and-half, Gouda cheese, pine nuts, tarragon, the 1 tablespoon chives, and black pepper.

3. Spoon about 1 heaping teaspoon of the filling into each pastry-lined muffin cup. Bake for 25 to 30 minutes or until a knife inserted in centers comes out clean. Cool slightly in muffin cups. Carefully remove from muffin cups; place on a wire rack or serving platter. Top with chopped roasted red pepper and additional snipped chives. Serve warm.

Advance Preparation: Prepare as directed; cool quiches. Place in freezer container; cover. Freeze up to 3 months. To serve, thaw in refrigerator overnight. Arrange quiches on baking sheet. Heat in a 325°F oven for 10 to 15 minutes or until warm.

Per serving: 77 cal., 6 g total fat (4 g sat. fat), 25 mg chol., 53 mg sodium, 4 g carbo., 0 g fiber, 1 g pro.

Herb and Cheese Mini Quiches

Festive Deviled Eggs

A few small changes, such as using Dijon-style mustard instead of prepared mustard and adding sour cream, ham, and green onion, add a new flavor twist.

Start to Finish: 35 minutes **Makes:** 24 egg halves

- **12 Hard-Cooked Eggs**
- **¼ cup mayonnaise or salad dressing**
- **2 tablespoons dairy sour cream**
- **1½ teaspoons Dijon-style mustard**
- **¼ cup finely chopped cooked ham**
- **1 green onion, finely chopped**
- **Salt and ground black pepper**
- **Sliced green onion**
- **Fresh thyme sprigs**

1. Halve Hard-Cooked Eggs lengthwise and remove yolks. Set whites aside. Place yolks in a food processor. Add mayonnaise, sour cream, and mustard. Cover and process until smooth. (Or place yolks, mayonnaise, sour cream and mustard in a medium mixing bowl and beat with an electric mixer on medium speed until smooth.) Stir in ham and finely chopped green onion. Season to taste with salt and pepper.

2. Stuff egg white halves with yolk mixture. Cover and chill until serving time. Garnish with sliced green onion and thyme sprigs.

Advance Preparation: Prepare stuffed eggs as directed. Place in an airtight container; cover. Refrigerate up to 24 hours.

Hard-Cooked Eggs: Place eggs in a single layer in an extra-large saucepan or kettle (do not stack eggs). Add enough cold water to cover eggs by at least 1 inch. Bring to a rapid boil over high heat (water will have large rapidly breaking bubbles). Remove from heat, cover, and let stand for 15 minutes; drain. (Let extra-large eggs stand in the boiled water for 18 minutes.) Run cold water over eggs or place them in ice water until cool enough to handle; drain. To peel eggs, gently tap each egg on the countertop. Roll the egg between the palms of your hands. Peel off shell, starting at large end.

Per egg-half serving: 60 cal., 5 g total fat (1 g sat. fat), 108 mg chol., 95 mg sodium, 0 g carbo., 0 g fiber, 3 g pro.

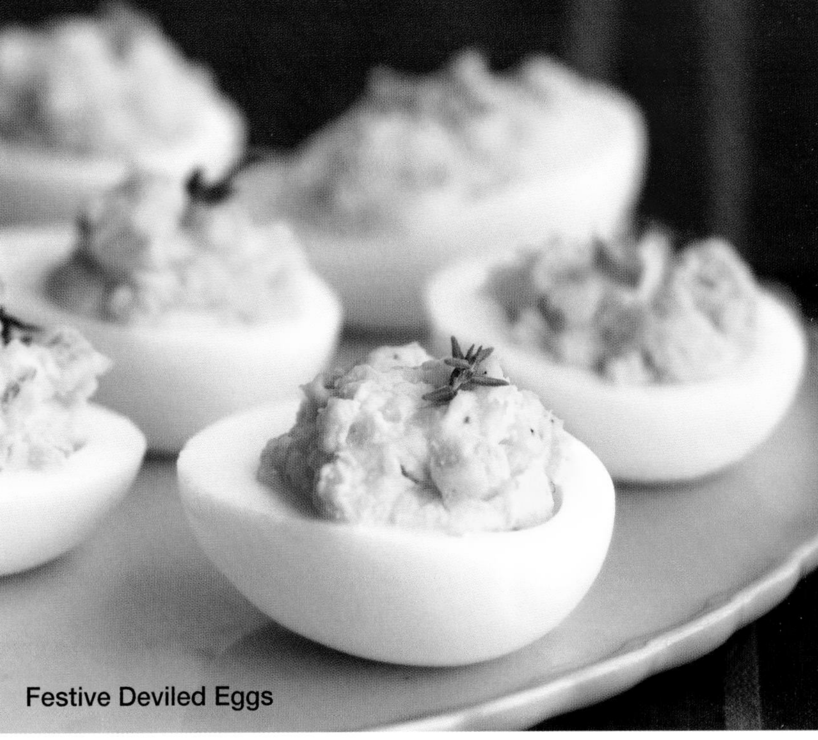
Festive Deviled Eggs

Horseradish-Stuffed Mushrooms

To clean fresh mushrooms, wipe them with a clean, damp cloth or rinse them lightly, then dry gently with paper towels.

Prep: 30 minutes **Bake:** 13 minutes **Oven:** 425°F
Makes: 24 mushrooms

- **24 large (1½ to 2 inches in diameter) white or cremini mushrooms**
- **3 tablespoons olive oil**
- **⅓ cup chopped onion**
- **2 3-ounce packages cream cheese, cut up**
- **3 to 4 teaspoons prepared horseradish**
- **Garnishes, such as snipped fresh chives, Italian (flat-leaf) parsley, basil, or cooked bacon pieces**

1. Preheat oven to 425°F. Clean mushrooms and remove stems. Chop stems; reserve ¾ cup of the stems (discard remaining stems). Lightly brush mushroom caps using 1 tablespoon of the olive oil. Place mushroom caps, stem side down, on a 15×10×1-inch baking pan. Bake for 5 minutes. Carefully place mushroom caps, stem side down, on a double thickness of paper towels to drain while preparing filling. Set aside.

2. For filling, in a large skillet cook chopped mushroom stems and onion in remaining 2 tablespoons olive oil over medium heat about 8 minutes or until onion is tender, stirring occasionally. Remove from heat; add cream cheese and horseradish. Let stand for 2 minutes. Stir until combined.

3. Place mushroom caps, stem side up, in the same baking pan. Use a spoon to mound filling into mushroom caps. Bake for 8 to 10 minutes or until heated through and cheese is slightly browned. Sprinkle with garnishes.

Advance Preparation: Clean mushrooms and chop stems and onions several hours ahead. Cover and chill until ready to use.

Per mushroom: 46 cal., 5 g total fat (2 g sat. fat), 8 mg chol., 24 mg sodium, 1 g carbo., 0 g fiber, 1 g pro.

Ripe Olive Cheese Balls

Ripe Olive Cheese Balls

For a festive presentation, display the cheese balls on a bed of fresh basil leaves.

Prep: 15 minutes **Stand:** 45 minutes
Chill: 4 hours **Makes:** 2 balls (3½ cups, fifty-six 1-tablespoon servings)

- **2 8-ounce packages cream cheese**
- **½ cup butter**
- **½ cup crumbled blue cheese (2 ounces)**
- **1 4¼-ounce can sliced pitted ripe olives, drained**
- **2 tablespoons chopped green onion or snipped fresh chives**
- **Assorted crackers, flat bread, dried dates and/or dried apricots, and walnut halves**

1. Place cream cheese, butter, and blue cheese in a large mixing bowl; let stand for 30 minutes to reach room temperature. With an electric mixer beat mixture on low speed until smooth. Stir in olives and green onion. Cover and chill at least 4 hours or up to 24 hours.

2. Shape mixture loosely into 2 balls; cover and chill until serving time. Serve cheese balls with assorted crackers and/or dried fruits.

Advance Preparation: Prepare as directed. Place in freezer container; cover. Freeze up to 3 months. Let thaw in refrigerator overnight before serving.

Per 1-tablespoon serving: 55 cal., 6 g total fat (3 g sat. fat), 14 mg chol., 69 mg sodium, 1 g carbo., 0 g fiber, 1 g pro.

Chili-Toasted Pecans with Dried Cherries

Present guests their own serving-size portions by offering these spicy nuts in foil bake cups.

Prep: 15 minutes **Bake:** 12 minutes
Oven: 325°F **Makes:** about 2½ cups

- **1 tablespoon vegetable oil**
- **¼ teaspoon bottled hot pepper sauce**
- **2 cups pecan halves (8 ounces)**
- **1½ teaspoons chili powder**
- **1 teaspoon ground black pepper**
- **¾ teaspoon salt**
- **½ teaspoon ground cumin**
- **¼ teaspoon dried oregano, crushed**
- **¾ cup dried cherries or combination of raisins and dried cranberries (4 ounces)**

1. Preheat oven to 325°F. In a large bowl combine oil and hot pepper sauce. Add pecans; toss to coat evenly. Set aside.

2. In a small bowl combine chili powder, black pepper, salt, cumin, and oregano. Add to pecans; toss well to coat.

3. Spread pecans in a 15×10×1-inch baking pan. Bake for 12 to 15 minutes or until toasted, stirring every 5 minutes. Stir in dried cherries. Serve warm or cooled to room temperature.

Advance Preparation: Transfer cooled nut mixture to an airtight container; cover. Store at room temperature up to 1 week.

Per ¼ cup: 196 cal., 17 g total fat (2 g sat. fat), 0 mg chol., 182 mg sodium, 11 g carbo., 3 g fiber, 2 g pro.

Crunchy Nut Snack Mix

The cereals and pecans soak up the maple and cinnamon flavors as they roast, producing a flavor-packed punch in every bite.

Prep: 10 minutes **Bake:** 45 minutes
Oven: 300°F **Makes:** 7½ cups

- **2 cups round toasted multigrain cereal or round toasted oat cereal**
- **2 cups bite-size wheat or rice square cereal**
- **2 cups bite-size corn or oat square cereal**
- **1½ cups coarsely chopped pecans**
- **½ cup butter**
- **½ cup packed brown sugar**
- **⅓ cup maple-flavor syrup**
- **¼ teaspoon ground cinnamon**
- **1 teaspoon vanilla**

1. Preheat oven to 300°F. In a 3-quart rectangular baking pan, combine cereals and pecans; set aside.

2. In a medium saucepan combine butter, brown sugar, syrup, and cinnamon. Cook and stir over medium heat until sugar dissolves. Stir in vanilla. Pour over cereal mixture in pan; toss to coat well.

3. Bake for 45 minutes, stirring every 15 minutes. Spread baked mixture on foil to cool. Break into bite-size pieces.

Advance Preparation: Prepare as directed. Transfer snack mix to an airtight container; cover. Store at room temperature up to 5 days.

Per ½ cup: 232 cal., 15 g total fat (4 g sat. fat), 17 mg chol., 175 mg sodium, 25 g carbo., 2 g fiber, 2 g pro.

Chili-Toasted Pecans with Dried Cherries

Buffalo-Style Chicken Fingers

Buffalo-Style Chicken Fingers

Since the first spicy wings flew from Buffalo to parties across the country, countless variations have appeared. This neat-to-eat chicken breast version is sure to be a holiday favorite.

Prep: 25 minutes **Bake:** 18 minutes
Oven: 425°F **Makes:** 12 servings

- **2 cups crushed cornflakes**
- **2 tablespoons finely snipped fresh parsley**
- **½ teaspoon salt**
- **1 pound skinless, boneless chicken breast halves**
- **⅓ cup bottled blue cheese salad dressing**
- **2 teaspoons water**
- **1 to 2 teaspoons bottled hot pepper sauce**
- **Celery sticks**
- **Bottled blue cheese salad dressing**

1. Preheat oven to 425°F. In a shallow bowl or pie plate combine crushed cornflakes, parsley, and salt. Cut chicken breasts into strips about ¾-inch wide and 3 inches long. In a large bowl combine ⅓ cup dressing, water, and hot pepper sauce. Add chicken; stir to coat. Roll chicken pieces individually in crumb mixture to coat.

2. Place chicken strips in a single layer on a lightly greased 15×10×1-inch baking pan. Bake for 18 to 20 minutes or until chicken is no longer pink and crumbs are golden. Serve warm with celery sticks and additional blue cheese dressing for dipping.

Advance Preparation: Prepare as directed through Step 1. Place coated chicken strips on a foil-lined baking sheet. Freeze about 2 hours or until firm. Place frozen strips in a freezer container; cover. Freeze up to 1 month. To serve, bake as directed in Step 2.

Per serving: 184 cal., 12 g total fat (2 g sat. fat), 26 mg chol., 408 mg sodium, 9 g carbo., 0 g fiber, 11 g pro.

Curry-Coconut Shrimp with Mango Dipping Sauce

Curry-Coconut Shrimp with Mango Dipping Sauce

If you don't own a food processor, finely chop the coconut and cashews.

Prep: 30 minutes **Cook:** 3 minutes per batch
Oven: 200°F **Makes:** 10 to 12 servings

- **24 fresh or frozen jumbo shrimp in shells**
- **1 teaspoon curry powder**
- **2 cups shredded coconut**
- **½ cup chopped cashews**
- **⅓ cup all-purpose flour**
- **½ teaspoon salt**
- **¼ teaspoon ground black pepper**
- **2 eggs, lightly beaten**
- **1 tablespoon lime juice**
- **Vegetable oil for deep-fat frying**
- **1 recipe Mango Dipping Sauce**

1. Thaw shrimp, if frozen. Peel and devein shrimp, leaving tails intact. Rinse shrimp and pat dry with paper towels. Sprinkle shrimp with ½ teaspoon of the curry powder.

2. In a food processor combine coconut and cashews. Cover and pulse until finely chopped. Place mixture in a shallow bowl.

3. In another shallow bowl combine flour, remaining ½ teaspoon curry powder, salt, and pepper. In another shallow bowl combine the beaten eggs and lime juice.

4. Dip each shrimp, one at a time, into the flour mixture, shaking off any excess. Dip into egg mixture, then into coconut mixture to coat. Pat coconut mixture in place as necessary to adhere.

5. Preheat oven to 200°F. In a large saucepan heat 1½ inches of vegetable oil to 350°F. Cook shrimp, four to six at a time, in hot oil about 3 minutes or until golden brown. Drain on paper towels. Keep warm on a baking sheet in oven while frying remaining shrimp. Carefully skim and discard any coconut that falls in oil between batches.

6. Serve warm with Mango Dipping Sauce.

Mango Dipping Sauce: In a small bowl combine ½ cup mango chutney (snip any large pieces), ½ cup dairy sour cream, and ½ teaspoon curry powder. Makes 1 cup.

Advance Preparation: Place peeled and deveined shrimp on ice; cover. Chill up to 24 hours. Place cashew mixture in an airtight container; cover. Store at room temperature up to 1 week. Cover and chill Mango Dipping Sauce up to 24 hours.

Per serving: 148 cal., 11 g total fat (4 g sat. fat), 48 mg chol., 125 mg sodium, 7 g carbo., 1 g fiber, 5 g pro.

Ricotta Puffs

Ricotta Puffs

Using puff pastry makes it easy to prepare these flaky appetizers. They're oozing with Italian ricotta cheese.

Prep: 30 minutes **Bake:** 20 minutes
Cool: 5 minutes **Oven:** 400°F **Makes:** 18 puffs

- 1 17.3-ounce package frozen puff pastry (2 sheets), thawed
- ½ cup ricotta cheese
- ½ cup chopped roasted red sweet peppers
- 3 tablespoons grated Romano or Parmesan cheese
- 1 tablespoon snipped fresh parsley
- 1 teaspoon dried oregano, crushed
- ½ teaspoon black pepper
- Milk
- Grated Romano cheese

1. Preheat oven to 400°F. On a lightly floured surface, unfold the pastry sheets. Use a sharp knife to cut each pastry sheet into nine 3-inch squares.

2. For ricotta filling, in a medium bowl stir together ricotta cheese, roasted sweet peppers, 3 tablespoons Romano cheese, parsley, oregano, and black pepper.

3. Moisten the edges of each pastry square with milk. Spoon about 2 teaspoons filling onto one-half of each pastry square. Fold the other half of the pastry over the filling, forming a rectangle. Seal edges by pressing with the tines of a fork. With a sharp knife cut slits in the top of each pastry bundle. Brush with milk; sprinkle with additional Romano cheese. Arrange pastry bundles on an ungreased baking sheet.

4. Bake about 20 minutes or until golden brown. Transfer to a wire rack; cool before serving.

Advance Preparation: Prepare through Step 3. Place unbaked puffs in an airtight container; cover. Freeze up to 1 month. Thaw puffs in refrigerator about 4 hours. Place on an ungreased baking sheet. Brush with milk and Romano cheese, and bake as directed.

Per puff: 137 cal., 10 g total fat (1 g sat. fat), 3 mg chol., 137 mg sodium, 10 g carbo., 0 g fiber, 3 g pro.

Cheese-and-Walnut-Stuffed Mushroom Bundles

Layers of flaky phyllo encase a savory garlic-and-herb cheese filling in these luscious appetizers.

Prep: 30 minutes **Bake:** 10 minutes
Cook: 6 minutes **Oven:** 400°F **Makes:** 12 bundles

- 12 mushrooms (about 1½ inches in diameter)
- 8 sheets frozen phyllo dough (9×14 inches), thawed
- ¼ cup butter, melted
- ½ of a 5.2-ounce package semisoft cheese with garlic and herb (about ⅓ cup)
- ¼ cup chopped walnuts, toasted

1. Preheat oven to 400°F. Remove stems from mushrooms; discard or set aside for another use. Cook mushroom caps in a small amount of boiling water in a covered saucepan for 6 to 8 minutes or until soft. Drain and invert caps on paper towels.

2. Unfold phyllo dough; keep covered with plastic wrap, removing sheets as needed. Brush one phyllo sheet with melted butter. Top with a second sheet; brush with melted butter. Layer with two more phyllo sheets and melted butter. Use a sharp knife to cut phyllo stack in half lengthwise; cut each half crosswise into three squares, making six squares. Repeat with remaining phyllo and butter to make 12 squares total.

3. Place a mushroom, stem side up, on each phyllo square; top each mushroom with about 1 teaspoon each cheese and walnuts. Bring corners of phyllo together on top of mushrooms and filling and pinch to seal. Place bundles on an ungreased baking sheet. Brush with remaining melted butter. Bake for 10 to 12 minutes or until pastry is golden. Serve warm.

Advance Preparation: Place unbaked phyllo bundles in a single layer in an airtight container; cover. Freeze up to 1 month. Bake as directed (do not thaw before baking).

Per bundle: 114 cal., 8 g total fat (4 g sat. fat), 16 mg chol., 89 mg sodium, 8 g carbo., 1 g fiber, 2 g pro.

Warming Wassail

Toast the season with this hot spiced cider that fills the kitchen with a cinnamon and clove aroma.

Prep: 20 minutes **Cook:** 30 minutes
Makes: about 16 (8-ounce) servings

- 1 1-gallon bottle apple cider
- 1 cup lemon juice
- ⅓ cup sugar
- 10 2-inch cinnamon sticks, broken in half
- 6 oranges
- Whole cloves
- Orange wedges and cinnamon sticks (optional)

1. In a 6-quart kettle combine apple cider, lemon juice, and sugar. Add 10 cinnamon sticks. Stud each orange with cloves; cut each orange into 6 wedges. Add orange wedges to cider mixture.

2. Bring to boiling; reduce heat. Cover and simmer for 30 minutes. If desired, remove orange wedges and cinnamon sticks with slotted spoon. If desired, garnish each serving with additional orange wedges and cinnamon sticks.

Per serving: 136 cal., 0 g total fat, 0 mg chol., 8 mg sodium, 34 g carbo., 0 g fiber, 0 g pro.

Warming Wassail

Spiced Cranberry Tea

Spiced Cranberry Tea

With its crimson color and refreshing taste, this hot drink goes great with sweet and savory snacks at holiday parties.

Prep: 10 minutes **Cook:** 25 minutes
Makes: 6 (8-ounce) servings

- **4 cups cranberry juice**
- **2 2- to 3-inch cinnamon sticks**
- **2 cups orange juice**
- **½ cup sugar**
- **¼ cup lemon juice**
- **Lemon slices (optional)**
- **Fresh cranberries (optional)**

1. In a 3-quart saucepan combine cranberry juice and cinnamon; bring mixture to a simmer over medium heat. Cover and simmer for 20 minutes.

2. Stir in orange juice, sugar, and lemon juice. Cook and stir until sugar dissolves and mixture is heated through. If desired, garnish each serving with a lemon slice and fresh cranberries.

Per serving: 195 cal., 0 g total fat, 0 mg chol., 4 mg sodium, 49 g carbo., 0 g fiber, 1 g pro.

White Hot Chocolate

A small amount of coffee rounds out the flavor of this favorite hot beverage.

Start to Finish: 15 minutes
Makes: 4 (5½-ounce) servings

- **3 ounces white chocolate baking squares with cocoa butter, chopped**
- **2 cups milk, half-and-half, or light cream**
- **⅓ cup hot strong-brewed coffee**
- **½ teaspoon vanilla**
- **Vanilla ice cream (optional)**
- **Grated nutmeg or chocolate-flavor sprinkles**

1. In a medium saucepan combine white chocolate and ⅓ cup of the milk. Cook and stir over low heat until chocolate melts. Add remaining milk. Stir until mixture is heated through. Add coffee and vanilla. If desired, top each serving with a scoop of vanilla ice cream. Sprinkle each serving with nutmeg or chocolate sprinkles.

Per serving: 183 cal., 9 g total fat (6 g sat. fat), 17 mg chol., 80 mg sodium, 18 g carbo., 0 g fiber, 6 g pro.

Peppermint-Cocoa Warmer

A splash of peppermint schnapps makes this soothing concoction hard to resist.

Start to Finish: 30 minutes
Makes: 8 (5- to 6-ounce) servings

- **6 tablespoons sugar**
- **6 tablespoons unsweetened cocoa powder**
- **Dash salt**
- **2½ cups whole milk**

2½ cups half-and-half or light cream
½ teaspoon vanilla
Dash ground cinnamon
Whipped cream
8 tablespoons peppermint schnapps (optional)
Peppermint sticks (optional)
Marshmallows (optional)

1. In a medium saucepan combine sugar, cocoa powder, and salt. Whisk in milk. Cook and stir over medium heat until sugar and cocoa powder dissolve. Stir in half-and-half, vanilla, and cinnamon; heat through (do not boil).

2. Serve in mugs topped with whipped cream. If desired, add 1 tablespoon peppermint schnapps to each serving. If desired, serve with peppermint sticks and marshmallows.

Per serving: 223 cal., 14 g total fat (9 g sat. fat), 46 mg chol., 82 mg sodium, 18 g carbo., 0 g fiber, 6 g pro.

Peppermint-Cocoa Warmer

Orange-Kissed Eggnog

Orange-Kissed Eggnog

Add rays of holiday cheer by using a star-shaped cutter on a piece of orange peel to garnish this drink.

Prep: 5 minutes **Makes:** 8 (5-ounce) servings

1 quart eggnog
1 cup pulp-free orange juice
Whipped cream
Orange peel stars (optional)

1. Combine eggnog and orange juice. Top each serving with whipped cream and, if desired, an orange peel star.

Per serving: 211 cal., 12 g total fat (7 g sat. fat), 85 mg chol., 72 mg sodium, 21 g carbo., 0 g fiber, 5 g pro.

breakfast and brunch

After the excitement of opening presents, an easygoing sit-down breakfast or help-yourself buffet is a relaxed way to celebrate Christmas morning. Select from oven-ready egg dishes, cakes fresh from the griddle, or colorful fruit compotes to warm guests' spirits on this festive day.

Apple Butter Hot Cakes,
page 60

Cheddar-Bacon Wake-Up Casserole

Cheddar-Bacon Wake-Up Casserole

This dish is perfect for entertaining brunch guests. Make it oven-ready up to 24 hours in advance to ease the last-minute crunch when serving a crowd.

Prep: 25 minutes **Bake:** 25 minutes
Stand: 5 minutes **Chill:** 8 hours **Oven:** 350°F
Makes: 6 servings

4 ounces dry French bread, cut into ¾-inch cubes (4 cups)
1½ cups shredded cheddar cheese (6 ounces)
4 slices bacon, crisp-cooked, drained and crumbled, or 1 cup diced cooked ham
2 cups milk
4 eggs, lightly beaten
2 tablespoons snipped fresh Italian (flat-leaf) parsley
½ teaspoon prepared mustard
¼ teaspoon ground black pepper
⅛ teaspoon onion powder

1. In a large bowl toss together the bread cubes, cheddar cheese, and cooked bacon. Divide among six 10-ounce individual casseroles or place all of the mixture in a 2-quart baking dish.

2. In a medium bowl whisk together milk, eggs, parsley, mustard, pepper, and onion powder. Pour over the bread mixture in the individual casseroles or 2-quart baking dish. Cover and chill at least 8 hours or up to 24 hours.

3. Preheat oven to 350°F. Bake, uncovered, for 25 to 30 minutes for individual casseroles (about 40 minutes for 2-quart dish) or until a knife inserted near center comes out clean. Let stand for 5 minutes before serving.

Per serving: 287 cal., 17 g total fat (9 g sat. fat), 183 mg chol., 507 mg sodium, 15 g carbo., 1 g fiber, 18 g pro.

Mushroom-Sweet Pepper Variation: Cook 2 cups sliced fresh mushrooms and ¼ cup chopped onion in 1 tablespoon hot olive oil over medium heat for 5 minutes or until onion is tender, stirring occasionally. Stir mushroom mixture and ¼ cup chopped roasted red sweet pepper into bread mixture before putting into casseroles or baking dish. Continue as directed.

Sausage and Provolone Variation: Substitute 1½ cups shredded provolone cheese or shredded Italian cheese blend for the cheddar, and 1 cup chopped fully cooked turkey Italian sausage links for the bacon. Substitute basil for the parsley.

Greek Variation: Omit the bacon and substitute 6 ounces feta cheese. Substitute ¼ cup shredded Parmesan cheese for the cheddar cheese. Stir in 1 cup drained and chopped canned or marinated artichoke hearts, ¼ cup chopped green onions, and 2 tablespoons chopped kalamata olives (optional) into bread mixture before pouring mixture into casseroles or baking dish.

Hearty Potato and Sausage Casserole

Herbs, onions, and cheese spruce up sliced potatoes and sausage. This dish makes a great partner for scrambled eggs. Add fruit and cinnamon rolls to round out the meal.

Prep: 30 minutes **Bake:** 20 minutes
Cook: 12 minutes **Oven:** 350°F **Makes:** 8 servings

- **3 large long white potatoes (about 1½ pounds), peeled and cut into ¼-inch slices (about 5 cups)**
- **3 tablespoons butter or margarine**
- **2 cups chopped onion**
- **1 tablespoon dried parsley flakes, crushed**
- **½ teaspoon garlic salt**
- **½ teaspoon ground black pepper**
- **½ teaspoon dried thyme, crushed**
- **½ teaspoon dried sage, crushed**
- **¼ teaspoon dried rosemary, crushed**
- **1 pound bulk pork sausage**
- **2 cups shredded Swiss cheese (8 ounces) or 8 ounces sliced Swiss cheese**

1. In a covered large saucepan cook potatoes in lightly salted, boiling water for 12 to 15 minutes or just until tender. Drain.

2. Preheat oven to 350°F. In a large heavy skillet, melt butter over medium-high heat. Add potatoes and onion; cook until potatoes are lightly browned, turning often. Add parsley flakes, garlic salt, pepper, thyme, sage, and rosemary; toss lightly. Spoon mixture into an ungreased 3-quart rectangular baking pan.

3. In the same skillet cook sausage over medium-low heat until cooked through, using a wooden spoon to break up sausage as it cooks; drain off fat. Spread the cooked sausage over potato mixture. Sprinkle evenly with shredded cheese, or arrange cheese slices over sausage.

4. Bake, uncovered, for 20 to 25 minutes or until heated through.

Per serving: 423 cal., 29 g total fat (13 g sat. fat), 76 mg chol., 549 mg sodium, 24 g carbo., 2 g fiber, 16 g pro.

Eggs, Sausage, and Polenta with Pomodoro Sauce

The red Pomodoro Sauce imparts a holiday look to this one-dish meal.

Prep: 25 minutes **Bake:** 35 minutes
Cook: 10 minutes **Chill:** 4 to 24 hours
Oven: 350°F **Makes:** 8 servings

- **8 eggs**
- **1 16-ounce tube refrigerated cooked polenta (desired flavor), cut in ½-inch slices**
- **6 ounces bulk hot or Italian sausage**
- **1 recipe Pomodoro Sauce**
- **Shaved Parmesan cheese (optional)**
- **Snipped fresh thyme (optional)**
- **Salt and ground black pepper (optional)**

1. Lightly grease a very large skillet. Half-fill the skillet with water. Bring water to boiling; reduce heat to simmering (bubbles should begin to break the surface of the water). Break one of the eggs into a measuring cup. Holding the lip of the cup as close to the water as possible, carefully slide egg into simmering water. Repeat with remaining eggs, allowing each egg an equal amount of space.

2. Simmer eggs, uncovered, for 3 to 5 minutes or until the whites are completely set and yolks begin to thicken but are not hard. Use a slotted spoon to immediately transfer eggs to a baking dish half-filled with ice water. When cooled, use the slotted spoon to transfer eggs to a plate.

3. Grease a 3-quart rectangular baking dish. Place polenta slices in prepared pan or dish. Top polenta slices with sausage pieces, Pomodoro Sauce, and cooked eggs. Cover with plastic wrap and chill for at least 4 hours or up to 24 hours.

4. To serve, preheat oven to 350°F. Remove plastic wrap from baking dish; recover with foil. Bake, covered, for 35 to 40 minutes or until heated through. If desired, garnish with Parmesan cheese and sprinkle with thyme, salt, and pepper.

Pomodoro Sauce: In a medium saucepan cook 1 medium chopped onion and 3 cloves minced garlic in 1 tablespoon hot olive oil until tender. Stir in one 14½-ounce can undrained diced tomatoes, 1 tablespoon balsamic vinegar, 1 teaspoon crushed Italian seasoning, ¼ teaspoon salt, and ¼ teaspoon crushed red pepper. Bring to boiling; reduce heat and simmer about 20 minutes or to desired consistency. Let cool. Makes about 2 cups.

Per serving: 230 cal., 13 g total fat (5 g sat. fat), 220 mg chol., 639 mg sodium, 17 g carbo., 3 g fiber, 11 g pro.

Spinach Breakfast Casserole

Spinach and carrots add extra colorful nutrients to this make-ahead favorite. For variety, substitute frozen kale or chopped broccoli for spinach.

Prep: 30 minutes **Bake:** 55 minutes
Stand: 10 minutes **Chill:** 8 to 24 hours
Oven: 325°F **Makes:** 12 servings

- **4 cups seasoned croutons (about 7 ounces)**
- **1 pound bulk pork sausage, cooked and well drained**
- **1 10-ounce package frozen chopped spinach, thawed and well drained**
- **½ cup coarsely shredded carrot**
- **4 eggs, beaten**
- **2 cups milk**
- **1 10¾-ounce can condensed cream of mushroom soup**
- **1 cup shredded cheddar cheese (4 ounces)**
- **1 cup shredded Monterey Jack cheese (4 ounces)**
- **1 4-ounce can (drained weight) sliced mushrooms, drained**
- **¼ teaspoon dry mustard**
- **Shredded cheddar and/or Monterey Jack cheese (optional)**

1. Spread croutons in an ungreased 3-quart rectangular baking pan. Spread sausage over croutons. Sprinkle spinach and carrot over sausage.

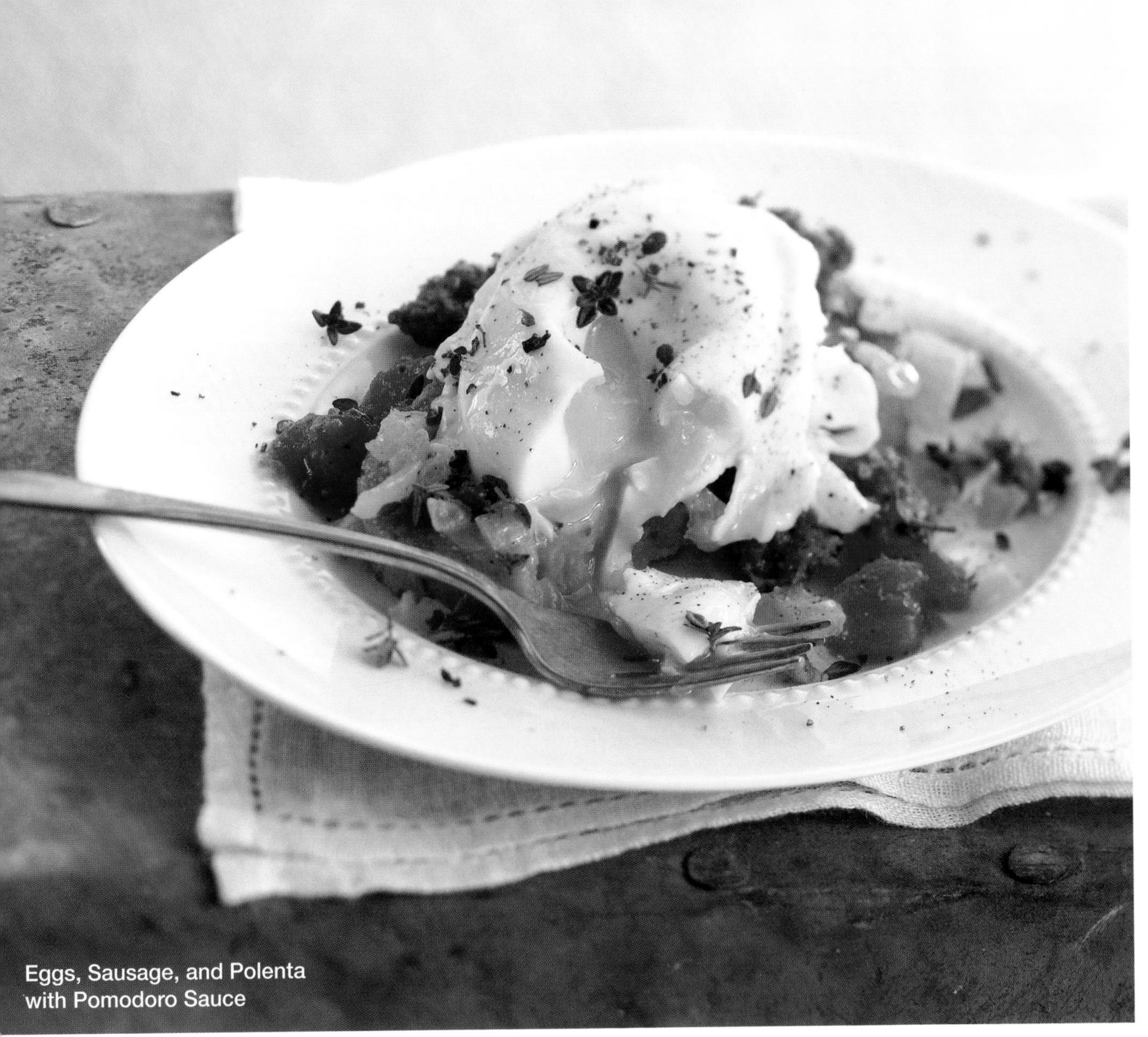

Eggs, Sausage, and Polenta with Pomodoro Sauce

2. In a medium bowl stir together eggs, milk, cream of mushroom soup, the 1 cup cheddar cheese, the 1 cup Monterey Jack cheese, mushrooms, and dry mustard until well mixed. Pour egg mixture evenly over ingredients in pan or dish. Press down lightly with a rubber spatula or the back of a large spoon to moisten all of the croutons. Cover and chill at least 8 hours or up to 24 hours.

3. Preheat oven to 325°F. Bake, uncovered, for 45 minutes. If desired, sprinkle with additional cheese. Bake about 10 minutes or until edges are bubbly and center is heated through. Let stand for 10 minutes before serving.

Per serving: 346 cal., 24 g total fat (10 g sat. fat), 115 mg chol., 754 mg sodium, 15 g carbo., 2 g fiber, 15 g pro.

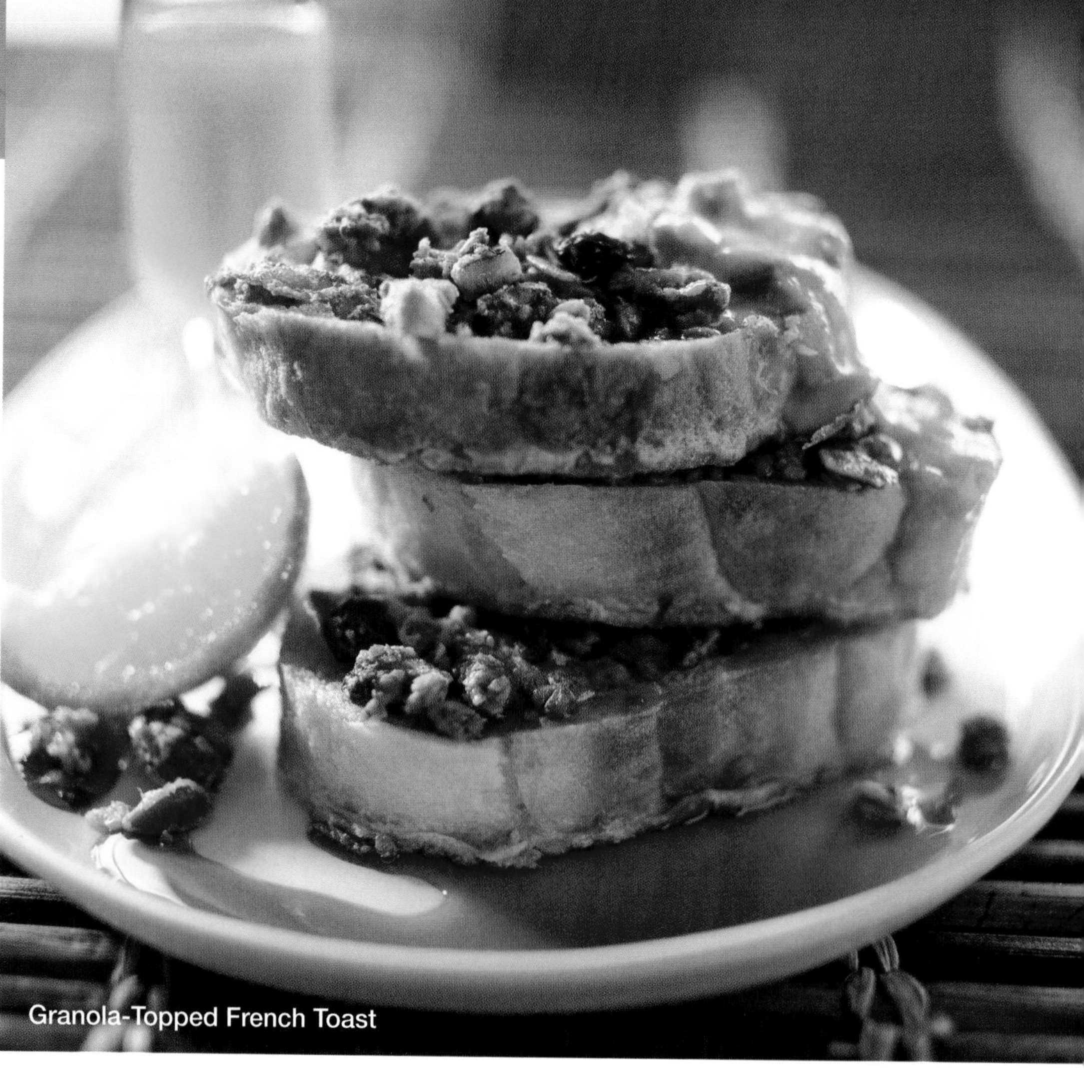

Granola-Topped French Toast

Granola-Topped French Toast

The granola develops a nutty, toasted flavor as the bread cooks. Flip the slices and serve them granola sides up.

Start to Finish: 40 minutes **Makes:** 4 servings

- **3 eggs, lightly beaten**
- **¾ cup milk**
- **1 tablespoon sugar**
- **1 tablespoon finely shredded orange peel**
- **½ teaspoon vanilla**
- **¼ teaspoon ground cinnamon**
- **12 ½-inch bias slices baguette-style French bread**
- **2 tablespoons butter**
- **1 cup granola, coarsely crushed**
- **1 recipe Cinnamon-Yogurt Sauce**
- **Maple syrup**

1. In a shallow bowl whisk together eggs, milk, sugar, 1½ teaspoons of the orange peel, vanilla, and cinnamon. Dip bread slices into egg mixture, coating both sides.

2. In a skillet or on a griddle melt 1 tablespoon of the butter over medium heat; add half of the bread slices. Sprinkle some of the granola on top of each bread slice in the skillet, pressing each slice gently with a spatula so granola sticks. Cook for 2 to 3 minutes or until bottom is golden brown. Turn over each slice, pressing lightly with the spatula. Cook for 2 minutes or until golden brown. Remove from pan and turn each slice so granola side is up.

3. Repeat with remaining butter, bread slices, and granola. Serve immediately with Cinnamon-Yogurt Sauce, remaining orange peel, and maple syrup.

Cinnamon-Yogurt Sauce: In a small bowl combine one 6-ounce carton plain low-fat yogurt, 1 tablespoon honey, ¼ teaspoon ground cinnamon, and ¼ teaspoon vanilla. Makes about ¾ cup.

Advance Preparation: Combine ingredients for the Cinnamon-Yogurt Sauce. Place in an airtight container and chill up to 24 hours.

Per serving: 679 cal., 17 g total fat (8 g sat. fat), 180 mg chol., 780 mg sodium, 110 g carbo., 4 g fiber, 22 g pro.

Pumpkin Waffles with Maple-Pecan Cream

Preheat your oven to 300°F at the same time you preheat your waffle baker. As you pull completed waffles from the baker, transfer them to the oven to stay warm until serving time.

Prep: 25 minutes **Bake:** according to waffle baker directions **Oven:** 300°F **Makes:** 12 to 14 servings

- **4 cups all-purpose flour**
- **¼ cup packed brown sugar**
- **2 tablespoons baking powder**
- **1 teaspoon ground cinnamon**
- **½ teaspoon ground ginger**
- **½ teaspoon ground nutmeg**
- **4 eggs**
- **3 cups milk**
- **1 15-ounce can pumpkin puree**
- **¼ cup butter, melted**
- **1 recipe Maple-Pecan Cream**

1. Lightly grease waffle baker. Preheat waffle baker. Preheat oven to 300°F.

2. In a large bowl stir together flour, brown sugar, baking powder, cinnamon, ginger, nutmeg, and 1 teaspoon *salt.* Make a well in the center of the flour mixture. In another bowl beat eggs lightly; stir in milk, pumpkin, and butter. Add pumpkin mixture all at once to flour mixture. Stir just until moistened (batter should be slightly lumpy).

3. Pour 1 to 1¼ cups batter (or amount suggested in waffle baker directions) onto grids of the preheated waffle baker. Close lid quickly; do not open until done. Bake according to manufacturer's directions. When baked, use a fork to lift waffle off grid. Reserve in oven until all waffles are baked. Repeat with remaining batter. Serve warm with Maple-Pecan Cream.

Maple-Pecan Cream: In a medium saucepan melt 1 tablespoon butter over medium heat. Add ¾ cup coarsely chopped pecans. Cook and stir for 1 to 2 minutes or until pecans are toasted. Stir in 1½ cups pure maple syrup and ½ cup whipping cream; heat through. Makes 2½ cups.

Per serving: 465 cal., 17 g total fat (7 g sat. fat), 102 mg chol., 408 mg sodium, 70 g carbo., 3 g fiber, 10 g pro.

Sausage and Fontina Frittata

If you don't have a broilerproof skillet, wrap the handle with foil before broiling.

Start to Finish: 30 minutes **Makes:** 4 servings

- **Nonstick cooking spray**
- **½ cup thinly sliced fennel**
- **8 ounces bulk Italian sausage**
- **½ of a medium red sweet pepper, cut into bite-size strips**
- **2 cloves garlic, minced**
- **8 eggs, lightly beaten**
- **¼ cup half-and-half, light cream or milk**
- **1 tablespoon chopped fresh marjoram or 1 teaspoon dried marjoram, crushed**
- **2 ounces fontina cheese, shredded**

1. Preheat broiler. Coat a large broilerproof skillet with nonstick cooking spray. Heat skillet over medium heat. Cook fennel 5 minutes. Add sausage, sweet pepper, and garlic to the skillet. Cook and stir 10 minutes or until sausage is no loner pink and vegetables are tender. Drain fat, if necessary.

2. Meanwhile, in a medium bowl beat together eggs, half-and-half, and marjoram. Stir in cheese. Pour egg mixture over sausage mixture in skillet. Cook over medium heat. As mixture sets, run a spatula around the skillet edge, lifting egg mixture so uncooked portion flows underneath. Continue cooking and lifting edges until egg mixture is almost set (surface will be moist). Reduce heat as necessary to prevent overcooking.

3. Broil 4 to 5 inches from heat for 1 to 2 minutes or until top is set. Cut into quarters to serve.

Per serving: 429 cal., 32 g total fat (15 g sat. fat), 483 mg chol., 772 mg sodium, 6 g carbo., 1 g fiber, 29 g pro.

Puff Pancake with Minted Grapes and Nectarines

Puff Pancake with Minted Grapes and Nectarines

This puff pancake deflates after baking to form a bowl just right for filling with luscious fresh fruit.

Prep: 10 minutes **Bake:** 20 minutes
Oven: 400°F **Makes:** 6 servings

- ¼ cup butter
- 3 eggs
- ½ cup all-purpose flour
- ½ cup milk
- ¼ teaspoon salt
- 2 tablespoons packed brown sugar
- ½ teaspoon finely shredded lemon peel
- 1½ cups red seedless grapes, halved
- 2 small nectarines, pitted and sliced (1½ cups)
- 1 teaspoon snipped fresh mint
- Powdered sugar (optional)

1. Preheat oven to 400°F. Place 2 tablespoons of the butter in a 10-inch ovenproof skillet. Place in oven for 3 to 5 minutes or until butter melts. Meanwhile, for batter, in a medium bowl use a wire whisk or rotary beater to beat eggs until combined. Add flour, milk, and salt; beat until mixture is smooth. Immediately pour batter into the hot skillet. Bake for 20 to 25 minutes or until edges are puffed and pancake is well browned.

2. Meanwhile, in a medium saucepan melt remaining 2 tablespoons butter over medium-low heat. Stir in brown sugar and lemon peel, stirring until sugar dissolves. Stir in grapes, nectarines and mint; heat through. Fill pancake with fruit mixture. Cut into wedges and serve warm. If desired, top with powdered sugar.

Per serving: 200 cal., 11 g total fat (6 g sat. fat), 128 mg chol., 197 mg sodium, 21 g carbo., 1 g fiber, 5 g pro.

Strawberry-Cream Cheese-Stuffed French Toast

Any fruit combination can be used for this extraordinary french toast. Try raspberries, peaches, and apricots.

Prep: 20 minutes **Cook:** 4 minutes per batch
Oven: 250°F **Makes:** 10 to 12 slices (5 or 6 servings)

- **1 8-ounce package cream cheese, softened**
- **3 tablespoons strawberry preserves**
- **¼ teaspoon almond extract**
- **½ cup chopped almonds, toasted**
- **1 16-ounce loaf French bread**
- **4 eggs, lightly beaten**
- **1 cup half-and-half or light cream**
- **1 tablespoon amaretto or ¼ teaspoon almond extract**
- **3 cups sliced fresh strawberries**
- **¼ cup powdered sugar**
- **Powdered sugar**

1. Preheat oven to 250°F. In a medium bowl beat cream cheese, strawberry preserves, and almond extract with an electric mixer on medium speed until fluffy. Stir in almonds; set aside.

2. Cut bread into 10 to 12 one-inch-thick slices. Cut a pocket in the top crust of each bread slice, about 2 inches deep, being careful not to cut all the way to the sides. Divide cream cheese mixture evenly among pockets. Set aside.

3. In a medium bowl whisk together eggs, half-and-half, and amaretto. Using tongs, quickly dip the filled bread slices in the egg mixture, allowing excess mixture to drip off (making sure not to squeeze out the filling). Cook on a lightly greased griddle over medium heat about 4 minutes or until golden brown, turning once. Keep warm in oven while cooking the remaining slices.

4. In a medium bowl toss together sliced strawberries and ¼ cup powdered sugar. Let stand until sugar dissolves and forms a syrup. Spoon strawberries over French toast. Sift additional powdered sugar over each serving.

Per serving: 699 cal., 32 g total fat (15 g sat. fat), 237 mg chol., 805 mg sodium, 82 g carbo., 5 g fiber, 23 g pro.

Tropical Breakfast Ambrosia

Island fruits and nuts are a natural combination for this ambrosia. When heated, they become even more fragrant and are a perfect accompaniment to muffins or scones.

Prep: 25 minutes **Bake:** 30 minutes
Oven: 350°F **Makes:** 8 to 10 servings

- **1 medium fresh pineapple, peeled, cored, and cut into bite-size pieces (about 4½ cups)**
- **1 11-ounce can mandarin oranges, drained**
- **1 medium mango, peeled, seeded, and cut into ½-inch pieces**
- **1 cup frozen unsweetened pitted dark sweet cherries, thawed**
- **2 tablespoons amaretto (optional)**
- **2 medium bananas, cut into ½-inch slices**
- **1 cup flaked coconut**
- **½ cup chopped macadamia nuts or sliced almonds**

1. Preheat oven to 350°F. In a large bowl combine pineapple, mandarin oranges, mango, cherries, and, if desired, amaretto. Spoon pineapple mixture into an ungreased 3-quart rectangular baking pan.

2. Bake, uncovered, for 15 minutes. Stir in bananas. Sprinkle with coconut and macadamia nuts. Bake about 15 minutes or until fruit is heated through and coconut and nuts are golden brown. Serve warm, spooning some of the liquid in the pan or dish over fruit.

Per serving: 241 cal., 12 g total fat (6 g sat. fat), 0 mg chol., 71 mg sodium, 36 g carbo., 5 g fiber, 3 g pro.

Honey-Rum Fruit Compote

Honey-Rum Fruit Compote

A dressing of mint, lime juice, rum, and honey bathes fresh fruits with pick-me-up flavor.

Prep: 25 minutes **Stand:** 15 minutes
Makes: 8 servings

- **¼ cup snipped fresh mint**
- **¼ cup lime juice**
- **¼ cup rum or orange juice**
- **¼ cup honey**
- **1 large cantaloupe or honeydew melon**
- **1 16-ounce container fresh strawberries, hulled and halved or quartered**
- **1½ cups green and/or red seedless grapes**
- **4 kiwifruits and/or golden kiwifruits, peeled and cut into ½-inch pieces**

1. For dressing, in a large bowl whisk together mint, lime juice, rum, and honey; set aside.

2. Cut cantaloupe in half and remove the seeds. Use a melon baller to scoop out pulp. Add melon balls, strawberries, grapes, and kiwifruits to dressing; toss lightly to coat. Let stand for 15 minutes to allow flavors to blend. Serve in glasses or small bowls.

Advance Preparation: Prepare as directed. Cover and chill up to 3 hours.

Per serving: 135 cal., 1 g total fat (0 g sat. fat), 0 mg chol., 14 mg sodium, 30 g carbo., 3 g fiber, 2 g pro.

Morning Pecan Casserole

A crunchy, praline layer tops this easy, make-ahead brunch dish. The recipe features pieces of sausage patties in a raisin bread strata.

Prep: 25 minutes **Bake:** 45 minutes
Stand: 15 minutes **Chill:** 8 to 24 hours
Oven: 350°F **Makes:** 10 servings

- **1 7-ounce package brown-and-serve sausage patties**
- **12 slices raisin bread, cubed (about 8 cups)**
- **6 eggs**
- **3 cups milk**
- **1 teaspoon vanilla**
- **¼ teaspoon ground nutmeg**
- **¼ teaspoon ground cinnamon**
- **1 cup coarsely chopped pecans**
- **½ cup packed brown sugar**
- **¼ cup butter, softened**
- **2 tablespoons pure maple syrup or maple-flavor syrup**

1. Lightly grease a 3-quart rectangular baking pan; set aside. Brown the sausage patties according to package directions. Cut sausage patties into bite-size pieces. Spread bread cubes evenly in prepared pan or dish. Top with sausage pieces.

2. In a large bowl whisk together eggs, milk, vanilla, nutmeg, and cinnamon. Pour egg mixture evenly over bread and sausage. Press down lightly with a rubber spatula or the back of a large spoon to moisten all of the bread. Cover and chill for at least 8 hours or up to 24 hours.

3. Preheat oven to 350°F. For topping, in a small bowl combine pecans, brown sugar, butter, and syrup. Drop by teaspoonfuls over top of egg mixture.

4. Bake, uncovered, for 45 to 50 minutes or until a knife inserted near the center comes out clean (170°F). Let stand for 15 minutes before serving.

Per serving: 408 cal., 24 g total fat (7 g sat. fat), 162 mg chol., 386 mg sodium, 36 g carbo., 2 g fiber, 14 g pro.

Hot Biscuits and Sausage Gravy

Here is a good, hearty, stick-to-your-ribs Southern breakfast that will have everyone clamoring for more.

Prep: 30 minutes **Bake:** 10 minutes **Oven:** 450°F
Makes: 6 servings (10 biscuits)

- **3 cups all-purpose flour**
- **4 teaspoons baking powder**
- **1 tablespoon sugar**
- **1 teaspoon salt**
- **¾ teaspoon cream of tartar**
- **¾ cup butter (1½ sticks) or ½ cup butter (1 stick) and ¼ cup shortening**
- **1¼ cups buttermilk or sour milk* or 1 cup milk**
- **1 recipe Sausage Gravy**

1. Preheat oven to 450°F. In a large bowl stir together flour, baking powder, sugar, salt, and cream of tartar. Use a pastry blender to cut in butter until mixture resembles coarse crumbs. Make a well in the center of the flour mixture. Add buttermilk all at once. Use a fork to stir just until moistened.

2. Turn dough out onto a lightly floured surface. Knead dough by folding and gently pressing it for 4 to 6 strokes or just until dough holds together. Pat or lightly roll dough to ¾ inch thick. Cut dough with a floured 2½-inch biscuit cutter; reroll scraps as necessary and dip cutter into flour between cuts.

3. Place biscuits 1 inch apart on an ungreased baking sheet. Bake for 10 to 12 minutes or until golden. Remove biscuits from baking sheet.

4. To serve, split biscuits and place on serving plates. Top with Sausage Gravy. (Store remaining biscuits overnight in airtight container or bag.)

Sausage Gravy: In a heavy large skillet or cast-iron skillet, cook 12 ounces bulk pork sausage and 1 medium onion, chopped (½ cup), over medium-high heat until meat is brown and onion is tender, stirring occasionally. Do not drain; leave pan juices in skillet. Sprinkle 2 tablespoons all-purpose flour over meat mixture. Whisk the flour into the meat mixture. Cook and stir over medium heat for 1 minute. While whisking, gradually add 1½ cups milk. Cook and stir until thickened and bubbly. Cook and stir for 1 minute. Season to taste with salt and black pepper. Makes about 3 cups.

***Test Kitchen Note:** To make 1¼ cups sour milk, place 4 teaspoons lemon juice or vinegar in a glass measuring cup. Add enough milk to make 1¼ cups total liquid; stir. Let mixture stand for 5 minutes before using.

Per serving: 506 cal., 32 g total fat (16 g sat. fat), 81 mg chol., 1,027 mg sodium, 40 g carbo., 1 g fiber, 11 g pro.

Apple Butter Hot Cakes

Make the flavored butter and cherry sauce ahead, then set the butter out and warm the sauce while cooking the hot cakes. *Pictured on page 49.*

Prep: 25 minutes **Cook:** 4 minutes per batch
Makes: 32 to 40 mini size or 8 to 10 standard size hot cakes

- **½ cup butter, softened**
- **¼ cup honey**
- **¼ teaspoon ground cinnamon**
- **1 12-ounce package frozen pitted light or dark sweet cherries**
- **½ cup cherry jam or cherry preserves**
- **1 teaspoon finely shredded orange peel**
- **1½ cups packaged regular or buttermilk pancake mix (not the just-add-water pancake mix)**
- **¾ cup milk**
- **2 tablespoons vegetable oil**
- **2 eggs, lightly beaten**
- **½ cup purchased apple butter**

1. For honey- and cinnamon-flavored butter, use a small whisk to combine softened butter, honey, and cinnamon. Whisk until well combined. Set aside.

2. For cherry sauce, in a medium saucepan combine frozen cherries, cherry jam, and orange peel. Bring to boiling over medium heat, stirring frequently; reduce heat. Simmer, uncovered, for 10 minutes or until sauce thickens slightly. Cover and set aside; keep warm.

3. In a medium bowl stir together pancake mix, milk, vegetable oil, eggs, and apple butter. Stir just until moistened (batter should still be lumpy). For mini-size hot cakes, spread about 1 tablespoon batter into a 1½-inch circle onto a hot lightly greased griddle or heavy skillet. (For standard-size hot cakes, spread about ¼ cup batter into a 4-inch circle.) Cook over medium heat about 2 minutes on each side or until hot cakes are golden brown, turning to second sides when hot cake surface bubbles and edges are slightly dry. Serve warm with flavored butter and cherry sauce.

Per hot cake: 114 cal., 4 g total fat (2 g sat. fat), 21 mg chol., 100 mg sodium, 18 g carbo., 1 g fiber, 1 g pro.

Caramel Apple Punch

The mellow-sweet taste of this brunch drink will remind you of a caramel apple. Be sure to use caramel sauce; it is a little thicker and richer in flavor than ice cream topping.

Prep: 10 minutes **Makes:** 8 servings

- **1½ cups apple cider, chilled**
- **3 tablespoons caramel-flavor dessert sauce**
- **1 tablespoon lemon juice**
- **1 750-milliliter bottle sparkling cider, chilled**
- **Apple wedges (optional)**

1. In a small pitcher stir together apple cider, caramel sauce, and lemon juice. Divide mixture among eight fluted glasses. Pour sparkling cider into glasses. If desired, garnish with apple wedges. Serve immediately.

Per serving: 101 cal., 0 g total fat, 0 mg chol., 22 mg sodium, 25 g carbo., 0 g fiber, 1 g pro.

Caramel Apple Punch

Chai

Offer breakfast guests steaming cups of this chocolaty rich spiced milk-and-tea favorite.

Start to Finish: 15 minutes **Makes:** 8 servings

- **2 cups water**
- **4 black tea bags, such as orange pekoe, English breakfast, Lapsang souchong, or Darjeeling**
- **4 3-inch pieces stick cinnamon**
- **8 cups milk**
- **½ cup raw sugar or honey**
- **1 tablespoon vanilla**
- **½ teaspoon ground ginger**
- **½ teaspoon ground cardamom**
- **Ground cinnamon (optional)**
- **Stick cinnamon (optional)**

1. In a large saucepan combine the water, tea bags, and cinnamon sticks. Bring to boiling. Remove from heat. Let stand, covered, for 5 minutes. Remove and discard tea bags and cinnamon sticks.

2. Stir milk, sugar, vanilla, ginger, and cardamom into tea. Cook and stir over medium heat just until mixture is heated through (do not boil). To serve, pour hot mixture into warm mugs. If desired, sprinkle with ground cinnamon and add a cinnamon stick.

Per about 10-ounce serving: 175 cal., 5 g total fat (3 g sat. fat), 18 mg chol., 124 mg sodium, 24 g carbo., 0 g fiber, 8 g pro.

Chocolate Chai: Prepare as directed, except stir 1 tablespoon unsweetened Dutch-process cocoa powder in with the milk and spices. Heat through. Serve with whipped cream. If desired, sprinkle with ground nutmeg.

Chai

Triple Berry-Lime Smoothies

Make as few or as many batches of this refreshing drink as needed, depending on the number of guests.

Start to Finish: 10 minutes **Makes:** 2 servings

- **1 to 1½ cups cranberry juice, chilled**
- **1 cup frozen unsweetened raspberries**
- **1 cup frozen unsweetened whole strawberries**
- **1 tablespoon lime juice**
- **1 to 2 tablespoons honey**

1. In a blender combine cranberry juice, raspberries, strawberries, lime juice, and honey. Cover and blend until smooth.

Per serving: 149 cal., 1 g total fat (0 g sat. fat), 0 mg chol., 20 mg sodium, 38 g carbo., 2 g fiber, 1 g pro.

holiday breads

Fill your kitchen with the aroma of fresh bread baking. Start with tender muffins and coffee cakes, ooey gooey sticky rolls, and flavorful nut breads that are perfect for brunches, family feasts, and even gift giving. Make-ahead directions streamline baking during this busy season.

Jumbo Coffee Cake Muffins, page 66

Blueberry Streusel Coffee Cake

Blueberry Streusel Coffee Cake

Try other seasonal fruits, such as sliced peeled apples or pears in this moist, tender quick bread. Use just enough sliced fruit to cover the entire surface of the cake batter and then top with the streusel.

Prep: 30 minutes **Bake:** 35 minutes
Oven: 350°F **Makes:** 16 servings

- **1½ cups packed brown sugar**
- **1 cup coarsely chopped nuts**
- **4 teaspoons ground cinnamon**
- **1 8-ounce carton dairy sour cream**
- **1 teaspoon baking soda**
- **¾ cup granulated sugar**
- **½ cup butter, softened**
- **3 eggs**
- **1 teaspoon vanilla**
- **2 cups all-purpose flour**
- **1½ teaspoons baking powder**
- **2 cups fresh or frozen blueberries, thawed**
- **1 recipe Powdered Sugar Icing**

1. Preheat oven to 350°F. For topping, in a small bowl stir together brown sugar, nuts, and cinnamon. Set aside. In another small bowl stir together sour cream and baking soda. Set aside. Grease a 13×9×2-inch baking pan; set aside.

2. In a large mixing bowl beat granulated sugar and butter with an electric mixer on medium speed until well mixed. Beat in eggs and vanilla. Beat in flour and baking powder until well mixed. Add the sour cream mixture; beat until combined.

3. Spread half of the batter evenly in the prepared pan. Sprinkle blueberries over batter. Sprinkle half of the topping over the blueberries. Drop remaining batter into large mounds on top of filling. Carefully spread batter over the topping and blueberries. Sprinkle the remaining topping over batter.

4. Bake for 35 to 40 minutes or until a wooden toothpick inserted near the center comes out clean. Drizzle with Powdered Sugar Icing. Serve warm or let cool on a wire rack.

Powdered Sugar Icing: Stir together ½ cup powdered sugar, 2 teaspoons milk, and ¼ teaspoon vanilla. Stir in enough additional milk, 1 teaspoon at a time, to make an icing of drizzling consistency.

Advance Preparation: Prepare and bake as directed. Cool completely; do not add icing. Cover pan with heavy foil. Freeze up to 1 month. Bake, covered, in a 350°F oven for 25 to 30 minutes or until heated. Drizzle with icing as directed.

Per serving: 345 cal., 14 g total fat (6 g sat. fat), 61 mg chol., 184 mg sodium, 51 g carbo., 2 g fiber, 4 g pro.

Dreamy Cinnamon Breakfast Rolls

No one will suspect these rolls are made using a cake mix!

Prep: 30 minutes **Rise:** 1 hour **Bake:** 25 minutes
Stand: 40 minutes **Chill:** 8 to 24 hours
Oven: 350°F **Makes:** 32 rolls

- **1 package 2-layer French vanilla cake mix**
- **5½ to 6 cups all-purpose flour**
- **2 packages active dry yeast**
- **2½ cups warm water (120°F to 130°F)**
- **¼ cup butter, softened**
- **¾ cup granulated sugar**
- **1 tablespoon ground cinnamon**
- **1⅓ cups packed brown sugar**
- **1 cup butter**
- **2 tablespoons light-color corn syrup**
- **1½ cups chopped walnuts**

1. In a large bowl combine dry cake mix, 2 cups of the flour, the yeast, and 1 teaspoon *salt.* Add warm water; beat with electric mixer on low speed until combined, scraping side of bowl. Beat on high speed for 3 minutes.

2. Stir in as much of the remaining flour as possible. Turn dough out onto a floured surface. Knead in enough of the remaining flour to make a smooth dough (about 3 minutes total; dough will still be slightly sticky). Place dough in a large greased bowl. Cover and let rise in a warm place until double in size (about 1 hour).

3. Punch down dough. Turn dough out onto a well-floured surface. Divide dough in half. Cover and let stand for 10 minutes. Roll each dough portion into a 9×16-inch rectangle. Spread each rectangle with half of the ¼ cup butter. Combine granulated sugar and cinnamon; sprinkle over top. Starting from a long side, roll each rectangle into a spiral. Pinch seams to seal. Cut each spiral into 1-inch slices.

4. In a saucepan combine brown sugar, 1 cup butter, and corn syrup. Bring to boiling. Remove from heat; divide between two 13×9×2-inch baking pans. Sprinkle nuts evenly over syrup mixture. Place half of dough slices, cut side down, into each pan. Cover; chill at least 8 hours or up to 24 hours.

5. Let pans or dishes of rolls stand at room temperature for 30 minutes. Meanwhile, preheat oven to 350°F. Bake, uncovered, about 25 minutes or until golden brown. Let cool in pans on wire racks for 10 minutes. Turn out onto foil. Serve warm or cool.

Advance Preparation: Prepare and bake as directed. Cool completely. Cover and store at room temperature up to 8 hours or wrap and freeze up to 3 months. Thaw rolls, if frozen, before serving.

Per roll: 298 cal., 13 g total fat (0 g sat. fat), 21 mg chol., 258 mg sodium, 43 g carbo., 1 g fiber, 4 g pro.

Dreamy Cinnamon Breakfast Rolls

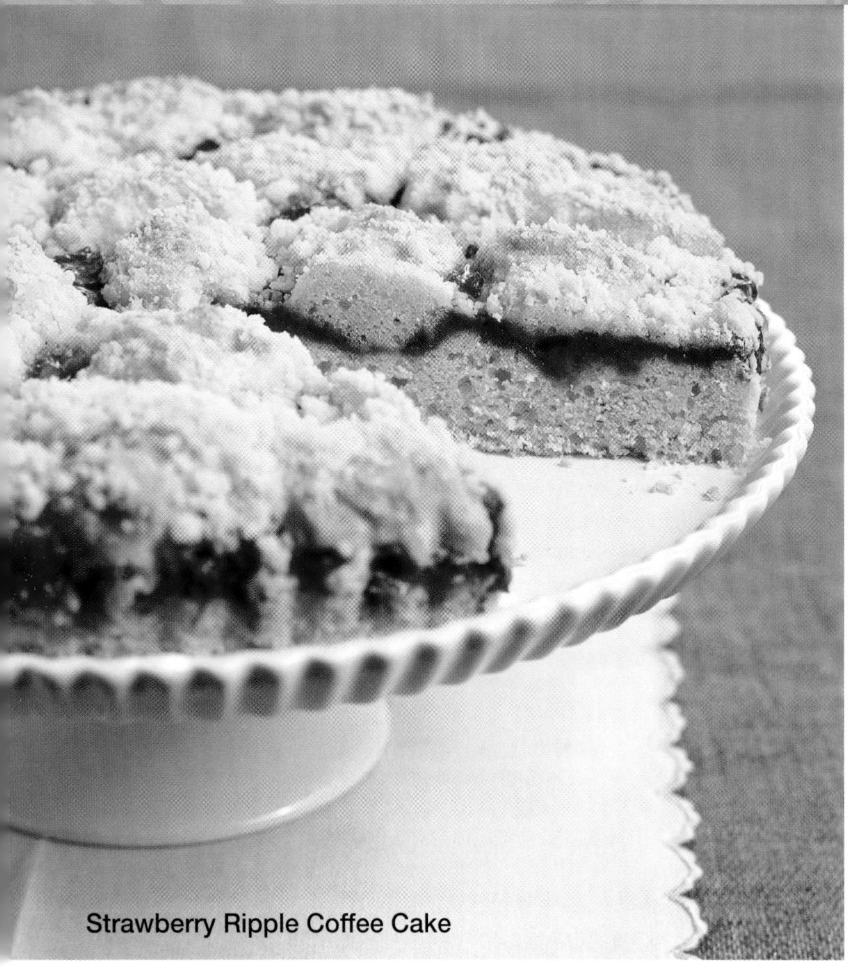
Strawberry Ripple Coffee Cake

Strawberry Ripple Coffee Cake

Enjoy this classic cake and berry combination in the winter months by using frozen sweetened strawberries in the filling.

Prep: 30 minutes **Bake:** 30 minutes
Oven: 350°F **Makes:** 12 servings

- **1 10-ounce package frozen sweetened sliced strawberries, thawed**
- **1 tablespoon cornstarch**
- **2¼ cups all-purpose flour**
- **¾ cup sugar**
- **¾ cup cold butter**
- **½ teaspoon baking powder**
- **½ teaspoon baking soda**
- **⅛ teaspoon salt**
- **1 egg**
- **¾ cup buttermilk**

1. Preheat oven to 350°F. Grease a 11×7×1½-inch baking pan; set aside.

2. For filling, in a small saucepan combine undrained strawberries and cornstarch. Cook and stir over medium heat until thickened and bubbly. Remove from heat. Set aside to cool slightly.

3. In a large bowl stir together flour and sugar. Use a pastry blender to cut in butter until mixture resembles coarse crumbs. Set aside ½ cup of the crumb mixture for the topping. Stir baking powder, baking soda, and salt into remaining crumb mixture; mix well. Make a well in the center of the crumb mixture.

4. In a small bowl beat egg lightly with a fork; stir in buttermilk. Add egg mixture all at once to crumb mixture. Stir just until moistened. Remove and set aside ½ cup of the dough. Spread remaining dough into the bottom of the prepared pan. Carefully spread the strawberry filling on top of the dough in the pan. Spoon the reserved dough in small mounds on top of the filling. Sprinkle with the reserved crumb topping.

5. Bake for 30 to 35 minutes or until a wooden toothpick inserted near the center comes out clean. Cool slightly in pan on a wire rack. Cut into squares and serve warm.

Advance Preparation: Prepare and bake as directed. Cool completely. Cover and store in refrigerator up to 3 days. To serve, let stand at room temperature for 45 minutes.

Per serving: 278 cal., 13 g total fat (8 g sat. fat), 49 mg chol., 191 mg sodium, 38 g carbo., 1 g fiber, 4 g pro.

Jumbo Coffee Cake Muffins

A rich ribbon of streusel fills the centers and decorates the tops of these muffins, pictured on page 63.

Prep: 20 minutes **Bake:** 25 minutes
Cool: 15 minutes **Oven:** 350°F **Makes:** 6 muffins

- **Nonstick cooking spray**
- **1½ cups all-purpose flour**
- **2 teaspoons baking powder**
- **¼ teaspoon baking soda**
- **¼ teaspoon salt**

¼ cup shortening
1 8-ounce carton dairy sour cream or plain yogurt
½ cup granulated sugar
½ cup milk
1 beaten egg
¼ cup packed brown sugar
¼ cup chopped nuts
2 tablespoons granulated sugar
1 teaspoon ground cinnamon

1. Preheat oven to 350°F. Lightly coat six jumbo (3½-inch) muffin cups with cooking spray or line with paper bake cups. Set aside.

2. In a mixing bowl combine flour, baking powder, baking soda, and salt. Use a pastry blender to cut in shortening until the mixture is crumbly. In another bowl stir together sour cream, the ½ cup granulated sugar, milk, and egg. Add to the flour mixture and stir just until combined.

3. In a small bowl stir together the brown sugar, nuts, the 2 tablespoons sugar, and cinnamon. Set aside.

4. Spoon half the batter into prepared muffin cups. Sprinkle half of the nut mixture into cups. Top with remaining batter and the remaining nut mixture. Bake for about 25 minutes or until a wooden toothpick inserted in center comes out clean. Cool for 15 minutes in pan on wire rack. Remove from pan and serve warm.

Advance Preparation: Prepare and bake as directed. Cool completely. Cover and store at room temperature up to 8 hours or wrap and freeze up to 3 months. Place frozen muffins on a baking sheet and bake in a 350°F oven for 10 minutes.

Per muffin: 436 cal., 21 g total fat (0 g sat. fat), 54 mg chol., 328 mg sodium, 56 g carbo., 1 g fiber, 7 g pro.

Standard Muffin Variation: Use twelve 2½-inch muffin cups; divide batter evenly among cups. Bake in a 400°F oven for 15 to 18 minutes. Cool for 5 minutes. Remove from pans and serve warm.

Pumpkin Currant Scones

Buttermilk has a thick creamy texture and rich buttery taste that make baked goods tender. For a sour milk substitute, mix 1½ teaspoons lemon juice with enough milk to equal ½ cup.

Prep: 25 minutes **Bake:** 12 minutes/batch
Oven: 400°F **Makes:** 18 scones

2½ cups all-purpose flour
¾ cup packed brown sugar
4 teaspoons pumpkin pie spice
2 teaspoons baking powder
½ teaspoon baking soda
½ cup butter
2 eggs
¾ cup canned pumpkin puree
½ cup dried currants or snipped raisins
½ cup buttermilk
1 egg white, lightly beaten
1 tablespoon water
Coarse or granulated sugar

1. Preheat oven to 400°F. Lightly grease two baking sheets; set aside. Stir together flour, brown sugar, pumpkin pie spice, baking powder, baking soda, and ½ teaspoon *salt.* Cut in butter until mixture resembles coarse crumbs. Make a well in the center of the flour mixture; set aside.

2. In a medium bowl stir together whole eggs, pumpkin puree, currants, and buttermilk. Add egg mixture to flour mixture all at once. Use a fork to stir just until moistened.

3. Drop dough in ¼-cup portions two inches apart on the prepared baking sheets. In a small bowl stir together egg white and water. Lightly brush scones with egg white mixture and sprinkle with coarse sugar. Bake about 12 minutes or until light brown. Remove scones from baking sheet; serve warm.

Advance Preparation: Prepare and bake as directed. Cool completely. Place scones in freezer container; cover. Freeze up to 3 months. Place frozen scones on a baking sheet and bake in a 400°F oven for 5 to 8 minutes or until warm.

Per scone: 173 cal., 6 g total fat (4 g sat. fat), 37 mg chol., 186 mg sodium, 27 g carbo., 1 g fiber, 4 g pro.

Apple-Walnut Scones

Remove scones easily from the baking sheet with the nonstick, smooth surface of parchment paper. For safety, trim the parchment paper to fit the baking sheet so it doesn't touch the oven rack or wall.

Prep: 15 minutes **Bake:** 15 minutes
Cool: 5 minutes **Oven:** 375°F **Makes:** 16 scones

- **2 cups all-purpose flour**
- **3 tablespoons sugar**
- **1 teaspoon ground cinnamon**
- **½ teaspoon baking powder**
- **⅛ teaspoon salt**
- **½ cup butter, chilled and cut into pieces**
- **1 cup chopped apple**
- **¾ cup chopped walnuts, toasted**
- **2 beaten eggs**
- **⅔ cup whipping cream**
- **1 beaten egg yolk**
- **1 tablespoon whipping cream**
- **Sugar**

Apple-Walnut Scones

1. Preheat oven to 375°F. Line a large baking sheet with parchment paper; set aside. In a large bowl combine flour, 3 tablespoons sugar, cinnamon, baking powder and salt. Use a pastry blender to cut in butter until mixture resembles coarse crumbs. Stir in apple and nuts.

2. In a small bowl combine 2 eggs and the ⅔ cup whipping cream. Add to flour mixture and stir until just moistened.

3. Use a ¼-cup ice cream scoop to scoop dough and place on prepared baking sheet. Don't flatten.

4. In a small bowl combine the egg yolk and 1 tablespoon whipping cream. Brush over the top of the scones. Sprinkle some additional sugar over the scones.

5. Bake for 15 to 17 minutes or until scones are lightly browned. Remove from baking sheet. Cool on wire rack 5 minutes; serve warm.

Advance Preparation: Prepare and bake as directed. Cool completely. Place scones in freezer container; cover. Freeze up to 3 months. Place frozen scones on a baking sheet and bake in a 350°F oven for 10 minutes or until warm.

Per scone: 208 cal., 14 g total fat (7 g sat. fat), 70 mg chol., 81 mg sodium, 17 g carbo., 1 g fiber, 4 g pro.

Orange-Date Muffins

Dates have a deep, rich flavor and texture that make them a wonderful sweetener. Shredded orange peel and orange juice play up the citrus theme, adding brightness and lightness to these breakfast breads.

Prep: 25 minutes **Bake:** 15 minutes
Oven: 375°F **Makes:** 12 muffins

- **1½ cups all-purpose flour**
- **½ cup sugar**
- **1 teaspoon baking powder**

½ **teaspoon baking soda**
½ **teaspoon salt**
1 **egg, lightly beaten**
½ **cup butter, melted**
2 **teaspoons finely shredded orange peel**
½ **cup orange juice**
½ **cup finely snipped pitted dates**

1. Preheat oven to 375° F. Line twelve 2½-inch muffin cups with paper bake cups. Set aside.

2. In a medium mixing bowl combine flour, sugar, baking powder, baking soda, and salt. Make a well in center of mixture.

3. In another bowl combine egg, melted butter, orange peel, and juice. Add egg mixture all at once to the dry mixture. Stir just until moistened (batter should be lumpy). Fold in dates. Spoon the muffin batter into the prepared muffin cups, filling each cup two-thirds full with batter.

4. Bake for 15 to 18 minutes or until golden and a wooden toothpick inserted in centers of muffins comes out clean. Cool in muffin cups on a wire rack for 5 minutes. Remove from muffin cups and serve warm.

Advance Preparation: Prepare and bake as directed. Cool completely. Layer muffins between sheets of waxed paper in an airtight container; cover. Freeze up to 3 months. Wrap muffins in heavy foil and reheat in 300°F oven for 15 to 18 minutes or until warm.

Per fruit-filled muffin: 188 cal., 8 g total fat (5 g sat. fat), 38 mg chol., 231 mg sodium, 27 g carbo., 1 g fiber, 2 g pro.

Peanut Butter-Streusel Muffins

For a hint of crunch, opt for chunky peanut butter rather than creamy.

Prep: 30 minutes **Bake:** 22 minutes
Oven: 375°F **Makes:** 12 muffins

1¼ **cups all-purpose flour**
¾ **cup packed brown sugar**
2 **tablespoons peanut butter**
3 **tablespoons butter**
¼ **cup chopped peanuts**
¼ **cup miniature semisweet chocolate pieces**
¼ **cup peanut butter**
½ **cup milk**
1 **egg**
1 **teaspoon baking powder**
¼ **teaspoon baking soda**
¼ **teaspoon salt**
¼ **cup miniature semisweet chocolate pieces**

1. Preheat oven to 375°F. Line twelve 2½-inch muffin cups with paper bake cups; set aside. For streusel topping, in a small bowl combine ¼ cup of the flour and ¼ cup of the brown sugar. Use a pastry blender to cut in the 2 tablespoons peanut butter and 1 tablespoon of the butter until crumbly. Stir in chopped peanuts and the ¼ cup miniature chocolate pieces; set aside.

2. In a large mixing bowl combine the remaining 2 tablespoons butter and the ¼ cup peanut butter; beat with an electric mixer on medium to high speed about 30 seconds or until combined. Add about ½ cup of the remaining flour, the remaining ½ cup brown sugar, half of the milk, egg, baking powder, baking soda, and salt. Beat with an electric mixer on low speed until combined, scraping the bowl constantly. Add the remaining ½ cup flour and the remaining ¼ cup milk. Beat on low to medium speed just until combined. Stir in the ¼ cup miniature chocolate pieces.

3. Spoon batter into prepared muffin cups, filling each two-thirds full. Sprinkle with the streusel topping. Bake for 22 to 25 minutes or until a wooden toothpick inserted near centers comes out clean.

4. Cool in muffin cups on a wire rack for 5 minutes. Remove from muffin cups and serve warm.

Advance Preparation: Prepare and bake as directed. Layer completely cooled muffins between sheets of waxed paper in an airtight container; cover. Freeze up to 3 months. To serve, remove muffins from airtight container; wrap muffins in foil. Bake in a 350°F oven for 20 to 25 minutes or until warm.

Per muffin: 255 cal., 12 g total fat (5 g sat. fat), 26 mg chol., 191 mg sodium, 33 g carbo., 1 g fiber, 6 g pro.

Crazy-About-Cranberry Bread

Crazy-About-Cranberry Bread

Not too sweet, this biscuit-style quick bread is studded with our favorite holiday berry. When selecting cranberries, opt for firm red fruits.

Prep: 25 minutes **Bake:** 1 hour for large loaf; 40 minutes for small loaves **Oven:** 350°F
Makes: 16 servings

- **2 cups all-purpose flour**
- **1 cup sugar**
- **1½ teaspoons baking powder**
- **½ teaspoon salt**
- **¼ teaspoon baking soda**
- **⅓ cup butter**
- **1 beaten egg**
- **1 teaspoon finely shredded orange peel**
- **⅔ cup orange juice**
- **1½ cups fresh cranberries, halved**
- **1 cup coarsely chopped nuts**

1. Preheat oven to 350°F. Lightly grease a 9×5×3-inch loaf pan, two 7½×3½×2-inch loaf pans, or three 5¾×3×2-inch mini loaf pans.

2. In a large bowl stir together flour, sugar, baking powder, salt, and baking soda. Use a pastry blender to cut in butter until the mixture is crumbly.

3. Add egg, orange peel, and juice to bowl, stirring just until combined. Fold in cranberries and nuts.

4. Spoon batter into pan(s). Bake for 1 hour to 1 hour and 10 minutes for the large loaf, or 40 to 50 minutes for the small loaves. A wooden toothpick inserted in center should come out clean.

5. Cool in pan(s) on a wire rack for 10 minutes. Remove from pan(s) and cool completely on wire rack. Wrap in plastic wrap. The bread is best if eaten the day after baking.

Advance Preparation: Prepare and bake as directed. Cool completely. Cover and store in refrigerator up to 3 days or wrap and freeze up to 1 month. Thaw bread, if frozen, before serving.

Per serving: 198 cal., 9 g total fat (0 g sat. fat), 24 mg chol., 175 mg sodium, 26 g carbo., 1 g fiber, 6 g pro.

Walnut-Pear Sour Cream Coffee Cake

Use a springform pan to make removing the cake easy after cooling.

Prep: 30 minutes **Bake:** 55 minutes
Cool: 1 hour 10 minutes **Oven:** 350°F
Makes: 12 servings

- **1 cup broken walnuts**
- **⅓ cup packed brown sugar**
- **1 teaspoon ground cinnamon**
- **¼ cup butter**
- **⅓ cup all-purpose flour**
- **2 medium pears, peeled, cored, and sliced (about 2 cups)**
- **2 teaspoons lemon juice**
- **1¾ cups all-purpose flour**
- **¾ teaspoon baking powder**
- **½ teaspoon baking soda**
- **¼ teaspoon salt**
- **½ cup butter, softened**
- **1 cup granulated sugar**
- **1 teaspoon vanilla**
- **2 eggs**
- **1 8-ounce carton dairy sour cream**
- **½ cup broken walnuts (optional)**
- **Sweetened whipped cream (optional)**

1. Preheat oven to 350°F. Grease a 9-inch springform pan or a 9×9×2-inch baking pan; set aside. For nut mixture, in a small bowl stir together 1 cup walnuts, the brown sugar, and cinnamon. For topping, in another small bowl use a pastry blender to cut the ¼ cup butter into the ⅓ cup flour until mixture resembles coarse crumbs. Stir in ¾ cup of the nut mixture. Set topping and the remaining nut mixture aside.

2. In a small bowl toss pears with lemon juice; set aside. In a medium bowl stir together the 1¾ cups flour, baking powder, baking soda, and salt; set aside. In a large mixing bowl, beat the ½ cup butter with an electric mixer on medium to high speed for 30 seconds. Beat in the granulated sugar and vanilla. Add eggs, one at a time, beating well after each addition. Add flour mixture and sour cream alternately to egg mixture, beating on low speed after each addition until combined.

3. Spread two-thirds of the batter evenly in the prepared pan. Sprinkle with reserved nut mixture. Layer pears over nut mixture. Gently spread remaining batter over pears. Sprinkle with the reserved topping.

4. Bake for 10 minutes. If desired, sprinkle with the ½ cup walnuts. Bake for 45 to 50 minutes more or until a wooden toothpick inserted near the center comes out clean. Cool in pan on a wire rack for 10 minutes. Run a thin metal spatula or knife around edge of cake. Remove sides of springform pan, if using. Cool for at least 1 hour. If desired, serve warm with whipped cream.

Advance Preparation: Prepare and bake as directed. Cool completely. Wrap and freeze up to 1 month. Thaw at room temperature. Or reheat by placing freezer wrapped cake in 300°F oven for 20 to 30 minutes or until warm.

Per serving: 396 cal., 23 g total fat (10 g sat. fat), 75 mg chol., 260 mg sodium, 45 g carbo., 2 g fiber, 5 g pro.

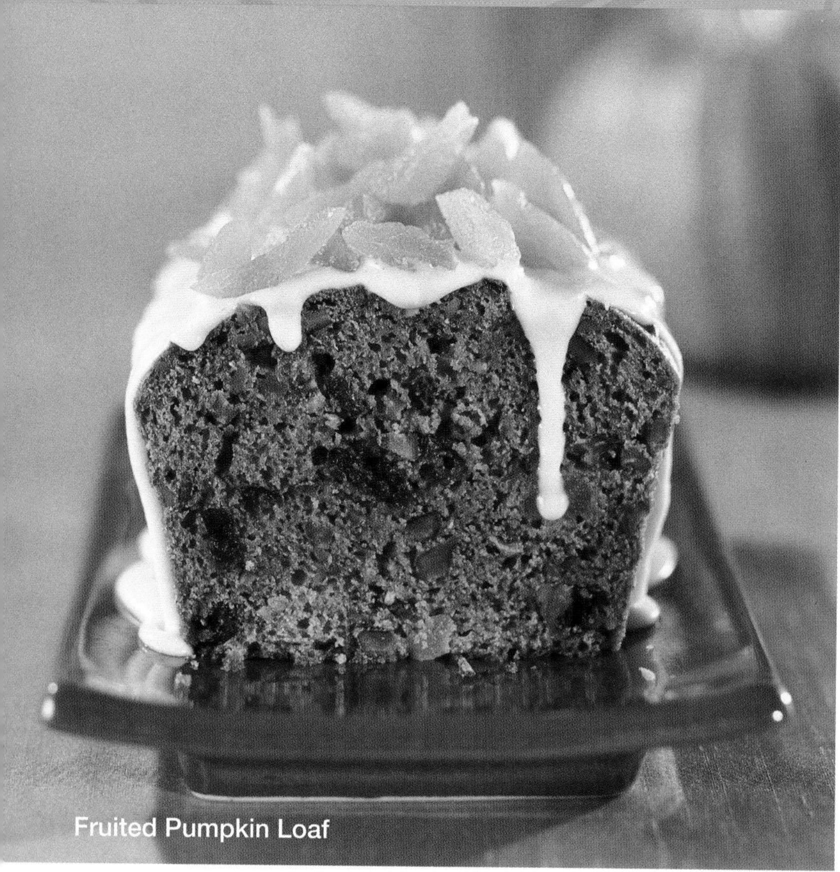
Fruited Pumpkin Loaf

Fruited Pumpkin Loaf

Dried apricots, cranberries, and apricot nectar elevate a pumpkin quick bread mix to new heights. Bake it in a single loaf to enjoy over a weekend, or in three mini loaf pans to share with friends and neighbors.

Prep: 20 minutes **Bake:** 55 minutes for large loaf; 30 minutes for small loaves **Oven:** 350°F
Makes: 1 large or 3 small loaves (16 to 18 servings)

- **2 eggs**
- **⅔ cup water**
- **½ cup apricot nectar**
- **3 tablespoons vegetable oil**
- **1 14-ounce package pumpkin quick bread mix**
- **1 cup chopped pecans, toasted**
- **½ cup snipped dried apricots**
- **½ cup dried cranberries**
- **1 recipe Apricot Icing (optional)**
- **Snipped dried apricots (optional)**

1. Preheat oven to 350°F. Grease the bottom and ½ inch up sides of an 8×4×2-inch loaf pan or three 5¾×3×2-inch loaf pans; set aside.

2. In a large bowl beat eggs with a whisk; whisk in water, nectar, and oil. Use a wooden spoon to stir pumpkin quick bread mix into egg mixture until combined. Stir in pecans, the ½ cup apricots, and the cranberries.

3. Spoon batter into prepared pan(s); spread evenly. Bake 8×4×2-inch pan for 55 to 65 minutes; 5¾×3×2-inch pans for 30 to 35 minutes or until a wooden toothpick inserted near the center comes out clean.

4. Cool in pan(s) on wire rack(s) for 10 minutes. Remove from pan(s). Cool completely on wire rack(s). Wrap and store overnight before slicing. If desired, pour Apricot Icing over bread and sprinkle with additional snipped apricots.

Apricot Icing: In a small bowl stir together ¾ cup powdered sugar and enough apricot nectar (3 to 4 teaspoons) to reach drizzling consistency.

Advance Preparation: Prepare and bake as directed. Cool completely. Wrap and freeze (without icing) up to 1 month. Thaw at room temperature for several hours. Drizzle with icing.

Per serving: 202 cal., 9 g total fat (1 g sat. fat), 26 mg chol., 153 mg sodium, 27 g carbo., 2 g fiber, 3 g pro.

Orange Biscuit Ring

For impressive results with minimum effort, coat refrigerated biscuits with citrus butter and orange-infused sugar, then arrange them in a wreath.

Prep: 20 minutes **Bake:** 35 minutes
Cool: 30 minutes **Oven:** 350°F **Makes:** 10 servings

- **1¼ cups sugar**
- **1 tablespoon finely shredded orange peel**
- **⅓ cup orange juice**
- **¼ cup butter, melted**
- **2 12-ounce packages refrigerated biscuits (20 biscuits)**
- **Kumquats (optional)**
- **Fresh cranberries (optional)**
- **Fresh herbs (optional)**

1. Preheat oven to 350°F. Grease a 10-inch fluted tube pan; set aside.

2. In a small bowl combine sugar and orange peel, breaking up any orange peel clumps with a fork. In another small bowl combine orange juice and melted butter.

3. Separate biscuits. Dip each biscuit into the orange juice mixture, then roll in the sugar mixture to coat. Place biscuits on edge in the prepared pan. Pour remaining orange juice mixture over biscuits.

4. Bake for 35 to 40 minutes or until top is golden brown. Cool in pan on a wire rack for 1 minute. Invert pan onto a serving platter with slightly raised sides; remove pan. Cool for 30 to 45 minutes. Serve warm. If desired, garnish center of biscuit ring with kumquats, cranberries, and fresh herbs.

Per serving: 240 cal., 6 g total fat (2 g sat. fat) 13 mg chol., 410 mg sodium, 44 g carbo., 0 g fiber, 3 g pro.

Orange Biscuit Ring

Cherry-Pecan Bread

These sweet loaves are perfect for a holiday tea. If you prefer a vanilla glaze, substitute 3 to 5 teaspoons water and 1 teaspoon vanilla for the maraschino cherry juice.

Prep: 25 minutes **Bake:** 1 hour **Oven:** 325°F
Makes: 2 loaves (28 servings)

- **Nonstick cooking spray**
- **1 10-ounce jar maraschino cherries**
- **2 cups all-purpose flour**
- **½ cup coarsely chopped pecans**
- **½ cup flaked coconut**
- **1 8-ounce package cream cheese, softened**
- **¾ cup butter, softened**
- **2 cups granulated sugar**
- **4 eggs**
- **1½ teaspoons baking powder**
- **1½ teaspoons vanilla**
- **1 cup powdered sugar**

Cherry-Pecan Bread

1. Preheat oven to 325°F. Lightly coat two 8×4×2-inch loaf pans with nonstick cooking spray. Set aside. Drain the maraschino cherries, reserving 2 tablespoons of the juice. Chop the cherries to yield about ¾ cup. In a medium bowl combine the chopped cherries, ¼ cup of the flour, the pecans, and coconut; set aside.

2. In a large mixing bowl combine cream cheese and butter; beat with an electric mixer on medium speed until smooth. Gradually add granulated sugar, beating until light and fluffy. Add eggs, one at a time, beating well after each addition. In a small bowl combine the remaining 1¾ cups flour and the baking powder; gradually add to cream cheese mixture. Beat in vanilla. Fold in maraschino cherry mixture. Spread batter into prepared pans.

3. Bake 1 hour or until a wooden toothpick inserted near the center comes out clean. Cool in pans on wire racks 10 minutes. Remove from pans; cool. For easier slicing, wrap and store overnight.

4. In a small bowl stir together powdered sugar and enough of the reserved maraschino cherry juice to make a glaze. Spread glaze over bread.

Advance Preparation: Prepare and bake as directed. Cool completely. Wrap and freeze up to 1 month. Thaw at room temperature for several hours. To reheat, wrap bread in foil. Heat in 350°F oven for 20 minutes or until warm. Spread glaze over bread.

Per serving: 228 cal., 11 g total fat (6 g sat. fat), 52 mg chol., 88 mg sodium, 31 g carbo., 1 g fiber, 3 g pro.

Fruit Stollen

Fruit Stollen

This rich, fruit-filled German bread is rolled and folded like a giant Parker House roll.

Prep: 35 minutes **Rise:** 2¼ hours **Bake:** 20 minutes
Oven: 350°F **Makes:** 2 loaves (24 to 32 servings)

- **1 package active dry yeast**
- **¼ cup warm water (105°F to 115°F)**
- **½ cup milk**
- **¼ cup granulated sugar**
- **¼ cup butter**
- **½ teaspoon salt**
- **3 to 3½ cups all-purpose flour**
- **1 egg**
- **½ cup raisins**
- **¾ cup diced mixed candied fruits and peels (4½ ounces)**
- **Sifted powdered sugar**

1. In a large mixing bowl dissolve yeast in warm water; let stand for 5 minutes. Meanwhile, in a small saucepan heat and stir milk, granulated sugar, butter, and salt just until warm (105°F to 115°F) and butter starts to melt. Add 1⅓ cups of flour, the milk mixture, and egg to yeast mixture. Beat with an electric mixer on low speed for 30 seconds, scraping sides of bowl constantly. Beat on high speed for 3 minutes more. Stir in raisins, candied fruits, and as much of the remaining flour as possible with a wooden spoon.

2. Turn dough out onto a lightly floured surface. Knead in enough remaining flour to make a moderately soft dough that is smooth and elastic (3 to 5 minutes). Place dough in a greased bowl, turning once to grease surface of dough. Cover and let rise in a warm place until double (about 1½ hours).

3. Punch down dough. Divide dough in half. Cover and let rest for 10 minutes. Grease a large baking sheet; set aside. Press or roll each half of dough into a 9×5-inch oval. Without stretching, fold lengthwise in half; press edges to lightly seal. Place loaves on prepared baking sheet. Cover and let rise until nearly double (about 45 minutes).

4. Preheat oven to 350°F. Bake about 20 minutes or until bread is golden brown and sounds hollow when lightly tapped. Remove from baking sheet and cool on wire racks. Sprinkle with powdered sugar before serving.

Advance Preparation: Prepare and bake as directed. Cool completely. Wrap and freeze up to 1 month. Thaw in refrigerator overnight. Let stand at room temperature for 1 hour. Sprinkle with powdered sugar as directed.

Per serving: 110 cal., 2 g total fat (1 g sat. fat), 15 mg chol., 77 mg sodium, 20 g carbo., 0 g fiber, 0 g pro.

Rosemary-Chive Parker House Rolls

Rosemary-Chive Parker House Rolls

For 30 rolls, plan to reroll the dough scraps. Rolls from rerolled dough will be as light and tender as the others.

Prep: 30 minutes **Rise:** 1½ hours **Bake:** 12 minutes
Oven: 375°F **Makes:** about 30 rolls

- **3 to 3½ cups all-purpose flour**
- **1 package active dry yeast**
- **3 tablespoons snipped fresh chives**
- **1 tablespoon snipped fresh rosemary**
- **¾ cup water**
- **¼ cup butter**
- **1 teaspoon sugar**
- **½ teaspoon salt**
- **1 egg**
- **¼ cup mashed potatoes**
- **3 tablespoons butter, melted**

1. In a large mixing bowl combine 1 cup of the flour, yeast, chives, and rosemary. In a small saucepan heat and stir water, ¼ cup butter, sugar, and salt until warm (120°F to 130°F) and butter almost melts. Add butter mixture to flour mixture. Add egg and mashed potatoes. Beat with an electric mixer on low to medium speed for 30 seconds, scraping bowl constantly. Beat on high speed for 3 minutes. Use a wooden spoon to stir in as much of the remaining flour as possible.

2. Turn dough out onto a lightly floured surface. Knead in enough of the remaining flour to make a moderately stiff dough that is smooth and elastic (6 to 8 minutes). Shape dough into a ball. Place in a lightly greased bowl, turning once to grease surface. Cover; let rise in a warm place until double in size (about 1 hour).

3. Punch down dough. Turn out onto a lightly floured surface. Cover; let rest for 10 minutes. Grease two large baking sheets; set aside. Roll dough to ¼-inch thickness. Use a floured 2½-inch biscuit cutter to cut into rounds. Brush with some of the melted butter. Reroll scraps as necessary.

4. To shape rolls, fold dough rounds in half, making the crease slightly off center. Place rolls, larger halves on top, 2 inches apart on prepared baking sheets. Cover; let rise until nearly double in size (about 30 minutes).

5. Preheat oven to 375°F. Lightly brush tops of rolls with the 3 tablespoons melted butter. Bake for 12 to 15 minutes or until golden. Serve warm.

Advance Preparation: Prepare and bake rolls as directed. Cool completely. Place in an airtight container; cover. Freeze up to 1 month. Thaw at room temperature for several hours. To reheat, wrap rolls in a single layer in foil. Heat in a 350°F oven for 10 to 12 minutes or until warm.

Per roll: 75 cal., 3 g total fat (2 g sat. fat), 14 mg chol., 66 mg sodium, 10 g carbo., 0 g fiber, 2 g pro.

Checkerboard Rolls

Have all of the ingredients for the festive toppings ready before dipping the rolls into the melted butter, because the butter will set quickly.

Prep: 20 minutes **Bake:** 20 minutes
Stand: 45 minutes **Chill:** 8 to 24 hours
Oven: 375°F **Makes:** 16 rolls

- **2 tablespoons poppy seeds**
- **2 tablespoons sesame seeds**
- **1 teaspoon lemon-pepper seasoning**
- **2 tablespoons yellow cornmeal**
- **2 tablespoons grated or finely shredded Parmesan cheese**
- **3 tablespoons butter, melted**
- **16 pieces (1.3 ounces each) frozen white roll dough**

1. Grease a 9×9×2-inch square pan; set aside. In a shallow dish combine poppy seeds, sesame seeds, and lemon-pepper seasoning. In another shallow dish combine cornmeal and Parmesan cheese.

2. Place butter in a small dish. Working quickly, roll dough pieces in butter, then in one of the seasoning mixtures to lightly coat. (Coat half of the rolls with one seasoning mixture, and the remaining rolls with the other seasoning mixture.) Alternate rolls in prepared pan. Cover rolls with greased plastic wrap. Chill in refrigerator so rolls can thaw for at least 8 hours or up to 24 hours.

3. Remove pan from refrigerator; uncover and let stand at room temperature for 45 minutes. After 35 minutes, preheat oven to 375°F.

4. Bake rolls for 20 to 25 minutes or until golden. Remove rolls from pan to wire rack. Cool slightly.

Per roll: 136 cal., 5 g total fat (2 g sat. fat), 6 mg chol., 189 mg sodium, 19 g carbo., 1 g fiber, 4 g pro.

Garlic-Herb Checkerboard Rolls: Prepare as directed, except in Step 1 omit lemon-pepper seasoning. Substitute with 1 teaspoon dried Italian seasoning and ½ teaspoon garlic powder.

Bacon-Onion Biscuits

If you don't have a biscuit cutter, pat or lightly roll the dough into a ¾-inch-thick rectangle, cut into 12 square biscuits, and bake as directed.

Prep: 30 minutes **Bake:** 10 minutes
Oven: 450°F **Makes:** 12 biscuits

- **4 slices bacon, chopped**
- **1 large onion, chopped**
- **3 cups all-purpose flour**
- **1 tablespoon baking powder**
- **1 tablespoon sugar**
- **½ teaspoon salt**
- **¾ teaspoon cream of tartar**
- **¾ cup butter**
- **1 cup milk**

1. In a skillet cook bacon and onion until bacon is slightly crisp and onion is tender. Drain off and discard fat.

2. In a bowl stir together flour, baking powder, sugar, salt, and cream of tartar. Use a pastry blender to cut in butter until mixture resembles coarse crumbs. Make a well in the center of the flour mixture. Combine milk and bacon mixture; add all at once to flour mixture. Use a fork to stir just until moistened.

3. Preheat oven to 450°F. Turn dough out onto a lightly floured surface. Knead dough by folding and gently pressing dough for four to six strokes or just until dough holds together. Pat or lightly roll dough to a ¾-inch thickness. Cut dough with a floured 2½-inch biscuit cutter, rerolling dough scraps as necessary. Place biscuits on an ungreased baking sheet.

4. Bake about 10 minutes or until golden. Serve warm.

Advance Preparation: Prepare through Step 3. Place unbaked biscuits on a baking sheet; freeze 1 hour. Transfer to a resealable freezer bag. Freeze up to 1 month. To bake, place frozen biscuits 1 inch apart on an ungreased baking sheet. Bake in a 350°F oven for 25 to 30 minutes or until golden.

Per biscuit: 294 cal., 18 g total fat (10 g sat. fat), 41 mg chol., 354 mg sodium, 27 g carbo., 1 g fiber, 6 g pro.

dressed-up desserts

In the spirit of abundance that permeates the holidays, home-baked cakes, pies, and other tempting desserts hit the spot at celebrations. Create these show-stoppers even if time is limited. Make-ahead tips and presentation ideas are especially useful for wowing guests with little effort.

Triple Chocolate-Pistachio
Layer Cake, page 94

Mango Raspberry Lemon Trifle

one-third of the raspberries and mangos. Top with one-third of the lemon curd mixture. Repeat layers twice. Cover and chill for 4 to 24 hours.

4. Before serving, in a chilled medium bowl combine remaining ½ cup whipping cream, powdered sugar, and vanilla. Beat until soft peaks form. Top trifle with whipped cream and sprinkle with sliced almonds.

Advance Preparation: Prepare as directed through Step 3. Cover and chill up to 24 hours. Serve as directed.

Per serving: 381 cal., 17 g total fat (8 g sat. fat), 68 mg chol., 176 mg sodium, 56 g carbo., 6 g fiber, 3 g pro.

Mango Raspberry Lemon Trifle

Take the easy route to recreate a traditional holiday trifle. A boxed cake mix and purchased lemon curd save time while fresh mango and raspberries add luscious fruit flavor.

Prep: 30 minutes **Chill:** 4 to 24 hours
Makes: 8 servings

- **1 9-ounce package white cake mix**
- **1 cup whipping cream**
- **1 10-ounce jar purchased lemon curd**
- **3 tablespoons dry sherry**
- **2 cups fresh raspberries**
- **1 cup chopped fresh mango or bottled mango slices, drained and chopped**
- **2 tablespoons powdered sugar**
- **½ teaspoon vanilla**
- **¼ cup sliced almonds, toasted**

1. Prepare cake mix according to package directions. Cool completely on a wire rack. Cut into 1-inch cubes; set aside.

2. In a chilled medium mixing bowl beat ½ cup of the whipping cream until soft peaks form using an electric mixer. Gently fold lemon curd into whipping cream until combined.

3. Place one-third of the cake cubes in the bottom of a 2-quart glass trifle bowl or serving bowl. Drizzle with 1 tablespoon of the sherry. Top with

Maple Crème Brûlée with Cranberries and Hazelnuts

Every bite of this dessert delivers sweet-tooth satisfaction. Fresh rosemary and cranberries make a lovely holiday garnish.

Prep: 35 minutes **Bake:** 30 minutes **Chill:** 1 hour
Oven: 350°F **Makes:** 6 servings

- **Nonstick cooking spray**
- **2 cups whipping cream**
- **3 tablespoons sugar**
- **6 egg yolks**
- **⅓ cup pure maple syrup or maple-flavor syrup**
- **1½ teaspoons vanilla**
- **⅛ teaspoon salt**
- **¼ cup chopped hazelnuts or almonds, toasted**
- **2 tablespoons snipped dried cranberries**
- **¼ cup sugar**

1. Preheat oven to 350°F. Lightly coat six 6-ounce custard cups or soufflé dishes with nonstick cooking spray. Place cups or dishes in a 3-quart rectangular baking dish; set aside. In a heavy small saucepan combine whipping cream and 3 tablespoons sugar; heat over medium heat just until bubbly, stirring occasionally. Remove from heat; set aside.

2. Meanwhile, in a large bowl combine egg yolks, maple syrup, vanilla, and salt. Beat with a wire whisk or rotary beater until just combined. Slowly whisk hot whipping cream mixture into the egg yolk mixture.

3. Divide custard mixture among prepared custard cups or soufflé dishes. Place baking dish on oven rack. Pour enough boiling water into the baking dish to reach halfway up the sides of the custard cups or soufflé dishes.

4. Bake for 30 to 35 minutes or until custards appear set when gently shaken. Remove custard cups or soufflé dishes from water; cool on a wire rack. Cover and chill for at least 1 hour or up to 24 hours.

5. Before serving, let custards stand at room temperature for 20 minutes. If desired, run a thin spatula or knife around the edge of each custard; invert custards onto serving plates. Sprinkle with toasted hazelnuts and dried cranberries.

6. Meanwhile, for caramelized sugar, in a heavy 8-inch skillet heat ¼ cup sugar over medium-high heat until sugar begins to melt, shaking skillet occasionally to heat sugar evenly. Do not stir. Once sugar starts to melt, reduce heat to low; cook about 5 minutes or until all of the sugar melts and is golden brown, stirring as needed with a wooden spoon. Quickly drizzle caramelized sugar over the custards. (If sugar starts to harden in the skillet, return to heat, stirring until melted.) Serve custards immediately.

Advance Preparation: Prepare as directed through Step 4. Cover and chill up to 24 hours. Before serving, continue as directed.

Per serving: 476 cal., 38 g total fat (20 g sat. fat), 314 mg chol., 89 mg sodium, 32 g carbo., 1 g fiber, 38 g pro.

Gingered Pear-Cherry Tart

Poach the pears and cherries in red wine to infuse with flavor.

Prep: 30 minutes **Bake:** 25 minutes
Cool: 30 minutes **Oven:** 425°F **Makes:** 8 servings

- **5 firm ripe Bosc pears, peeled, cored, and cut into ¾-inch pieces (about 5 cups)**
- **1 cup dried tart red cherries**
- **½ cup dry red wine**
- **½ cup packed brown sugar**
- **1 tablespoon grated fresh ginger**
- **⅛ teaspoon salt**
- **1 tablespoon cornstarch**
- **1 tablespoon lemon juice**
- **½ of a 15-ounce package rolled refrigerated unbaked piecrusts (1 crust)**
- **1 egg yolk, beaten**
- **2 teaspoons water**
- **Vanilla ice cream or sweetened whipped cream (optional)**

1. In a 4-quart saucepan combine pears, cherries, wine, brown sugar, ginger, and salt. Cook over medium heat for 20 minutes, stirring occasionally. In a small bowl whisk together cornstarch and lemon juice; add to pears. Cook and stir for 1 minute or until thickened. Cool slightly, about 30 minutes.

2. Preheat oven to 425°F. Unroll piecrust onto a lightly floured surface; roll with a floured rolling pin into a 17×11-inch rectangle (corners will be rounded). Fit dough into a 13½×4½-inch fluted rectangular tart pan with removable bottom. Trim dough 1 inch beyond edge of pan. Fold excess dough over onto sides of dough, pressing together. Reserve scraps. For egg wash, in a small bowl beat together egg yolk and water.

3. Use small cookie cutters to cut leaf shapes from dough scraps. Brush with egg wash.

4. Fill pastry shell with pear filling; scatter top with leaf cutouts. Place tart pan on a baking sheet. Bake for 25 to 30 minutes or until pastry is golden brown and juices bubble around fruit. Cool tart in pan on a wire rack. Serve warm or at room temperature. If desired, top with ice cream.

Advance Preparation: Prepare as directed. Place tart in airtight container; cover. Store in refrigerator overnight; let stand at room temperature for 30 minutes before serving.

Per serving: 325 cal., 8 g total fat (3 g sat. fat), 29 mg chol., 159 mg sodium, 62 g carbo., 5 g fiber, 1 g pro.

Chocolate Peppermint Cream Puffs

These puffs should be golden brown and crisp when the timer rings. Cutting a slit in each cooked puff allows steam to escape and prevents the puffs from becoming soggy.

Prep: 30 minutes **Bake:** 25 minutes per batch
Cool: 10 minutes **Oven:** 400°F
Makes: 48 mini desserts

- **1 cup water**
- **½ cup butter**
- **¼ teaspoon salt**
- **1 cup all-purpose flour**
- **4 eggs**
- **1 teaspoon peppermint extract or flavoring**
- **3 cups peppermint stick ice cream**
- **2 ounces bittersweet chocolate, chopped**
- **1 teaspoon shortening**
- **2 ounces white chocolate, chopped**

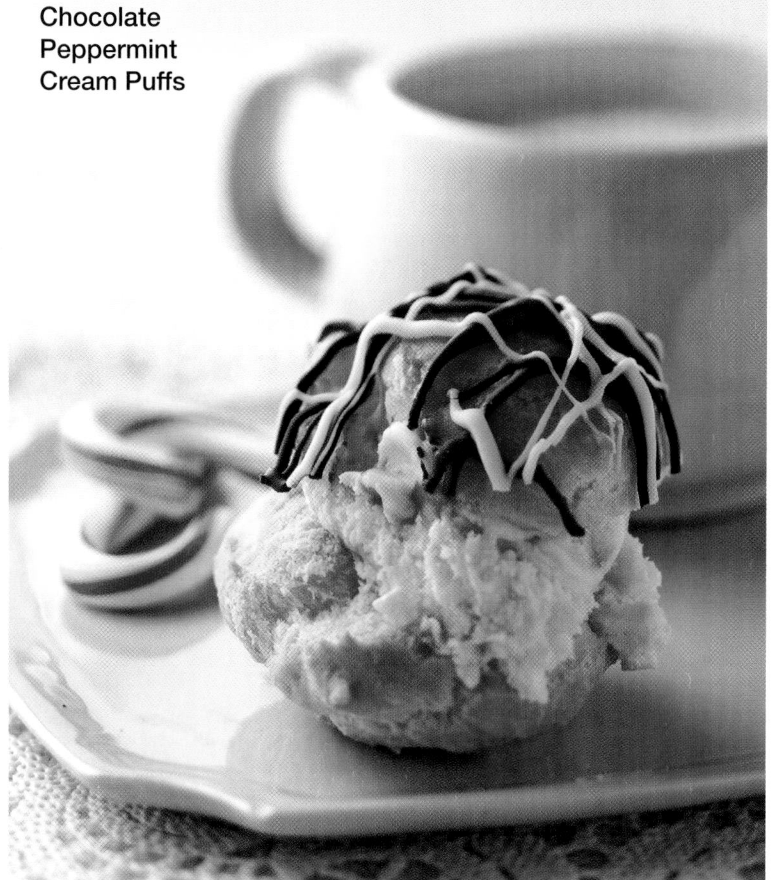

Chocolate Peppermint Cream Puffs

1. Preheat oven to 400°F. Grease a baking sheet; set aside. In a medium saucepan combine water, butter, and salt. Bring to boiling. Add flour all at once, stirring vigorously. Cook and stir until mixture forms a ball. Remove from heat. Cool for 10 minutes. Add eggs, one at a time, beating well with a wooden spoon after each addition. Beat in peppermint extract.

2. Drop dough by rounded teaspoons 2 inches apart onto prepared baking sheets. Bake one sheet at a time for 25 minutes (keep remaining dough covered while the first batch bakes). Cool.

3. Cut tops from puffs; remove soft dough from inside. Fill each with ice cream. Replace tops. Place in the freezer to firm, about 15 minutes.

4. In a small heavy saucepan melt bittersweet chocolate and ½ teaspoon of the shortening over low heat. Cool slightly. Place melted chocolate in a small self-sealing plastic bag. Snip off a tiny corner. Drizzle chocolate over puffs. Return puffs to freezer and freeze for 5 minutes or until chocolate sets. In another small saucepan melt white chocolate and remaining shortening over low heat; cool slightly. Place in a small self-sealing plastic bag. Snip off a tiny corner. Drizzle over the puffs. Return puffs to freezer and freeze until serving time.

Advance Preparation: Once chocolate sets, transfer to freezer container. Cover and store in refrigerator up to 1 week.

Per mini dessert: 65 cal., 4 g total fat (3 g sat. fat), 27 mg chol., 42 mg sodium, 6 g carbo., 0 g fiber, 1 g pro.

Eggnog Tiramisu

This variation of the traditional Italian dessert has just the right amount of eggnog flavor. It's easy to assemble and is perfect for the holiday dessert table.

Prep: 25 minutes **Chill:** 4 to 24 hours
Makes: 9 servings

- **2 8-ounce cartons mascarpone cheese**
- **½ cup powdered sugar**
- **1 cup eggnog**

- 4 tablespoons dark rum or 4 tablespoons eggnog plus ½ teaspoon rum extract
- 1 cup whipping cream
- 2 3-ounce packages ladyfingers, split
- ½ teaspoon freshly grated nutmeg or ¼ teaspoon ground nutmeg

1. In a medium bowl combine mascarpone cheese, powdered sugar, ⅓ cup of the eggnog, and 2 tablespoons of the rum. In a chilled small mixing bowl beat whipping cream with an electric mixer on medium speed until soft peaks form. Fold whipped cream into marscarpone mixture.

2. To assemble, arrange half of the ladyfinger halves in the bottom of a 2-quart square baking dish, cutting ladyfingers as necessary to fit. Drizzle with half of the remaining eggnog and 1 tablespoon of the remaining rum. Evenly spread half of the mascarpone mixture over the ladyfingers. Sprinkle half of the nutmeg. Repeat layers. Cover and chill 4 to 24 hours before serving.

Advance Preparation: Prepare as directed. Cover and chill up to 24 hours.

Per serving: 460 cal., 37 g total fat (21 g sat. fat), 159 mg chol., 82 mg sodium, 25 g carbo., 0 g fiber, 14 g pro.

Cherry Chip and Coconut Tartlets

If you can't find miniature cherry chips, chop regular-size cherry chips. Or try semisweet, lemon, or raspberry-chocolate chips for a different flavor twist.

Prep: 45 minutes **Bake:** 18 minutes
Oven: 325°F/350°F **Makes:** 36 tartlets

- ¾ cup butter, softened
- 1 8-ounce package cream cheese, softened
- 2 tablespoons sugar
- 1 teaspoon finely shredded lemon peel
- ⅛ teaspoon salt
- 1½ cups all-purpose flour
- ½ cup flaked coconut
- ½ cup white baking pieces, melted and cooled
- ⅓ cup lemon curd
- ¼ cup miniature cherry baking pieces

Cherry Chip and Coconut Tartlets

1. In a large mixing bowl beat butter and half of the cream cheese with an electric mixer on medium to high speed for 30 seconds. Add sugar, lemon peel, and salt. Beat until combined, scraping sides of bowl occasionally. Beat in as much flour as possible. Stir in any remaining flour. Shape dough into a ball. If necessary, cover and chill dough 30 minutes or until easy to handle.

2. Preheat oven to 325°F. Divide dough into 36 equal pieces. Press pieces evenly into bottoms and up the sides of 36 ungreased 1¾-inch muffin cups. Bake for 18 to 20 minutes or until lightly browned. Transfer pastry cups to a wire rack; cool.

3. Increase oven temperature to 350°F. Spread coconut in single layer on a shallow baking pan. Toast in oven for 5 to 10 minutes or until light golden brown, stirring occasionally. Remove from oven and cool.

4. For filling, in a bowl beat remaining cream cheese at medium to high speed for 30 seconds or until creamy. Beat in melted white baking pieces until smooth. Spoon about ½ teaspoon of the lemon curd into each pastry cup. Spoon cream cheese mixture over lemon curd, or transfer cream cheese mixture to a decorating bag fitted with a large star tip, and pipe over lemon curd. Sprinkle with toasted coconut and cherry baking pieces.

Advance Preparation: Place tartlets in a single layer in an airtight container; cover. Store in refrigerator up to 3 days. Do not freeze.

Per tartlet: 115 cal., 8 g total fat (5 g sat. fat), 20 mg chol., 65 mg sodium, 10 g carbo., 1 g fiber, 1 g pro.

Steamed Figgy Pudding

Steamed Figgy Pudding

Dried persimmon strips add a festive touch to this steamed dessert, redolent with dried fruit, rum, and an array of warm spices. When steaming the pudding, place a metal spoon in the kettle water. If there is enough water in the kettle, the spoon will rattle. If it stops, add water.

Prep: 25 minutes **Cook:** 1½ hours
Cool: 30 minutes **Makes:** 10 servings

- 1 cup finely chopped dried figs
- 1 cup mixed dried fruit bits
- ½ cup dried cranberries or dried cherries
- 1 tablespoon finely shredded orange peel
- ¾ cup orange juice
- ⅓ cup spiced rum, dark rum, or orange juice
- 1 cup all-purpose flour
- 1½ teaspoons apple pie spice
- 1 teaspoon baking powder
- ½ teaspoon salt
- ¼ teaspoon baking soda
- ½ cup butter, softened
- ¾ cup packed brown sugar
- 2 eggs
- 1½ teaspoons vanilla
- 1¾ cups lightly packed baguette-style French bread crumbs or soft white bread crumbs
- Honey
- Dehydrated persimmon strips
- 1 recipe Bourbon Custard Sauce

1. Grease a steamed pudding mold or a 1½-quart casserole; set aside. In a medium bowl combine figs, dried fruit bits, and dried cranberries. Stir in orange peel, orange juice, and rum; set aside.

2. Stir together flour, apple pie spice, baking powder, salt, and baking soda; set aside. In a large mixing bowl, beat butter on medium to high speed for 30 seconds. Add brown sugar; beat until combined. Beat in eggs and vanilla. Beat in flour mixture. Stir in bread crumbs and fruit mixture. Spoon batter into prepared pudding mold; cover tightly with greased foil.

3. Place pudding mold on a rack in a deep kettle. Add boiling water to kettle to a depth of 1 inch. Cover and bring to a gentle boil. Steam about 1½ hours or until a long wooden pick or skewer inserted in center of pudding comes out clean. Add more boiling water to kettle, as necessary.

4. Remove pudding mold from kettle. Remove foil. Cool on a wire rack for 30 minutes. Loosen edge of pudding from sides of mold; invert onto serving plate. Brush with honey. Garnish with persimmon strips. Serve with Bourbon Custard Sauce.

Advance Preparation: Prepare as directed. Place inverted pudding in airtight container; cover. Store in refrigerator overnight. Let stand at room temperature for 30 minutes and serve as directed.

Per serving: 444 cal., 15 g total fat (9 g sat. fat), 159 mg chol., 386 mg sodium, 69 g carbo., 2 g fiber, 7 g pro.

Bourbon Custard Sauce

Prep: 20 minutes **Chill:** 2 hours
Makes: about 1¼ cups sauce (10 servings)

- 4 egg yolks
- ¼ cup sugar
- ⅛ teaspoon salt
- 1 cup half-and-half or light cream
- 2 tablespoons bourbon (optional)
- ½ teaspoon vanilla

1. In a medium saucepan whisk egg yolks until combined. Whisk in sugar and salt; set aside. In a small saucepan heat half-and-half over medium heat just until tiny bubbles form around the edge.

2. Slowly stir the hot half-and-half into the egg yolk mixture. Cook and stir with a wooden spoon over medium heat just until the mixture thickens enough to coat the back of a clean metal spoon. Remove from heat. Stir in bourbon, if desired, and vanilla. Quickly cool mixture by placing saucepan in a large bowl of ice water for 1 to 2 minutes, stirring constantly.

3. Transfer sauce to a bowl; cover the surface with plastic wrap. Chill at least 2 hours.

Advance Preparation: Prepare sauce as directed. Cover and chill up to 3 days.

Per serving: 74 cal., 5 g total fat (2 g sat. fat), 94 mg chol., 42 mg sodium, 6 g carbo., 0 g fiber, 2 g pro.

Pumpkin Bread Pudding with Toffee Sauce

Give a favorite comfort food a holiday twist with pumpkin and spices. When buying canned pumpkin, read the label carefully to make sure you select pumpkin puree and not pumpkin pie filling.

Prep: 30 minutes **Bake:** 35 minutes
Cool: 30 minutes **Chill:** 1 to 4 hours
Oven: 350°F **Makes:** 8 servings

- 2 cups half-and-half or light cream
- 1 15-ounce can pumpkin puree
- 1 cup packed brown sugar
- 3 eggs
- 2 teaspoons vanilla
- 1½ teaspoons pumpkin pie spice
- 1½ teaspoons ground cinnamon
- 9 ounces French bread, torn into bite-size pieces (10 cups)
- ½ cup golden raisins
- ½ cup granulated sugar
- ½ cup evaporated milk
- 2 tablespoons butter
- 2 tablespoons light-color corn syrup
- ½ cup chocolate-covered toffee pieces

1. Lightly grease a 2-quart shallow baking dish; set aside. In a very large bowl combine half-and-half, pumpkin, brown sugar, eggs, vanilla, pumpkin pie spice, and cinnamon. Add bread pieces; stir to moisten evenly. Stir in raisins. Transfer mixture to the prepared baking dish. Cover and chill for 1 to 4 hours.

2. Meanwhile, for sauce, in a small saucepan combine granulated sugar, evaporated milk, butter, and corn syrup. Bring to boiling; reduce heat. Boil gently, uncovered, for 1 minute. Cool to room temperature. Transfer to a serving bowl. Stir in toffee pieces.

3. Preheat oven to 350°F. Bake bread pudding, uncovered, about 35 minutes or until a knife inserted in the center comes out clean. Cool on a wire rack for 30 minutes. Serve warm bread pudding with sauce.

Per serving: 539 cal., 18 g total fat (10 g sat. fat), 119 mg chol., 369 mg sodium, 86 g carbo., 3 g fiber, 10 g pro.

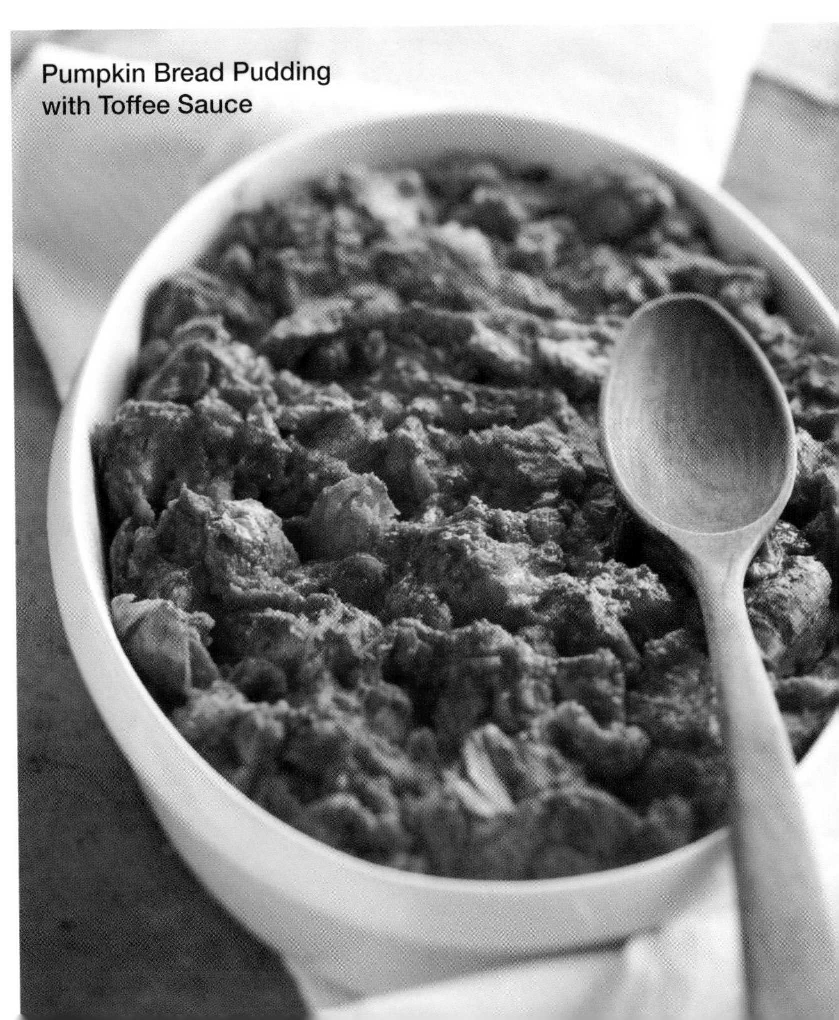
Pumpkin Bread Pudding with Toffee Sauce

Apple Cranberry Crostata

Apple Cranberry Crostata

Prep: 45 minutes **Bake:** 1 hour **Chill:** 30 minutes
Oven: 375°F **Makes:** 10 servings

1¾ cups all-purpose flour
⅓ cup sugar
¼ teaspoon salt
½ cup cold butter
3 egg yolks
4 teaspoons ice water
3 medium cooking apples such as Granny Smith or Braeburn, peeled, cored, and thinly sliced (2¾ cups)
1 cup fresh cranberries
1 cup sugar
2 tablespoons all-purpose flour
2 tablespoons butter, cut up
1 teaspoon finely shredded orange peel
1 tablespoon orange juice
½ cup fine dry bread crumbs
2 tablespoons sugar
¼ teaspoon ground cinnamon
⅛ teaspoon ground cloves
Sugared cranberries (optional)

1. In a bowl stir together 1¾ cups flour, ⅓ cup sugar, and salt. Use a pastry blender to cut in the ½ cup butter until pieces are pea size. Combine egg yolks and ice water; gradually add to flour mixture. Using your fingers, gently knead pastry just until a ball forms. Wrap pastry in plastic wrap; chill for 30 to 60 minutes or until pastry is easy to handle.

2. Preheat oven to 375°F. In a large bowl combine apples, cranberries, the 1 cup sugar, 2 tablespoons flour, the 2 tablespoons butter, orange peel, and orange juice. In a bowl combine bread crumbs, the 2 tablespoons sugar, cinnamon, and cloves.

3. Lightly flour a large piece of parchment paper. Use your hands to slightly flatten the pastry on the parchment. Roll pastry from center to edges into a circle 14 inches in diameter. Lift the parchment with the pastry and place on a very large baking sheet.

4. Sprinkle ⅓ cup of crumb mixture into a 9-inch circle in center of pastry. Arrange fruit mixture on top of the crumbs in the center of the dough. Sprinkle remaining crumb mixture over the fruit.

5. Lift parchment to bring pastry up and around fruit; press gently to form pleats. Bake for 1 hour or until crust is golden brown, fruit juices are bubbling, and fruit on top is brown on the edges. Cover with foil during the last 15 minutes of baking to prevent fruit from overbrowning. Cool on a wire rack. Serve warm or at room temperature. If desired, garnish with sugared cranberries made by tossing frozen cranberries with granulated sugar.

Per serving: 363 cal., 13 g total fat (8 g sat. fat), 93 mg chol., 187 mg sodium, 58 g carbo., 2 g fiber, 4 g pro.

Cherry Apricot Pistachio Baklava

This Greek pastry is divine with a mix of dried fruits and nuts, a splash of brandy, and warm spices.

Prep: 1 hour **Bake:** 40 minutes
Oven: 325°F **Makes:** 35 servings

- **1¼ cups sugar**
- **3 ¼-inch slices fresh ginger**
- **½ teaspoon finely shredded lemon peel**
- **½ cup honey**
- **2 tablespoons brandy or orange juice**
- **1 tablespoon lemon juice**
- **2 cups pistachios, finely chopped**
- **½ cup snipped dried apricots**
- **½ cup snipped dried cherries**
- **¼ cup sugar**
- **1 teaspoon ground ginger**
- **½ teaspoon ground cardamom**
- **1½ cups butter, melted**
- **1 16-ounce package frozen phyllo dough (9×14-inch sheets), thawed**

1. For syrup, in a medium saucepan stir together the 1¼ cups sugar, 1 cup *water,* fresh ginger, and lemon peel. Bring to boiling; reduce heat. Simmer, uncovered, over medium heat for 30 minutes, stirring occasionally. Remove from heat. Stir in honey, brandy, and lemon juice. Strain to remove lemon peel and ginger. Let syrup cool to room temperature (do not refrigerate).

2. Preheat oven to 325°F. For filling, in a large bowl combine pistachios, apricots, cherries, ¼ cup sugar, ground ginger, and cardamom. Set aside.

3. Brush the bottom of a 3-quart rectangular baking dish with some of the melted butter. Unfold phyllo dough. With a knife cut through stack of phyllo sheets to form a 13×9-inch rectangle. Discard extra pieces. Cover phyllo with plastic wrap, removing sheets as needed. One layer at a time, layer 10 phyllo sheets in dish, brushing each with melted butter. Sprinkle one-third of filling on phyllo layers. Repeat layering phyllo sheets and sprinkling filling twice. Layer remaining phyllo sheets on top, brushing each sheet with butter. Drizzle any remaining butter on top.

4. With a sharp knife make four straight cuts through all layers the length of the dish to make five rows. Then make eight diagonal cuts through all the layers to form diamonds. (Leave pieces in the dish). Bake 40 to 50 minutes or until golden brown. Cool slightly in dish on a wire rack. Spoon syrup over hot baklava. Cool completely or let set overnight at room temperature before serving.

Advance Preparation: Place baked baklava pieces between layers of waxed paper in an airtight container; cover. Store in refrigerator up to 1 week or freeze up to 3 months. Thaw in refrigerator.

Per serving: 213 cal., 12 g total fat (5 g sat. fat), 21 mg chol., 137 mg sodium, 26 g carbo., 1 g fiber, 3 g pro.

Cherry Apricot Pistachio Baklava

Chocolate-Hazelnut Tart

Chocolate-Hazelnut Tart

A serrated knife makes fast work of chopping chocolate for this intensely flavored dessert.

Prep: 30 minutes **Bake:** 43 minutes **Chill:** 30 minutes
Oven: 450°F/375°F **Makes:** 12 servings

1¼ cups all-purpose flour
¼ cup sugar
¼ teaspoon salt
½ cup cold butter, cut up
½ cup finely chopped hazelnuts, toasted
2 egg yolks, beaten
1 tablespoon ice water
1¼ cups whipping cream
2 tablespoons hazelnut liqueur
6 ounces semisweet chocolate, chopped
2 ounces unsweetened chocolate, chopped
1 egg yolk
1 3-ounce package cream cheese, softened
2 tablespoons sugar
1 tablespoon hazelnut liqueur
1 cup whipping cream
Chocolate-dipped toasted hazelnuts (optional)
Coarsely chopped dark chocolate (optional)

1. In a medium bowl stir together flour, ¼ cup sugar, and salt. Use a pastry blender to cut in butter until pieces are pea-size. Stir in nuts. In a small bowl stir together the 2 beaten yolks and ice water. Gradually stir egg yolk mixture into flour mixture. Use your fingers to gently knead the pastry just until a ball forms. Cover with plastic wrap and chill for 30 to 60 minutes or until pastry is easy to handle.

2. Preheat oven to 450°F. On a lightly floured surface, use your hands to slightly flatten the pastry. Roll pastry from center to edges into a circle 11 inches in diameter. Wrap pastry around the rolling pin. Unroll it into a 9-inch tart pan with a removable bottom. Press pastry into fluted sides of tart pan; trim edges. Line pastry with a double thickness of foil. Bake for 8 minutes. Remove foil. Bake for 5 to 6 minutes more or until golden. Reduce oven temperature to 375°F.

3. Meanwhile, in a medium saucepan combine the 1¼ cups whipping cream and 2 tablespoons hazelnut liqueur. Bring mixture just to simmering. Remove from heat. Stir in chopped chocolates until mixture is smooth. Stir in the 1 egg yolk just until combined. Pour mixture into baked tart shell. Bake for 25 minutes or until nearly set. Remove from oven; cool completely in pan on a wire rack.

4. Beat together cream cheese, 2 tablespoons sugar, and 1 tablespoon hazelnut liqueur on medium speed until smooth. Beat in 1 cup whipping cream just until soft peaks form. Spoon mixture into a pastry bag fitted with a large star tip. Pipe mixture on top of cooled tart. If desired, top with chocolate-dipped hazelnuts and chopped dark chocolate.

Advance Preparation: Prepare as directed through Step 3. Cover and chill up to 3 days. Before serving, let stand at room temperature about 1 hour and continue as directed.

Per serving: 477 cal., 39 g total fat (22 g sat. fat), 142 mg chol., 145 mg sodium, 30 g carbo., 3 g fiber, 6 g pro.

Scarlet-Swirl Cheesecake

Prep: 45 minutes **Bake:** 1 hour
Cool: 15 minutes + 30 minutes + 1 hour
Chill: 6 hours **Oven:** 350°F **Makes:** 16 servings

- ½ cup butter
- ¼ cup packed brown sugar
- ½ teaspoon vanilla
- 1¼ cups all-purpose flour
- ¼ cup finely chopped pecans
- 1 cup granulated sugar
- 2 tablespoons cornstarch
- 1½ cups fresh cranberries
- 1 cup orange juice
- 2 8-ounce packages cream cheese, softened
- 1 cup granulated sugar
- 1 8-ounce carton dairy sour cream
- 2 tablespoons all-purpose flour
- 4 eggs
- 1 cup whipping cream
- 1 teaspoon finely shredded orange peel
- 1 tablespoon orange juice
- 1 teaspoon vanilla
- ½ cup dairy sour cream

1. Preheat oven to 350°F. For crust, in a small bowl beat butter on medium speed for 30 seconds. Add brown sugar and the ½ teaspoon vanilla; beat until fluffy. Add the 1¼ cups flour and pecans. Beat just until combined (don't overbeat). With floured hands, press dough onto the bottom and 1½ inches up the side of a 9-inch springform pan. Bake for 10 to 12 minutes or until lightly browned. Cool on a wire rack while preparing filling.

2. For sauce, in a saucepan stir together 1 cup granulated sugar and cornstarch. Stir in cranberries and 1 cup orange juice. Cook and stir over medium heat until thickened and bubbly. Cook and stir 2 minutes. Remove half of the sauce (about 1 cup) and let stand at room temperature to cool slightly. Cover and chill remaining sauce until serving time.

3. Place the 1 cup cooled sauce in a food processor or blender. Cover and process or blend until smooth (you will have ¾ cup sauce). Set aside.

4. For filling, in large bowl combine cream cheese, 1 cup granulated sugar, the carton of sour cream, and 2 tablespoons flour. Beat on low to medium speed until combined. Add eggs. Beat just until combined (don't overbeat). Stir in whipping cream, orange peel, 1 tablespoon orange juice, and 1 teaspoon vanilla. Filling will be slightly thin.

5. Pour about half of the filling into the crust-lined pan. Drizzle pureed sauce over the filling in the pan. Carefully pour the remaining filling into the pan, covering the sauce as much as possible. Place springform pan in a shallow baking pan. Bake about 1 hour or until the center appears nearly set when gently shaken.

6. Cool in springform pan on a wire rack for 15 minutes. Use a small sharp knife to loosen sides of the pan. Cool for 30 minutes more. Remove sides of springform pan. Cool for 1 hour. Cover and chill for at least 6 hours.

7. Just before serving, top wedges of the chilled cheesecake with some of the chilled sauce and the ½ cup sour cream. Pass remaining sauce.

Advance Preparation: Prepare as directed through Step 6. Transfer cheesecake to airtight container. Cover and chill up to 24 hours or freeze up to 1 month. Thaw, if frozen and serve as directed.

Per serving: 435 cal., 28 g total fat (15 g sat. fat), 130 mg chol., 173 mg sodium, 43 g carbo., 1 g fiber, 5 g pro.

Graham Cracker-Pecan Sweet Potato Pie

Chilling the graham cracker-pecan crumb crust makes it firm for this sumptuous holiday dessert.

Prep: 50 minutes **Bake:** 55 minutes **Cool:** 1 hour
Chill: 4 hours **Oven:** 375°F/350°F **Makes:** 8 servings

- 3 tablespoons butter
- 3 tablespoons granulated sugar
- ¾ cup finely crushed graham crackers (about 10 squares)
- ½ cup finely chopped pecans
- 2 cups mashed, cooked sweet potatoes*
- ½ cup packed brown sugar
- ½ teaspoon ground ginger
- ½ teaspoon ground cinnamon
- ⅛ teaspoon salt
- ⅛ teaspoon ground nutmeg
- Dash cloves
- 2 eggs, lightly beaten
- 1 cup half-and-half or light cream
- 3 egg whites
- ¼ teaspoon cream of tartar
- ¼ teaspoon rum extract or vanilla
- 6 tablespoons granulated sugar

Graham Cracker-Pecan Sweet Potato Pie

1. In a medium saucepan melt butter; stir in the 3 tablespoons sugar. Add crushed crackers and pecans; toss to mix well. Spread in a 9-inch pie plate; press evenly onto bottom and up the sides. Chill about 1 hour.

2. Preheat oven to 375°F. For filling, in a large bowl stir together sweet potatoes, brown sugar, ginger, cinnamon, salt, nutmeg, and cloves. Add 2 eggs; beat lightly with a fork just until combined. Gradually stir in half-and-half until well combined.

3. Place the graham cracker crust on the oven rack. Pour filling into pie shell. To prevent overbrowning, cover edge of pie with foil. Bake 20 minutes. Uncover edge of pie. Bake pie 20 to 25 minutes or until a knife inserted in center comes out clean. Reduce oven temperature to 350°F.

4. Meanwhile, allow 3 egg whites to stand at room temperature for 30 minutes. In a large mixing bowl combine egg whites, cream of tartar, and rum extract. Beat with electric mixer on medium speed until soft peaks form (tips curl). Gradually add the 6 tablespoons granulated sugar, 1 tablespoon at a time, beating on high speed until mixture forms stiff, glossy peaks (tips stand straight) and sugar dissolves (rub a small amount between two fingers; it should feel completely smooth).

5. Immediately spread meringue over hot pie filling, carefully sealing to edge of crust to prevent shrinkage. Bake for 15 minutes. Cool on a wire rack for 1 hour. Chill for 3 to 6 hours before serving.

***Test Kitchen Note:** To make mashed, cooked sweet potatoes, peel and chop 3 medium sweet potatoes (about 1¼ pounds). In medium saucepan with cover, cook sweet potatoes in enough boiling water to cover about 10 minutes or until tender; drain. Or drain one 17.2-ounce can whole sweet potatoes and transfer to a medium bowl. Mash with potato masher or electric mixer on low speed. Measure 2 cups mashed sweet potato for pie.

Advance Preparation: Prepare crust as directed in Step 1; cover. Store in refrigerator up to 24 hours. Cook and mash sweet potatoes and store in refrigerator up to 24 hours.

Per serving: 355 cal., 15 g total fat (6 g sat. fat), 75 mg chol., 187 mg sodium, 52 g carbo., 3 g fiber, 6 g pro.

Pumpkin Walnut Praline Pie

Make the crimped crust with at least an inch of excess dough. Skimpy, thin crusts overbrown before the rest of the pie is done.

Prep: 40 minutes **Bake:** 25 minutes + 25 minutes
Chill: 30 minutes **Oven:** 375°F **Makes:** 10 servings

- **12 ounces cream cheese (four 3-ounce packages or one and one-half 8-ounce packages), softened**
- **⅓ cup granulated sugar**
- **1 egg**
- **1 teaspoon finely shredded orange peel**
- **1 recipe Pastry for a Single-Crust Deep-Dish Pie**
- **1 15-ounce can pumpkin puree**
- **¾ cup granulated sugar**
- **2 teaspoons pumpkin pie spice**
- **3 eggs**
- **¾ cup half-and-half or light cream**
- **¾ cup broken walnuts**
- **½ cup milk chocolate-covered toffee pieces or chopped chocolate-covered English toffee bars**
- **¼ cup packed brown sugar**
- **Hot fudge ice cream topping (optional)**
- **Whipped cream (optional)**
- **Pumpkin pie spice (optional)**

1. In a medium mixing bowl combine cream cheese and ⅓ cup granulated sugar; beat with an electric mixer on low to medium speed until smooth. Beat in the 1 egg; stir in orange peel. Cover and chill for 30 minutes.

2. Preheat oven to 375°F. Prepare Pastry for a Single-Crust Deep-Dish Pie. On a lightly floured surface, use your hands to slightly flatten pastry. Roll dough from center to edge into a circle about 13 inches in diameter. To transfer pastry, wrap it around the rolling pin. Unroll pastry into a 9½- to 10-inch deep-dish pie plate. Ease pastry into pie plate, taking care not to stretch pastry. Trim pastry to ½ inch beyond edge of pie plate. Fold under extra pastry. Crimp edge high. Do not prick pastry.

3. For pumpkin filling, in a large bowl combine pumpkin, ¾ cup granulated sugar, and the 2 teaspoons pumpkin pie spice. Add the 3 eggs and beat lightly. Gradually beat in half-and-half.

Pumpkin Walnut Praline Pie

Spread cream cheese mixture in pastry-lined pie plate. Carefully spoon pumpkin filling over cream cheese layer. To prevent overbrowning, cover edge of pie with foil. Bake for 25 minutes.

4. In a small bowl combine walnuts, toffee pieces, and brown sugar. Remove foil from pie. Sprinkle walnut mixture over pumpkin filling.

5. Bake for 25 to 30 minutes or until a knife inserted near the center comes out clean. Cool on a wire rack. Cover and chill pie within 2 hours. If desired, garnish individual servings with hot fudge topping, whipped cream, and additional pumpkin pie spice.

Pastry for a Single-Crust Deep-Dish Pie: In a medium bowl stir together 1½ cups all-purpose flour and ¼ teaspoon salt. Use a pastry blender to cut in 6 tablespoons shortening until pieces are pea-size. Sprinkle 1 tablespoon cold water over part of the mixture; gently toss with a fork. Push moistened dough to the side of the bowl. Repeat moistening dough, using 1 tablespoon cold water at a time, until all of the dough is moist (5 to 6 tablespoons cold water total). Form dough into a ball.

Per serving: 547 cal., 33 g total fat (13 g sat. fat), 133 mg chol., 255 mg sodium, 56 g carbo., 2 g fiber, 9 g pro.

Coconut-Cranberry Torte

Coconut-Cranberry Torte

Cooling a cake in the baking pan for 10 minutes allows the cake to take its shape and come out of the pan more easily.

Prep: 35 minutes **Bake:** 20 minutes **Cool:** 10 minutes
Oven: 375°F **Makes:** 10 to 12 servings

- **1 recipe Cranberry Filling**
- **¾ cup butter**
- **3 eggs**
- **2½ cups all-purpose flour**
- **2½ teaspoons baking powder**
- **1 teaspoon finely shredded orange peel**
- **½ teaspoon salt**
- **1¾ cups granulated sugar**
- **1½ teaspoons vanilla**
- **¾ cup milk**
- **½ cup orange juice**
- **1 8-ounce package cream cheese, softened**
- **½ cup butter, softened**
- **½ teaspoon coconut extract**
- **5½ to 6 cups powdered sugar**
- **½ cup coconut chips or shredded coconut**

1. Prepare Cranberry Filling. Allow the ¾ cup butter and eggs to stand at room temperature for 30 minutes. Grease the bottom of a 15×10×1-inch baking pan. Line bottom of pan with waxed paper. Grease and lightly flour pan; set aside. Stir together flour, baking powder, orange peel, and salt.

2. Preheat oven to 375°F. In a large bowl beat butter for 30 seconds. Gradually add granulated sugar; beat until combined. Beat 2 minutes more. Add eggs, one at a time, beating well after each addition. Beat in vanilla. Alternately add flour mixture and milk and orange juice, beating on low speed after each addition just until combined. Spread batter into prepared pan.

3. Bake for 20 to 25 minutes or until a wooden toothpick inserted near the center comes out clean. Cool cake in pan on a wire rack for 10 minutes. Remove cake from pan; remove waxed paper. Cool completely on wire rack. Slice cake crosswise into three 5-inch-wide sections; set aside.

4. For frosting, in a large bowl beat cream cheese, the ½ cup butter, and coconut extract until light and fluffy. Gradually beat in powdered sugar to reach spreading consistency.

5. Place one cake layer on a serving platter. Spread with half of the Cranberry Filling. Top with a second cake layer. Spread with the remaining cranberry filling. Top with remaining cake layer. Frost top and sides of the cake with frosting. Sprinkle coconut onto the top and sides of cake, pressing lightly to evenly coat.

Cranberry Filling: In a medium saucepan stir together a 12-ounce package cranberries, 1 cup sugar, ¼ cup cranberry juice, 2 teaspoons lemon juice, 1 teaspoon finely shredded orange peel, and ½ teaspoon apple pie spice. Bring to boiling; reduce heat. Simmer, uncovered, about 10 minutes or until thickened. Transfer filling to a medium bowl. Cover and chill for 2 hours. Stir in 1 cup shredded coconut. Transfer to a blender or food processor. Cover and blend or process until smooth.

Advance Preparation: Prepare as directed. Cover and chill up to 2 days.

Per serving: 970 cal., 37 g total fat (23 g sat. fat), 151 mg chol., 447 mg sodium, 156 g carbo., 4 g fiber, 8 g pro.

White Chocolate and Almond Pound Cake

Be sure to use white baking chocolate that contains cocoa butter (check the ingredient list on the package). Cocoa butter gives the white chocolate its hallmark ivory color and mild chocolate flavor.

Prep: 50 minutes **Bake:** 55 minutes **Cool:** 15 minutes
Oven: 350°F **Makes:** 16 to 20 servings

- **4 ounces white baking chocolate with cocoa butter, chopped**
- **3 cups all-purpose flour**
- **¼ cup blanched almonds, finely ground**
- **1 teaspoon baking powder**
- **½ teaspoon baking soda**
- **½ teaspoon salt**
- **1 cup butter, softened**
- **2 cups sugar**
- **6 eggs**
- **1 tablespoon vanilla**
- **1½ teaspoons almond extract**
- **1 8-ounce carton dairy sour cream**
- **4 ounces white baking chocolate with cocoa butter, chopped**
- **1 teaspoon shortening**
- **¼ cup sliced almonds, toasted and chopped**

1. Preheat oven to 350°F. Grease and flour a 10-inch fluted tube pan; set aside.

2. In a heavy small saucepan cook and stir the 4 ounces white chocolate over low heat until it melts. In a medium bowl combine flour, finely ground almonds, baking powder, baking soda, and salt. Set aside.

3. In a very large mixing bowl beat butter with an electric mixer on medium to high speed for 30 seconds. Gradually add sugar, beating about 10 minutes or until mixture is fluffy and lighter in color. Add eggs one at a time, beating about 1 minute after each addition and scraping sides of bowl frequently. Add vanilla, almond extract, and melted white chocolate; beat just until combined.

4. Alternately add flour mixture and sour cream to butter mixture, beating on low to medium speed after each addition just until combined. Do not overmix. Spread batter into prepared pan.

5. Bake for 55 to 60 minutes or until a wooden toothpick inserted near the center comes out clean. Cool cake in pan on a wire rack for 15 minutes. Remove cake from pan; cool on a wire rack.

6. For glaze, in a heavy small saucepan, combine the 4 ounces white chocolate and shortening. Cook and stir over low heat until melted. Spoon glaze over pound cake and sprinkle with the chopped almonds. Let stand until glaze is set.

Advance Preparation: Prepare cake as directed without glaze. Place in an airtight container; cover. Store at room temperature up to 3 days, or freeze up to 2 months. Before serving, thaw if frozen, and glaze as directed.

Per serving: 447 cal., 23 g total fat (13 g sat. fat), 120 mg chol., 270 mg sodium, 53 g carbo., 1 g fiber, 7 g pro.

White Chocolate and Almond Pound Cake

Triple Chocolate-Pistachio Layer Cake

Smooth chocolate mascarpone frosting nestles between cake layers containing chopped pistachio bark candy. Additional shards of candy piled on top of the cake add a festive final flourish. Also pictured on the cover.

Prep: 1 hour **Bake:** 25 minutes
Stand: 30 minutes **Cool:** 10 minutes
Oven: 350°F **Makes:** 12 to 14 servings

- **1 recipe Bittersweet-Pistachio Bark (recipe, page 117)**
- **4 eggs**
- **1¾ cups all-purpose flour**
- **1½ teaspoons baking powder**
- **½ teaspoon salt**
- **¼ teaspoon baking soda**
- **½ cup butter, softened**
- **⅓ cup shortening**
- **1¾ cups sugar**
- **1 teaspoon vanilla**
- **¾ cup buttermilk or sour milk***
- **1 recipe Chocolate Mascarpone Frosting**

Triple Chocolate-Pistachio Layer Cake

1. Prepare Bittersweet-Pistachio Bark. Chop 1 cup of bark; set aside. Break remaining bark into shards; set aside.

2. Separate eggs; allow egg yolks and egg whites in two small bowls to stand at room temperature for 30 minutes. Meanwhile, grease bottoms of three** 8×1½-inch round cake pans. Line bottoms of pans with waxed paper; grease and flour cake pans. Set aside. In a medium bowl stir together flour, baking powder, salt, and baking soda; set aside. Preheat oven to 350°F.

3. In a very large mixing bowl beat butter and shortening with an electric mixer on medium to high speed for 30 seconds. Add sugar; beat until well combined, scraping sides of bowl. Beat in egg yolks and vanilla. Alternately add flour mixture and buttermilk, beating on low speed after each addition just until combined. Fold in the chopped bark.

4. Thoroughly wash the beaters. In a clean large mixing bowl beat egg whites until stiff peaks form (tips stand straight). Stir about one-third of the egg whites into cake batter. Fold in remaining whites. Spread batter evenly among prepared pans.

5. Bake cake layers for 25 to 30 minutes or until tops spring back when gently touched. Cool in pans on wire racks for 10 minutes; remove cake layers from pans. Peel off waxed paper. Cool completely on racks.

6. When cool, place one cake layer on a serving plate. Spread top with ⅔ cup of the Chocolate Mascarpone Frosting. Top with a second cake layer. Spread top of second layer with ⅔ cup frosting. Top with third cake layer. Spread remaining frosting on top and sides of the cake. Garnish top with pistachio bark shards. Serve immediately or cover and chill until serving time.

Chocolate Mascarpone Frosting: Soften ½ cup butter. In a very large mixing bowl beat softened butter, one 8-ounce carton mascarpone cheese, ½ cup unsweetened cocoa powder, and 1½ teaspoons vanilla with an electric mixer until smooth. Gradually beat in 2 cups powdered sugar until well combined. Beat in 3 tablespoons milk until smooth. Gradually beat in 4 cups powdered sugar until smooth. If necessary, beat in additional milk, 1 teaspoon at a time, to make frosting of spreading consistency. Makes about 4 cups.

***Test Kitchen Note:** To make ¾ cup sour milk, place 2 teaspoons lemon juice or vinegar in a glass measuring cup. Add enough milk to make ¾ cup total liquid; stir. Let mixture stand for 5 minutes.

****Test Kitchen Tip:** If you do not have three cake pans, spread two-thirds of the batter into two cake pans and bake as directed. Cover and chill remaining cake batter while the first two cake layers bake. Remove baked cakes from pans as directed. Cool pans. Wash, dry, grease, and flour one pan. Spread remaining one-third of the chilled batter into prepared pan and bake as directed.

Advance Preparation: Prepare as directed. Cover and chill up to 2 days.

Per serving: 797 cal., 37 g total fat (19 g sat. fat), 136 mg chol., 327 mg sodium, 113 g carbo., 1 g fiber, 10 g pro.

Gingerbread with Caramel Pears and Pumpkin Ice Cream

Move over lemon sauce! Brandy-soaked cherries combined with buttery sautéed pears take classic gingerbread to new heights.

Prep: 50 minutes **Bake:** 55 minutes
Cool: 30 minutes **Oven:** 325°F
Makes: 12 to 16 servings

- **1 cup butter**
- **1 cup milk or water**
- **¾ cup packed dark brown sugar**
- **¾ cup unsulphured black strap molasses or dark-flavor molasses**
- **½ cup honey (full flavor)**
- **3 cups all-purpose flour**
- **2 teaspoons ground ginger**
- **2 teaspoons ground cinnamon**
- **1 teaspoon baking powder**
- **½ teaspoon baking soda**
- **¼ teaspoon salt**
- **⅛ teaspoon ground cloves**
- **3 eggs**
- **1 recipe Caramel Pears**
- **Pumpkin, cinnamon, or vanilla ice cream**

1. Preheat oven to 325°F. Grease a 9×9×2-inch pan; set aside. In a medium saucepan combine butter, milk, brown sugar, molasses, and honey. Cook and stir over low heat until butter melts. Remove from heat and transfer to a large mixing bowl; cool slightly.

2. In a medium bowl combine flour, ginger, cinnamon, baking powder, baking soda, salt, and cloves. Set aside.

3. With an electric mixer on medium speed, beat eggs, one at a time, into cooled butter mixture; beat well after each addition. Add flour mixture, 1 cup at a time, beating on low speed just until combined (batter may be lumpy). Pour batter into prepared pan. Bake for 55 to 60 minutes or until wooden toothpick inserted near the center comes out clean.

4. Cool 30 minutes on wire rack. Serve warm with Caramel Pears and ice cream.

Caramel Pears: Soak ¼ cup dried cherries in ¼ cup brandy or orange juice for 30 minutes or until softened. Meanwhile, in a large skillet, cook and stir 3 to 4 pears, thinly sliced, peeled, and cored, in 3 tablespoons butter and a pinch of sugar until golden brown and cooked. Drain cherries. Stir cherries into pear mixture before serving.

Advance Preparation: Prepare and bake gingerbread as directed. Completely cool in pan on rack. Cover and store at room temperature up to 3 days. For longer storage, place gingerbread in an airtight container; cover. Freeze up to 3 months. Prepare the caramel pears as directed. Cool for 15 minutes. Spoon into an airtight container; cover. Store in refrigerator up to 3 days. Reheat in saucepan over low heat just until warm.

Per serving: 641 cal., 28 g total fat (17 g sat. fat), 135 mg chol., 351 mg sodium, 89 g carbo., 3 g fiber, 9 g pro.

cookie tray treats

Chocolate, peanut butter, peppermint, and coconut—your baking adventures are about to begin! Get a jump on the season and fill your freezer with plenty of holiday goodies. Then beautiful, delicious bars and cookies are within reach to share with guests or package as gifts.

Coconut-Macadamia Drops,
page 101

Caramel-Cashew Cookies

Caramel-Cashew Cookies

These sophisticated treats boast a cashew shortbread base, ooze with a luscious caramel filling, and glisten with a shiny chocolate drizzle.

Prep: 1 hour **Bake:** 15 minutes per batch
Stand: 1 hour **Oven:** 325°F **Makes:** 48 cookies

- **1 cup butter, softened**
- **½ cup powdered sugar**
- **1 tablespoon water**
- **1 teaspoon vanilla**
- **2 cups all-purpose flour**
- **1½ cups finely chopped cashews**
- **16 vanilla caramels**
- **3 tablespoons whipping cream**
- **¼ cup coarsely chopped cashews**
- **¾ cup semisweet chocolate pieces**
- **2 teaspoons shortening**

1. Preheat oven to 325°F. In a mixing bowl beat butter with an electric mixer on medium to high speed for 30 seconds. Add powdered sugar and beat until combined, scraping sides of bowl occasionally. Beat in water and vanilla until combined. Beat in as much flour as you can with the mixer. Stir in any remaining flour and the finely chopped cashews.

2. Shape dough into 1-inch balls. Place balls 1½ inches apart on an ungreased cookie sheet. Press your thumb into the center of each ball. Bake about 15 minutes or until bottoms are lightly browned. Transfer to a wire rack and let cool.

3. In a heavy small saucepan heat and stir caramels and whipping cream over low heat until mixture is smooth. Add coarsely chopped cashews. Spoon some of the melted caramel mixture into indentation in each cookie. (If necessary, reheat caramel mixture so it is spoonable.)

4. In another heavy small saucepan heat and stir chocolate pieces and shortening over low heat until melted. Drizzle some of the chocolate mixture over caramel on each cookie. Let stand until chocolate is set.

Advance Preparation: Prepare as directed. Place cookies in single layer in airtight container; cover. Chill up to 3 days or freeze, unfilled, up to 3 months. Thaw cookies; fill and drizzle.

Per cookie: 115 cal., 8 g total fat (4 g sat. fat), 11 mg chol., 51 mg sodium, 11 g carbo., 1 g fiber, 2 g pro.

Spiced Gumdrop Snowballs

Before quartering the gumdrops, run water over the kitchen scissors to prevent them from sticking to the gumdrops. If necessary, toss cut pieces with 2 to 3 teaspoons sugar to keep them from sticking together.

Prep: 30 minutes **Bake:** 10 minutes per batch
Oven: 375°F **Makes:** 36 cookies

- **⅔ cup butter, softened**
- **½ cup sugar**
- **½ teaspoon ground cinnamon**
- **2 egg yolks**
- **1 teaspoon vanilla**
- **1½ cups all-purpose flour**
- **1 cup spiced red and green gumdrops, quartered**
- **⅓ to ½ cup white nonpareils**

1. Preheat oven to 375°F. Grease two large cookie sheets; set aside. In a large mixing bowl beat butter with an electric mixer on medium to high speed for 30 seconds. Add sugar and cinnamon. Beat until combined, scraping sides of bowl occasionally. Beat in egg yolks and vanilla until combined. Beat in as much of the flour as you can with the mixer. Stir in any remaining flour. Stir in gumdrops.

2. Shape dough into 1-inch balls; roll balls in nonpareils. Place balls 1 inch apart on the prepared cookie sheets. Press each ball slightly to flatten. Bake about 10 minutes or until edges are light brown. Transfer to a wire rack; cool.

Advance Preparation: Prepare as directed. Layer cookies between waxed paper in an airtight container; cover. Store at room temperature up to 3 days or freeze up to 3 months.

Per cookie: 90 cal., 4 g total fat (2 g sat. fat), 21 mg chol., 34 mg sodium, 13 g carbo., 0 g fiber, 1 g pro.

Chock-Full of Chips

With three kinds of chocolate, these exciting and indulgent cookies appeal to everyone.

Prep: 40 minutes **Bake:** 10 minutes per batch
Oven: 350°F **Makes:** about 48 cookies

- 2½ cups all-purpose flour
- 1 cup quick-cooking rolled oats
- 1 cup wheat flake cereal
- 1 teaspoon baking powder
- 1 teaspoon baking soda
- ¼ teaspoon salt
- 1 cup butter, softened
- 1 cup granulated sugar
- 1 cup packed brown sugar
- 2 eggs
- 1½ teaspoons vanilla
- 1 cup semisweet chocolate pieces
- ½ cup miniature candy-coated milk chocolate pieces
- ½ cup white baking pieces

1. Preheat oven to 350°F. In a medium bowl combine flour, oats, cereal, baking powder, baking soda, and salt; set aside. In a very large mixing bowl beat butter with an electric mixer on medium to high speed for 30 seconds. Add granulated sugar and brown sugar. Beat until combined, scraping sides of bowl occasionally. Beat in eggs and vanilla. Beat in as much of the flour mixture as you can with the mixer. Stir in any remaining flour mixture. Stir in the semisweet chocolate pieces, miniature candy-coated chocolate pieces, and white baking pieces.

2. Drop dough by rounded teaspoons 2 inches apart onto ungreased cookie sheet. Bake for 10 to 12 minutes or until cookies are golden brown. Cool for 1 minute on cookie sheet. Transfer to a wire rack; cool.

Advance Preparation: Prepare as directed. Layer cookies between waxed paper in airtight container; cover. Store at room temperature up to 3 days or freeze up to 3 months.

Per cookie: 146 cal., 7 g total fat (4 g sat. fat), 19 mg chol., 88 mg sodium, 21 g carbo., 1 g fiber, 2 g pro.

Chock-Full of Chips

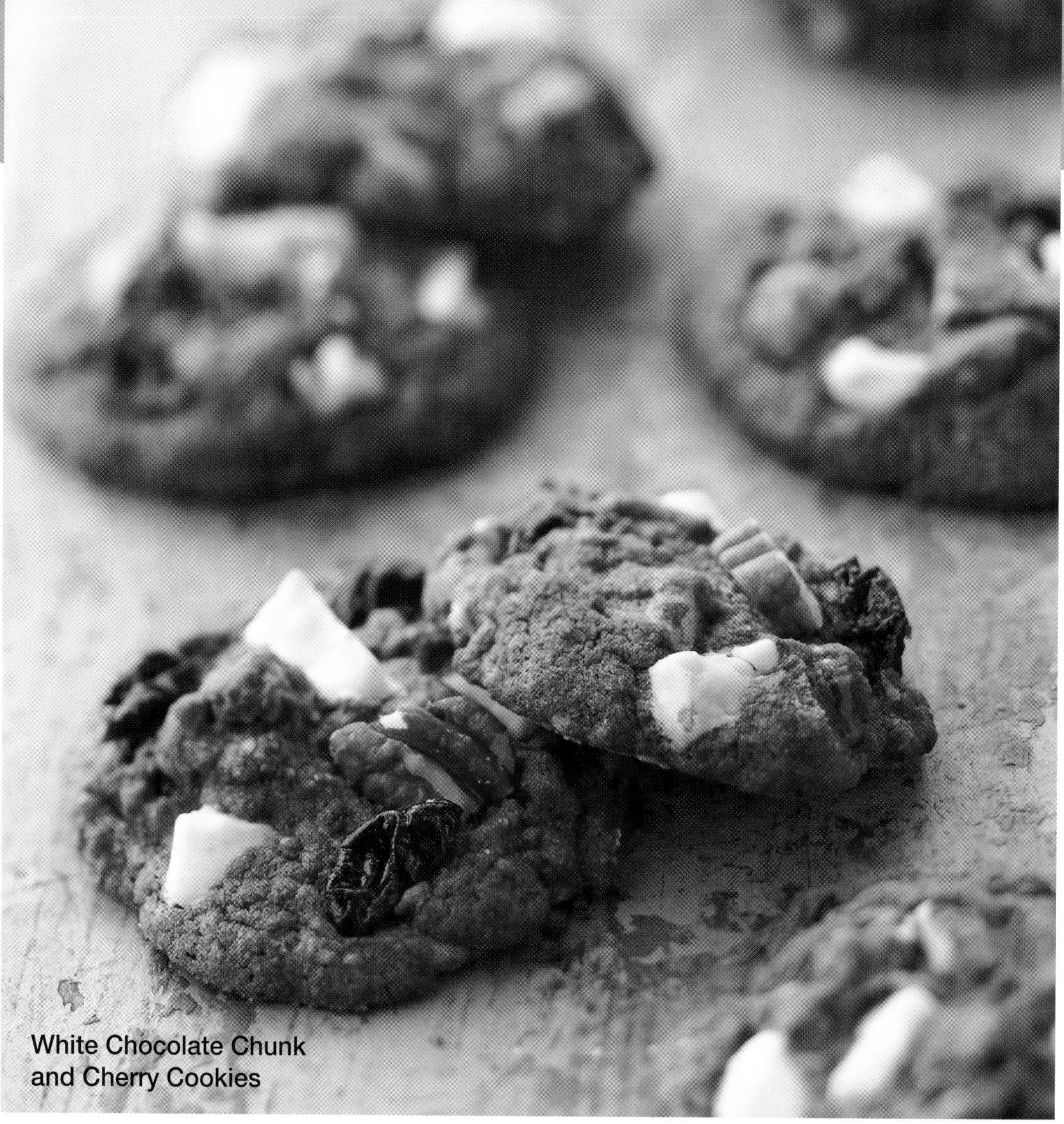
White Chocolate Chunk and Cherry Cookies

White Chocolate Chunk and Cherry Cookies

These cocoa drops are studded with chunks of white chocolate, dried cherries, and chopped pecans.

Prep: 40 minutes **Bake:** 7 minutes per batch
Oven: 350°F **Makes:** 60 cookies

- **2 cups all-purpose flour**
- **½ cup unsweetened cocoa powder**
- **2 teaspoons baking powder**
- **½ teaspoon salt**
- **1 cup butter, softened**
- **1½ cups sugar**
- **2 eggs**
- **1 teaspoon vanilla**
- **6 ounces white chocolate baking squares, coarsely chopped, or 1 cup white baking pieces**
- **1 cup coarsely chopped pecans, toasted if desired**
- **½ cup dried cherries**

1. Preheat oven to 350°F. Lightly grease cookie sheets; set aside. In a medium bowl combine flour, cocoa, baking powder, and salt. In a large mixing bowl, beat butter with an electric mixer on medium to high speed for about 30 seconds. Beat in sugar until light and fluffy. Beat in eggs and vanilla until combined. Beat in as much of the flour mixture as you can with the mixer; stir in any remaining flour mixture, white chocolate, pecans, and cherries.

2. Drop dough by rounded teaspoon 2 inches apart onto prepared cookie sheets. Bake for 7 to 9 minutes or until edges are just firm (do not overbake). Transfer cookies to wire racks to cool completely.

Advance Preparation: Prepare as directed. Layer cookies between waxed paper in airtight container; cover. Store at room temperature up to 3 days or freeze up to 3 months.

Per cookie: 100 cal., 6 g total fat (3 g sat. fat), 16 mg chol., 55 mg sodium, 11 g carbo., 0 g fiber, 1 g pro.

Toffee Fingers

For no-mess drizzling, transfer melted chocolate to a resealable bag; seal bag. Snip off a tiny piece of one corner of the bag and squeeze to drizzle the chocolate.

Prep: 30 minutes **Bake:** 20 minutes
Cool: 10 minutes **Oven:** 325°F **Makes:** 24 bars

- **1¼ cups all-purpose flour**
- **¾ teaspoon baking powder**
- **¼ teaspoon salt**
- **½ cup butter, softened**
- **¼ cup powdered sugar**
- **2 tablespoons packed brown sugar**
- **½ cup toffee pieces**
- **½ cup semisweet chocolate pieces**
- **1 teaspoon shortening**
- **¼ cup toffee pieces**

1. Preheat oven to 325°F. Line an 8×8×2-inch square baking pan with foil, leaving about 1 inch of foil extending over the ends of the pan; set aside.

2. In a small bowl stir together flour, baking powder, and salt; set aside. In a large mixing bowl beat butter with an electric mixer on medium to high speed for 30 seconds. Add powdered sugar and brown sugar. Beat until combined, scraping sides of bowl occasionally. Beat in flour mixture (combined mixture seems dry, but comes together during beating). Stir in the ½ cup toffee pieces. Press mixture evenly into the bottom of the prepared pan; prick dough with fork every ½ inch.

3. Bake about 20 minutes or until light brown. Cool slightly in pan on a wire rack.

4. Remove warm bars from pan, using the overhanging foil to lift bars. Place on cutting board. Cut into eight 1-inch strips. Cut each strip crosswise into three pieces, making 24 bars. Transfer bars to a wire rack placed over a sheet of waxed paper; cool completely.

5. In a small saucepan heat and stir chocolate pieces and shortening over low heat until smooth. Cool slightly. Drizzle bars with melted chocolate. Immediately sprinkle bars with the ¼ cup toffee pieces. Let bars stand until set.

Advance Preparation: Prepare as directed. Layer cookies between waxed paper in airtight container; cover. Store at room temperature up to 3 days or freeze, unfrosted, up to 3 months. Thaw cookies, then frost.

Per bar: 121 cal., 7 g total fat (4 g sat. fat), 11 mg chol., 80 mg sodium, 14 g carbo., 0 g fiber, 0 g pro.

Coconut-Macadamia Drops

For easy mixing, place the dough and ingredients in a resealable plastic bag and knead together. *Pictured on page 97.*

Prep: 30 minutes **Bake:** 14 minutes per batch
Oven: 350°F **Makes:** about 36 cookies

- **1 18-ounce package refrigerated sugar cookie dough**
- **4½ cups flaked coconut**
- **1 cup chopped macadamia nuts**
- **2 egg whites, lightly beaten**
- **2 to 3 teaspoons finely shredded lime peel**

1. Preheat oven to 350°F. Combine cookie dough, 2 cups of the flaked coconut, macadamia nuts, beaten egg whites, and lime peel. (Dough will be wet and sticky.)

2. Place the remaining 2½ cups flaked coconut in a bowl. Drop dough by rounded teaspoons into coconut. Roll dough around with spoons to coat. Place rolled dough pieces 2 inches apart on ungreased cookie sheet. Bake for 14 to 16 minutes or until edges are lightly browned and coconut is toasted. Transfer to a wire rack; cool.

Advance Preparation: Prepare as directed. Layer cookies between waxed paper in airtight container; cover. Store at room temperature up to 3 days or freeze up to 3 months.

Per cookie: 159 cal., 11 g total fat (6 g sat. fat), 4 mg chol., 113 mg sodium, 15 g carbo., 1 g fiber, 2 g pro.

Double Chocolate Diamonds

Double Chocolate Diamonds

Rich bittersweet chocolate finishes these cookies, giving crushed candy canes a dark backdrop.

Prep: 45 minutes **Bake:** 6 minutes per batch
Stand: 30 minutes **Oven:** 375°F
Makes: about 50 cookies

- ½ cup butter, softened
- 1 cup packed brown sugar
- ½ cup unsweetened cocoa powder
- 2 tablespoons milk
- 2 teaspoons vanilla
- ½ teaspoon baking soda
- 1⅓ cups all-purpose flour
- 1¼ cups bittersweet or semisweet chocolate pieces
- 1 tablespoon shortening
- ½ cup crushed candy canes (about 6)

1. In a large mixing bowl beat butter with an electric mixer on medium to high speed for 30 seconds. Add brown sugar, cocoa powder, milk, vanilla, and baking soda. Beat until combined, scraping sides of bowl occasionally. Beat in as much of the flour as you can with the mixer. Stir in any remaining flour. Shape dough into a smooth ball. If necessary, cover and chill dough about 30 minutes or until dough is easy to handle.

2. Preheat oven to 375°F. Divide dough in half. On a lightly floured surface, roll a portion of the dough ¼ inch thick. Use a 2½×1¾-inch diamond-shape cutter to cut out dough. Place cutouts 2 inches apart on ungreased cookie sheet. Bake for 6 to 8 minutes or until edges are firm. Cool for 1 minute on cookie sheet. Transfer to a wire rack and cool completely.

3. In a small saucepan combine chocolate pieces and shortening. Cook and stir mixture over low heat until melted. Dip half of each cookie into chocolate, allowing excess to drip off. Place on waxed paper. Sprinkle each cookie with crushed candy canes. Let stand about 30 minutes or until chocolate is set.

Advance Preparation: Prepare as directed. Layer undipped cookies between waxed paper in airtight container; cover. Store at room temperature up to 3 days. Or freeze, undipped, up to 3 months. Thaw cookies; dip and sprinkle.

Per cookie: 78 cal., 4 g total fat (2 g sat. fat), 5 mg chol., 28 mg sodium, 11 g carbo., 1 g fiber, 1 g pro.

Pistachio and Poppy Seed Shortbread

Dried fruit, boiled or dipped in sugar syrup, then sometimes into granulated sugar make up candied fruits. The most common candied fruits are cherries, pineapple, and citrus rinds. Store them in an airtight container in a cool, dry place.

Prep: 30 minutes **Bake:** 25 minutes
Oven: 325°F **Makes:** 16 wedges

- 1¼ cups all-purpose flour
- ⅓ cup sugar
- 3 tablespoons finely chopped pistachio nuts
- 2 teaspoons poppy seeds
- ⅔ cup butter
- 1 recipe Orange Glaze
- Diced candied citrus peel (optional)

1. Preheat oven to 325°F. Stir together flour, sugar, pistachios, and poppy seeds. Using a pastry blender, cut in butter until mixture resembles fine crumbs and starts to cling. Form mixture into a ball and knead until well combined.

2. On an ungreased cookie sheet pat or roll dough into an 8-inch circle. Crimp the edge. Cut circle into 16 wedges (do not separate). Bake for 25 minutes or until edges are lightly browned and the center is set. Cut circle into wedges again while still warm. Cool on the cookie sheet for 5 minutes. Transfer wedges to a wire rack; cool.

3. Drizzle wedges with Orange Glaze and, if desired, sprinkle with candied citrus peel.

Orange Glaze: Combine ¾ cup powdered sugar and enough orange juice (1 to 2 tablespoons) to make a mixture of glazing consistency.

Advance Preparation: Prepare as directed. Layer wedges between waxed paper in airtight container; cover. Store at room temperature up to 3 days or freeze up to 3 months. Thaw, then drizzle.

Per wedge: 151 cal., 9 g total fat (5 g sat. fat), 20 mg chol., 61 mg sodium, 18 g carbo., 0 g fiber, 1 g pro.

Jumbo Multigrain Cookies

Allow these cookies to stand a couple minutes after baking so they're easier to remove from the cookie sheet.

Prep: 30 minutes **Bake:** 12 minutes per batch
Oven: 350°F **Makes:** 24 cookies

- ⅔ cup butter, softened
- ¾ cup granulated sugar
- ½ cup packed brown sugar
- ½ teaspoon baking soda
- ½ teaspoon ground cinnamon
- 1 egg
- ⅓ cup vegetable oil
- ¼ cup honey
- 1 teaspoon vanilla
- 1¼ cups unbleached all-purpose flour or all-purpose flour
- ½ cup toasted wheat germ
- 2½ cups rolled oats
- 2 cups red and/or green candy-coated milk chocolate pieces

1. Preheat oven to 350°F. In a large mixing bowl beat butter with an electric mixer on medium to high speed for 30 seconds. Add granulated sugar, brown sugar, baking soda, and cinnamon; beat until combined. Beat in egg, oil, honey, and vanilla until combined. Beat in flour and wheat germ. Stir in oats and candies.

2. Place ¼-cup mounds of dough 4 inches apart on ungreased cookie sheets; flatten slightly. Bake about 12 minutes or until golden brown. Let cool for 2 minutes on cookie sheet. Transfer to wire racks; cool completely.

Advance Preparation: Prepare as directed. Layer cookies between waxed paper in airtight container; cover. Store at room temperature up to 3 days or freeze up to 3 months.

Per serving: 309 cal., 13 g total fat (6 g sat. fat), 25 mg chol., 78 mg sodium, 43 g carbo., 3 g fiber, 5 g pro.

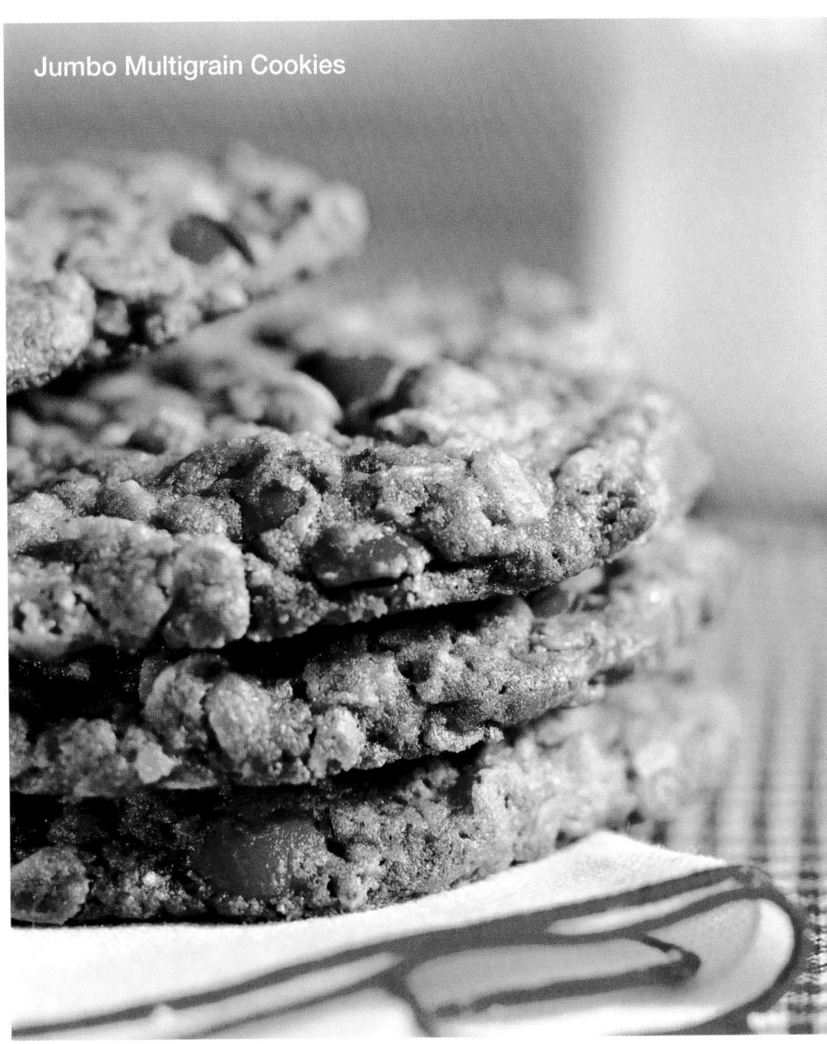
Jumbo Multigrain Cookies

Coconut-Raspberry Delights

Prep: 45 minutes **Bake:** 20 minutes per batch
Stand: 30 minutes **Oven:** 325°F
Makes: about 40 cookies

- **1 7-ounce package flaked coconut (2⅔ cups)**
- **⅔ cup sugar**
- **⅓ cup all-purpose flour**
- **3 egg whites, lightly beaten**
- **½ teaspoon almond extract**
- **4 ounces chocolate-flavor candy coating, chopped**
- **¼ cup seedless raspberry jam or preserves**

1. Preheat oven to 325°F. Line cookie sheets with parchment paper; set aside.

2. In a bowl stir together coconut, sugar, flour, and ¼ teaspoon *salt.* Stir in egg whites and almond extract. Drop coconut mixture by teaspoons 1 inch apart onto prepared cookie sheets, making ¾- to 1-inch mounds. Lightly flour your thumb and press an indentation into the center of each mound.

3. Bake about 20 minutes or until edges are golden. If necessary, use the rounded side of a teaspoon to press indentations again. Cool cookies completely on cookie sheets. Carefully remove cookies from cookie sheets.

4. In a heavy small saucepan heat and stir candy coating over low heat until melted. Carefully dip the bottom of each cooled cookie into the melted candy coating, letting excess drip off. Place cookies, candy coating sides up, on parchment paper or waxed paper; let stand about 30 minutes or until candy coating sets.

5. To fill cookies, just before serving spoon about ¼ teaspoon of the preserves into the indentation in each cookie.

Advance Preparation: Prepare as directed. Layer unfilled cookies between pieces of waxed paper in airtight container; cover. Chill up to 1 week or freeze up to 3 months. Thaw cookies, then fill.

Per cookie: 63 cal., 3 g total fat (2 g sat. fat), 0 mg chol., 33 mg sodium, 9 g carbo., 0 g fiber, 1 g pro.

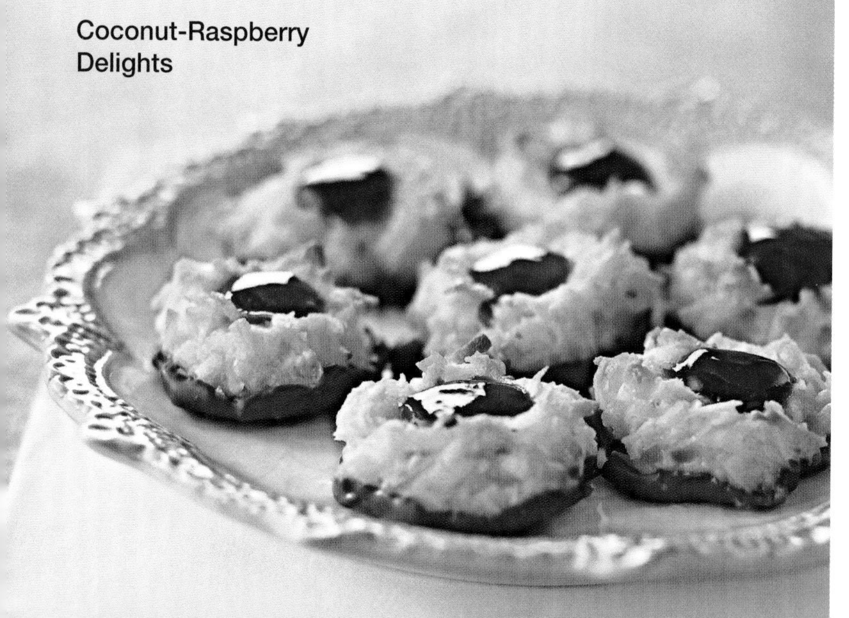

Coconut-Raspberry Delights

Mulling Spice and Coconut Cookies

Prep: 35 minutes **Bake:** 8 minutes per batch
Chill: 2 hours **Oven:** 375°F **Makes:** 60 cookies

- **½ cup canned coconut milk**
- **2 tablespoons mulling spice**
- **½ cup chopped pitted dates**
- **½ cup butter, softened**
- **½ cup shortening**
- **1½ cups granulated sugar**
- **2 teaspoons cream of tartar**
- **1 teaspoon baking soda**
- **¼ teaspoon salt**
- **2 eggs**
- **3 cups all-purpose flour**
- **1½ cups powdered sugar**
- **Milk**
- **1¼ cups flaked coconut (optional)**

1. In a small saucepan combine coconut milk and mulling spice. Bring just to boiling; reduce heat to low. Simmer, covered, over low heat for 5 minutes. Strain through a fine-mesh sieve; discard mulling spice. Reserve 2 tablespoons of the spiced coconut milk; cover and chill for use in frosting. Add dates to remaining spiced coconut milk. Cover; set aside.

2. For cookie dough, beat butter and shortening on medium to high speed for 30 seconds. Add granulated sugar, cream of tartar, baking soda, and salt. Beat until combined, scraping sides of bowl.

Beat in eggs until combined. Beat in as much flour as you can. Stir in any remaining flour. Add coconut milk and date mixture. Cover and chill dough 2 to 4 hours or until easy to handle.

3. Preheat oven to 375°F. Shape dough into 1-inch balls. Place balls 2 inches apart on an ungreased cookie sheet. Bake for 8 to 10 minutes or until light brown. Transfer to a wire rack; cool.

4. For frosting, combine powdered sugar and reserved spiced coconut milk. Stir in enough milk (1 to 2 teaspoons) to make a frosting of desired consistency. Spread or drizzle cooled cookies with frosting; if desired, sprinkle with coconut.

Advance Preparation: Prepare as directed. Layer cookies between waxed paper in airtight container; cover. Store at room temperature up to 3 days or freeze, unfrosted, up to 3 months. Thaw cookies, then frost.

Per cookie: 93 cal., 4 g total fat (2 g sat. fat), 11 mg chol., 45 mg sodium, 14 g carbo., 0 g fiber, 1 g pro.

Key Lime Spritz Cookies

Key Lime Spritz Cookies

Find key limes in Hispanic markets for this cookie-press treat. Also pictured on front and back covers.

Prep: 30 minutes **Bake:** 6 minutes per batch
Stand: 20 minutes **Oven:** 400°F
Makes: about 84 cookies

- **1 cup butter, softened**
- **¾ cup granulated sugar**
- **¼ teaspoon baking powder**
- **1 egg**
- **1 teaspoon finely shredded key lime or lime peel (set aside)**
- **2 teaspoons key lime or lime juice**
- **2½ cups all-purpose flour**
- **Green color sugar (optional)**
- **1 recipe Lime Icing (optional)**
- **Finely shredded lime peel (optional)**

1. In a bowl beat butter for 30 seconds. Add granulated sugar and baking powder. Beat until combined, scraping sides of bowl. Beat in egg and juice until combined. Beat in as much flour as you can. Stir in any remaining flour and the lime peel.

2. Preheat oven to 400°F. Place unchilled dough into cookie press fitted with template. Force dough through the press, forming desired shapes, 1 inch apart, onto ungreased cookie sheets. If desired, sprinkle cookies with green color sugar. Bake for 6 to 8 minutes or until edges are firm but not brown. Transfer cookies to wire racks and let cool. If desired, frost or pipe with Lime Icing; let stand 20 minutes or until set. If desired, sprinkle frosting with lime peel.

Lime Icing: Combine ¾ cup powdered sugar, 1½ teaspoons lime juice, and enough milk (2 to 3 teaspoons) to make drizzling consistency. If desired, tint with food coloring. Makes ⅓ cup.

Advance Preparation: Prepare as directed. Layer unfrosted cookies between waxed paper in airtight container; cover. Store at room temperature up to 3 days or freeze up to 3 months. Thaw cookies; frost, if desired.

Per cookie: 41 cal., 2 g total fat (1 g sat. fat), 8 mg chol., 9 mg sodium, 5 g carbo., 0 g fiber, 0 g pro.

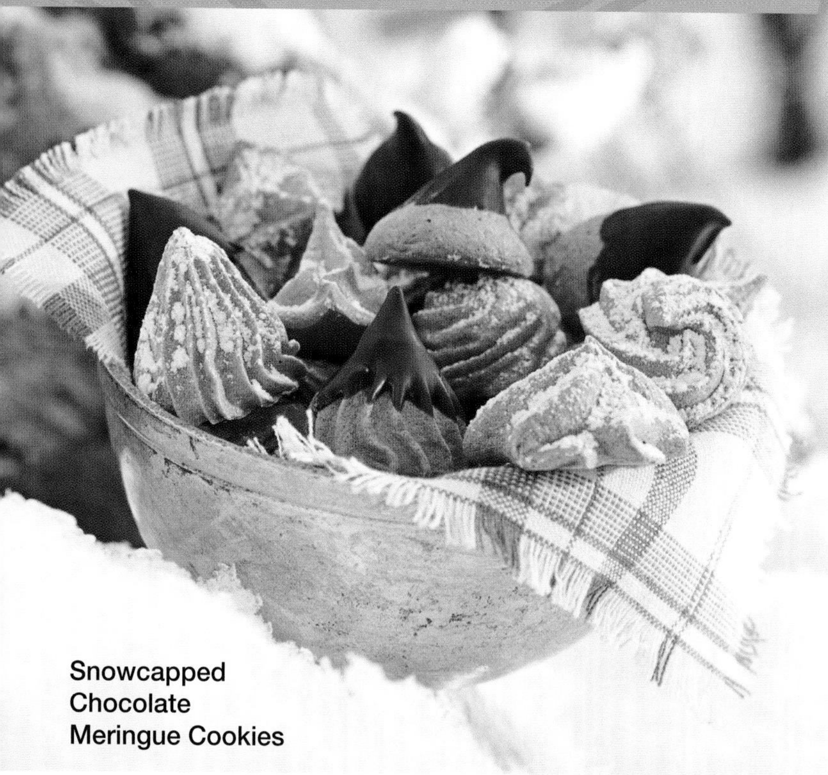
Snowcapped Chocolate Meringue Cookies

Snowcapped Chocolate Meringue Cookies

These melt-in-your-mouth treats are specialties of the San Sophia Inn in Telluride, Colorado. Their soft peaks resemble the snowcapped mountains outside the inn.

Prep: 30 minutes **Bake:** 15 minutes
Stand: 15 minutes **Oven:** 300°F **Makes:** 72 cookies

- **5 egg whites**
- **Dash salt**
- **½ cup granulated sugar**
- **¾ cup powdered sugar**
- **¼ cup unsweetened cocoa powder**
- **Powdered sugar (optional)**
- **1 cup semisweet chocolate pieces (optional)**
- **1 teaspoon shortening (optional)**

1. Allow egg whites to stand at room temperature for 30 minutes. Preheat oven to 300°F. Line two very large cookie sheets with parchment paper or foil; set aside. In a large bowl beat egg whites and salt with an electric mixer on medium speed until soft peaks form (tips curl). Gradually add granulated sugar, about 1 tablespoon at a time, beating on high speed until stiff peaks form (tips stand straight). In a medium bowl combine the powdered sugar and cocoa powder. Gently fold cocoa mixture into the beaten egg white mixture.

2. Spoon mixture into a decorating bag fitted with a star or open tip. Pipe mixture into 1½-inch shapes, about 2 inches apart, on prepared cookie sheets. (Or drop mixture by rounded teaspoons onto cookie sheets.) Bake both sheets on separate racks for 15 minutes. Turn off oven and let cookies dry in oven for 15 minutes more. Transfer cookies to a wire rack; cool completely.

3. If desired, sprinkle cookies with additional powdered sugar. Or if desired, in a small saucepan cook and stir chocolate pieces and shortening over low heat until mixture is melted and smooth. Dip tops of cookies into chocolate, allowing excess to drip off. Let stand until set.

Advance Preparation: Prepare as directed. Layer cookies between waxed paper in an airtight container; cover. Store at room temperature up to 3 days.

Per cookie: 12 cal., 0 g total fat (0 g sat. fat), 0 mg chol., 6 mg sodium, 3 g carbo., 0 g fiber, 0 g pro.

Northwest Pecan Treats

Your holiday guests are sure to love these pecan-pie bars topped with dried cherries.

Prep: 35 minutes **Bake:** 20 + 25 minutes
Oven: 350°F **Makes:** 48 bars

- **3 cups all-purpose flour**
- **½ cup sugar**
- **½ teaspoon salt**
- **1 cup cold butter**
- **4 eggs, lightly beaten**
- **1¼ cups dark-color corn syrup**
- **1¼ cups sugar**
- **3 tablespoons butter, melted**
- **2 teaspoons vanilla**
- **2½ cups chopped pecans**
- **⅓ cup dried cherries or cranberries, snipped**

1. Preheat oven to 350°F. Line a 15×10×1-inch baking pan with foil, extending foil over edges of pan. Grease the foil; set pan aside.

2. In a large bowl combine flour, the ½ cup sugar, and the salt. Use a pastry blender to cut in the 1 cup butter until mixture resembles coarse crumbs. Press mixture evenly into prepared pan. Bake for 20 minutes.

3. Meanwhile, in a mixing bowl whisk eggs, syrup, the 1¼ cups sugar, the 3 tablespoons melted butter, and the vanilla until combined.

4. Sprinkle pecans and dried cherries over hot crust. Slowly pour egg mixture over all. Bake for 25 to 30 minutes or until set. Cool completely in pan on a wire rack. Lift baked mixture from pan using the foil. Remove foil. Cut into bars.

Advance Preparation: Prepare as directed. Layer bars between waxed paper in airtight container; cover. Store at room temperature up to 3 days or freeze up to 3 months.

Per bar: 170 cal., 9 g total fat (3 g sat. fat), 30 mg chol., 76 mg sodium, 21 g carbo., 1 g fiber, 1 g pro.

Salted-Peanut Logs

A fun and delicious take on traditional peanut butter cookies, these peanut butter logs receive a piping of sweet butter frosting and a sprinkling of chopped salted peanuts.

Prep: 30 minutes **Bake:** 10 minutes per batch
Oven: 350°F **Makes:** 16 logs

- **⅓ cup butter, softened**
- **⅓ cup creamy peanut butter**
- **3 tablespoons packed brown sugar**
- **3 tablespoons milk**
- **½ teaspoon vanilla**
- **1¼ cups all-purpose flour**
- **1 recipe Butter Frosting**
- **¾ cup chopped dry roasted peanuts**

1. Preheat oven to 350°F. In a medium mixing bowl beat butter and peanut butter with an electric mixer on medium to high speed for 30 seconds. Add brown sugar, milk, and vanilla; beat until combined, scraping sides of bowl occasionally. Beat in flour.

2. Roll dough into a sixteen-inch log. Cut 1-inch slices of dough. Form each slice into a 3-inch log. Place logs 1 inch apart on an ungreased cookie sheet.

3. Bake for 10 to 12 minutes or until bottoms just begin to brown. Transfer cookies to a wire rack and let cool. Pipe or spread top of each log with Butter Frosting and sprinkle with peanuts.

Butter Frosting: In a bowl beat 2 tablespoons softened butter on medium to high speed for 30 seconds. Gradually beat in ¼ cup powdered sugar. Slowly beat in 2 teaspoons milk and ¼ teaspoon vanilla. Gradually beat in ¾ cup powdered sugar. If necessary, beat in additional milk to make a frosting of piping consistency.

Advance Preparation: Prepare as directed. Layer cookies between waxed paper in airtight container; cover. Store at room temperature up to 3 days or freeze, unfrosted, up to 3 months. Thaw cookies, then frost and sprinkle with peanuts.

Per log: 194 cal., 11 g total fat (4 g sat. fat), 14 mg chol., 120 mg sodium, 20 g carbo., 1 g fiber, 4 g pro.

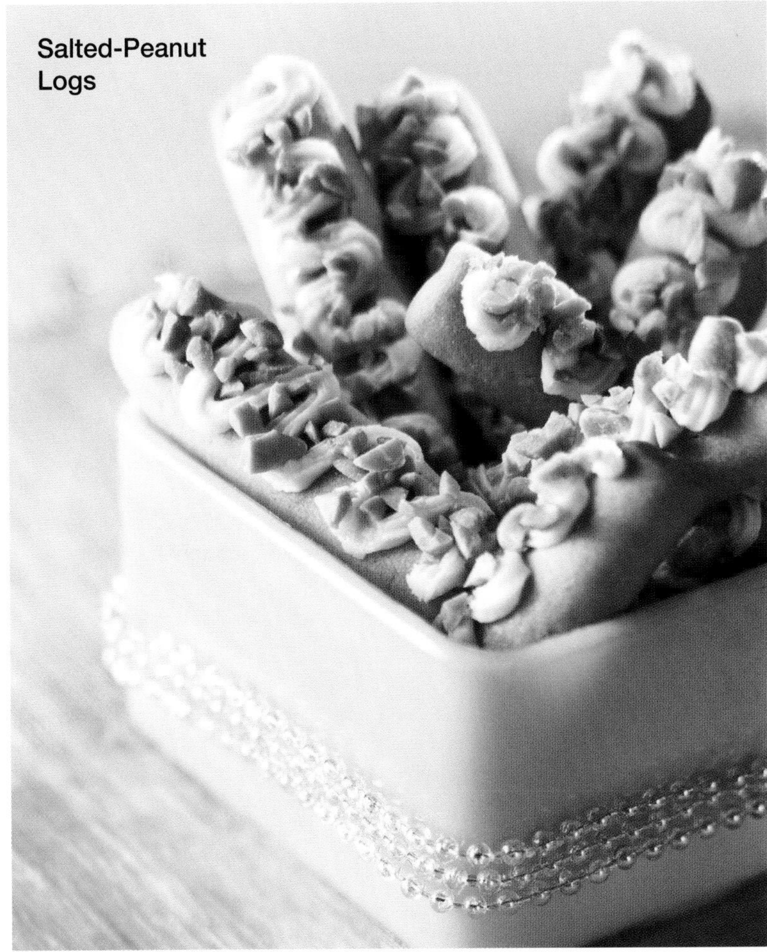
Salted-Peanut Logs

Gingery Pear-Pecan Cookies

Dried pears found near other dried fruit in the produce section of larger supermarkets lend a subtle sweetness to these cookies.

Prep: 40 minutes **Bake:** 8 minutes per batch
Oven: 350°F **Makes:** 60 cookies

- **3½ cups all-purpose flour**
- **1 tablespoon finely chopped crystallized ginger**
- **2 teaspoons ground ginger**
- **1½ teaspoons baking soda**
- **1 teaspoon ground cinnamon**
- **¼ teaspoon salt**
- **¼ teaspoon ground cloves**
- **¼ teaspoon ground nutmeg**
- **½ cup shortening**
- **½ cup butter, softened**
- **¾ cup granulated sugar**
- **¾ cup packed brown sugar**
- **2 eggs**
- **⅓ cup molasses**
- **½ cup chopped toasted pecans**
- **½ cup snipped dried pears**
- **½ cup coarse or granulated sugar**

Gingery Pear-Pecan Cookies

1. Preheat oven to 350°F. Stir together flour, crystallized ginger, ground ginger, baking soda, cinnamon, salt, cloves, and nutmeg; set aside.

2. In a mixing bowl beat shortening and butter on medium to high speed for 30 seconds. Add ¾ cup each granulated sugar and brown sugar. Beat until combined, scraping sides of bowl. Beat in eggs and molasses until combined. Beat in as much of the flour mixture as you can. Stir in any remaining flour mixture, pecans, and dried pears.

3. Shape dough into 1-inch balls. Roll balls in the ½ cup coarse sugar. Place balls 2 inches apart on an ungreased cookie sheet. Bake for 8 to 10 minutes or until tops are puffed and edges are set (do not overbake). Cool on cookie sheet for 1 minute. Transfer to a wire rack; cool.

Advance Preparation: Prepare as directed. Layer cookies between waxed paper in airtight container; cover. Store at room temperature up to 3 days or freeze up to 3 months.

Per cookie: 101 cal., 4 g total fat (2 g sat. fat), 11 mg chol., 56 mg sodium, 15 g carbo., 0 g fiber, 1 g pro.

Panettone Cookies

These fruit-studded cookies are reminiscent of the Italian sweet bread known by the same name that people celebrate at Christmas.

Prep: 25 minutes **Bake:** 8 minutes per batch
Oven: 375°F **Makes:** about 48 cookies

- **1 cup butter-flavor or plain shortening**
- **1 cup packed brown sugar**
- **½ cup granulated sugar**
- **1 teaspoon anise seeds, crushed**
- **1 teaspoon baking soda**
- **½ teaspoon salt**
- **2 eggs**
- **1 teaspoon vanilla**
- **2½ cups all-purpose flour**
- **½ cup golden or dark raisins**

½ **cup toasted pine nuts, chopped, if desired**
1 **to 2 tablespoons finely chopped candied citron**

1. Preheat oven to 375°F. In a large mixing bowl beat shortening on medium to high speed for 30 seconds. Add sugars, anise seeds, baking soda, and salt. Beat until combined, scraping sides of bowl. Beat in eggs and vanilla. Beat in as much flour as you can. Stir in any remaining flour. Stir in raisins, pine nuts, and citron.

2. Drop dough by rounded teaspoons 2 inches apart onto ungreased cookie sheet. Bake about 8 minutes or until edges are lightly browned. Transfer to a wire rack; cool.

Advance Preparation: Prepare as directed. Layer cookies between waxed paper in airtight container; cover. Store at room temperature up to 3 days or freeze up to 3 months.

Per cookie: 104 cal., 5 g total fat (1 g sat. fat), 9 mg chol., 56 mg sodium, 13 g carbo., 0 g fiber, 1 g pro.

Lime Shortbread Trees

Rolling and cutting the dough right on a cookie sheet creates extra tender trees. Also pictured on the cover.

Prep: 1 hour 15 minutes **Bake:** 15 minutes per batch
Cool: 10 minutes per batch **Oven:** 325°F
Makes: 30 cookies

1 **cup butter, softened**
½ **cup powdered sugar**
2 **teaspoons finely shredded lime peel**
2¼ **cups all-purpose flour**
1 **cup powdered sugar**
Milk
Green food coloring
Small candies

1. Beat butter for 30 seconds. Add sugar, lime peel, and ¼ teaspoon *salt.* Beat until combined, scraping sides of bowl. Beat in flour until dough just comes together. Divide dough in half. Cover and chill for 30 minutes or until dough is easy to handle.

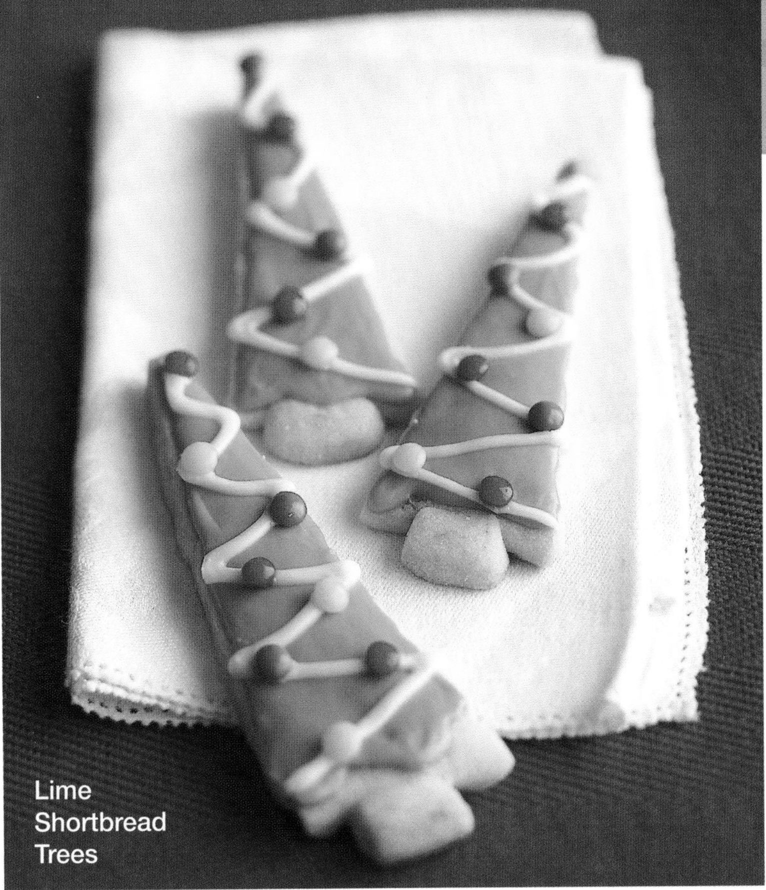

Lime Shortbread Trees

2. Preheat oven to 325°F. On a large ungreased cookie sheet roll one dough portion into 13×4-inch rectangle. Score one long side at 1½-inch intervals. Starting ¾ inch from the corner of the opposite long side, score at 1½-inch intervals. With a long knife, cut across the dough, connecting the scored marks and making 15 triangular trees; do not separate. Remove dough scraps from edges; shape into 15 small rectangles. Add to bottom of trees as trunks. Repeat with remaining dough portion.

3. Bake about 15 minutes or until edges just begin to brown. While still hot, recut trees with a long sharp knife. Cool for 10 minutes on cookie sheet. Transfer cookies to a wire rack; cool completely.

4. For frosting, combine powdered sugar and enough milk, 1 to 2 teaspoons at a time, until spreading consistency. Tint some of the frosting with green food coloring. Spread on cooled cookies. Pipe white icing on top and add candy decorations. Let stand for 20 minutes or until set.

Advance Preparation: Prepare as directed. Layer unfrosted cookies between waxed paper in an airtight container; cover. Store at room temperature up to 3 days or freeze up to 3 months. Thaw; frost.

Per serving: 128 cal., 8 g total fat (4 g sat. fat), 16 mg chol., 64 mg sodium, 14 g carbo., 1 g fiber, 2 g pro.

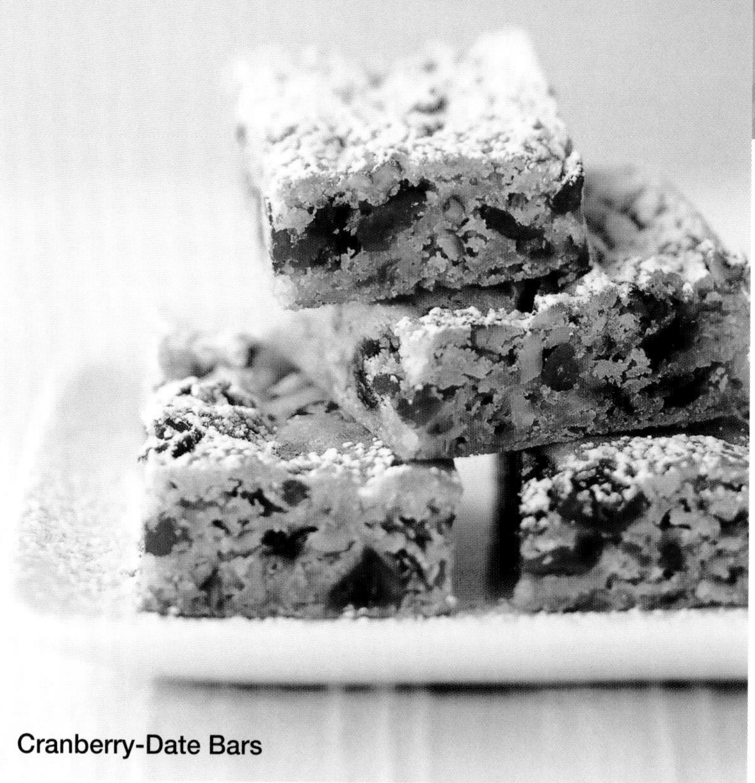

Cranberry-Date Bars

3. Spread dough evenly in prepared pan. Bake for 25 to 30 minutes or until top is lightly browned and a wooden toothpick inserted in center comes out clean. Cool in pan on a wire rack.

4. To serve, remove baked mixture from pan by lifting foil. Place on a cutting board; cut into bars. Dust with powdered sugar.

Advance Preparation: Prepare as directed. Place bars in single layer in airtight container; cover. Store at room temperature up to 3 days or freeze up to 3 months.

Per bar: 160 cal., 8 g total fat (4 g sat. fat), 23 mg chol., 165 mg sodium, 21 g carbo., 1 g fiber, 2 g pro.

Cranberry-Date Bars

Cardamom is known as the grain of paradise in India. Sample its woodsy, sweet scent in these moist, fruit-flecked bars.

Prep: 15 minutes **Bake:** 25 minutes
Oven: 350°F **Makes:** 20 bars

- Nonstick cooking spray
- 1⅔ cups packaged biscuit mix
- ¼ teaspoon ground cardamom
- ½ cup chopped dates
- ½ cup dried cranberries
- ½ cup chopped pecans
- ½ cup butter, softened
- ¾ cup granulated sugar
- 1 egg
- 1 teaspoon vanilla
- Powdered sugar

1. Preheat oven to 350°F. Line an 8-inch square baking pan with foil, extending foil over edges of pan. Lightly coat foil with cooking spray and set aside.

2. In a medium bowl combine biscuit mix and cardamom; stir in dates, cranberries, and pecans. Set aside. In a large bowl beat butter with an electric mixer on medium to high speed for 30 seconds. Add granulated sugar and beat until combined. Beat in egg and vanilla. Beat in dry mixture just until combined.

Holiday Seven-Layer Bars

Use kitchen scissors to snip the caramels into smaller pieces. If the caramels stick to the scissors, lightly coat the scissors with nonstick cooking spray.

Prep: 20 minutes **Bake:** 25 minutes
Oven: 350°F **Makes:** 30 bars

- ½ cup butter
- 2 cups finely crushed vanilla wafers (48) or shortbread cookies (33)
- 1 14-ounce can sweetened condensed milk
- 1 cup butterscotch-flavor pieces, candy-coated milk caramels (such as Sugar Babies), snipped vanilla caramels, semisweet chocolate pieces, or red and green candy-coated milk chocolate pieces
- 1 6-ounce package white baking chocolate, white confectionery bars, chopped, or 1 cup white baking pieces
- 1 cup mixed dried fruit bits, coarsely chopped dried apricots, golden raisins, dried cranberries, or dried cherries
- 1⅓ cups flaked or shredded coconut
- 1 cup unsalted mixed nuts or lightly salted roasted cashew pieces, coarsely chopped

1. Preheat oven to 350°F. Line a 13×9×2-inch baking pan with foil, extending foil over edges of pan. Place butter in prepared pan; place in oven about 5 minutes or until butter is melted. Tilt pan

to coat bottom evenly. Sprinkle with crushed vanilla wafers.

2. Drizzle crust evenly with sweetened condensed milk. Sprinkle with butterscotch-flavor pieces, chopped white chocolate, fruit bits, coconut, and nuts. Press down firmly with the back of a spoon.

3. Bake for 25 minutes or until edges are lightly browned. Cool in pan on a wire rack. Use foil to lift baked mixture out of pan. Cut into bars.

Advance Preparation: Prepare as directed. Place bars in single layer in airtight container; cover. Chill up to 3 days or freeze up to 3 months.

Per bar: 247 cal., 13 g total fat (8 g sat. fat), 13 mg chol., 94 mg sodium, 29 g carbo., 1 g fiber, 2 g pro.

Chocolate-Toffee Biscotti

Crisp biscotti are one of the country's most popular cookies and coffee-shop treats. Enjoy them the Italian way—dip them in coffee or tea.

Prep: 30 minutes **Bake:** 41 minutes
Oven: 350°F/325°F **Makes:** about 30 biscotti

- **¼ cup butter, softened**
- **½ cup granulated sugar**
- **½ cup packed brown sugar**
- **2½ teaspoons baking powder**
- **⅛ teaspoon salt**
- **3 eggs**
- **1 teaspoon vanilla**
- **2¾ cups all-purpose flour**
- **½ cup almond toffee pieces**
- **⅓ cup miniature semisweet chocolate pieces**
- **6 ounces semisweet chocolate, chopped**
- **4 teaspoons shortening**
- **Almond toffee pieces (optional)**

1. Preheat oven to 350°F. In a mixing bowl beat butter on medium to high speed for 30 seconds. Add sugars, baking powder, and salt; beat until combined. Beat in eggs and vanilla. Beat in as much of the flour as you can. Stir in any remaining flour. Stir in the ½ cup toffee pieces and chocolate pieces. Divide dough in half (dough will be sticky).

2. Use floured hands on a lightly floured surface to shape each dough portion into an 8-inch log. Place logs 5 inches apart on a greased cookie sheet.

3. Bake about 25 minutes or until golden brown and firm to the touch in the center (logs will spread during baking). Remove from the cookie sheet to a wire rack; cool for 1 hour.

4. Reduce oven temperature to 325°F. Transfer logs to a cutting board and cut each log crosswise diagonally into ½-inch slices. (Or cool completely; wrap and store overnight at room temperature before slicing.) Place slices, cut sides down, on the cookie sheet. Bake for 8 minutes. Turn slices over; bake 8 to 10 minutes more or until dry. Transfer slices to wire racks; cool.

5. In a heavy small saucepan heat and stir the 6 ounces chocolate and the shortening over low heat until melted and smooth. Dip one end of each biscotti into melted chocolate mixture. Arrange on a sheet of waxed paper. If desired, sprinkle with additional almond toffee pieces. Let stand until chocolate is set.

Advance Preparation: Prepare as directed. Layer between waxed paper in airtight container; cover. Store at room temperature up to 1 week. Or freeze, undipped, up to 3 months. Thaw; dip in chocolate.

Per biscotti: 143 cal., 6 g total fat (3 g sat. fat), 26 mg chol., 61 mg sodium, 20 g carbo., 1 g fiber, 2 g pro.

Chocolate-Toffee Biscotti

Swirls-of-Peppermint Cheesecake Bars

Add peppermint candies to the bars just before serving to prevent the candy from bleeding its color into the cheesecake.

Prep: 35 minutes **Bake:** 20 minutes **Cool:** 1 hour
Chill: 4 hours **Oven:** 350°F **Makes:** 32 bars

- **2 cups finely crushed chocolate wafer cookies (about 35 cookies)**
- **2 tablespoons sugar**
- **⅓ cup butter, melted**
- **2 8-ounce packages cream cheese, softened**
- **1 cup sugar**
- **1 teaspoon vanilla**
- **¼ cup milk**
- **5 eggs, lightly beaten**
- **½ teaspoon peppermint extract**
- **Red food coloring**
- **Peppermint pillow candies**

1. Preheat oven to 350°F. Grease the bottom of a 13×9×2-inch baking pan; set aside.

2. For crust, in a medium bowl combine crushed cookies, 2 tablespoons sugar, and the melted butter; stir until mixed. Press mixture evenly into bottom of prepared pan. Bake for 10 minutes.

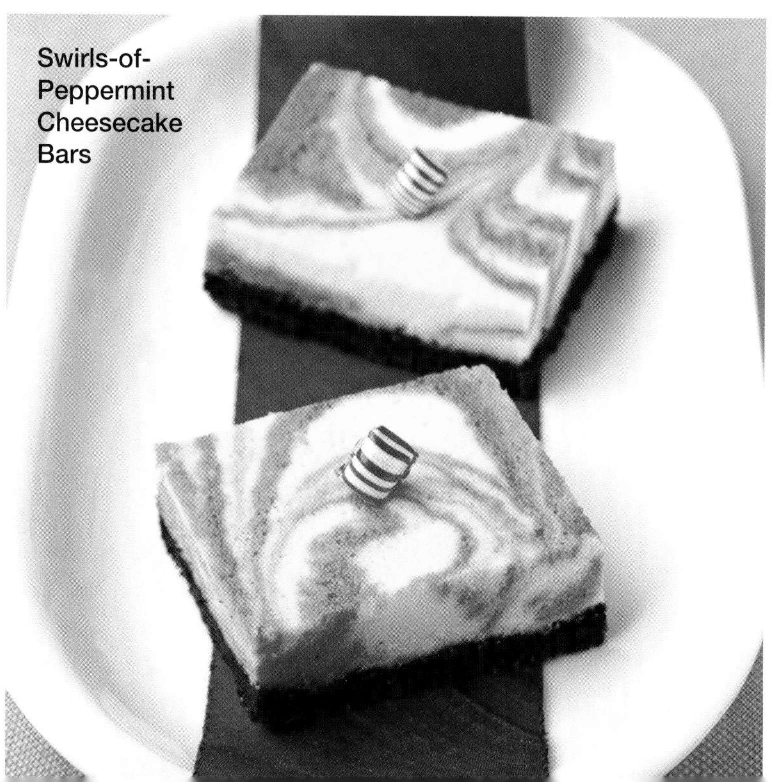

Swirls-of-Peppermint Cheesecake Bars

3. For filling, in a mixing bowl beat cream cheese, 1 cup sugar, and the vanilla on medium speed until smooth. Beat in milk until combined. Stir in eggs.

4. Transfer 1 cup of the cream cheese mixture to a small bowl; stir in peppermint extract and enough red food coloring for desired color. Pour the plain cream cheese mixture over partially baked crust, spreading evenly. Drizzle red cream cheese mixture over plain cream cheese mixture. Use a thin metal spatula to gently swirl the mixtures.

5. Bake about 20 minutes or until set. Cool in pan on a wire rack for 1 hour. Cover and chill for 4 to 24 hours. Cut into bars. Add peppermint pillow candies to the bars just before serving.

Advance Preparation: Prepare as directed. Place in single layer in airtight container; cover. Store in refrigerator up to 3 days or freeze up to 3 months.

Per bar: 147 cal., 9 g total fat (5 g sat. fat), 54 mg chol., 107 mg sodium, 15 g carbo., 0 g fiber, 3 g pro.

Triple Espresso Brownies

Prep: 30 minutes **Bake:** 20 minutes
Oven: 350°F **Makes:** 48 brownies

- **¼ cup water**
- **2 tablespoons instant espresso powder or instant coffee crystals**
- **1 cup butter**
- **1½ cups semisweet chocolate pieces**
- **1½ cups granulated sugar**
- **4 eggs, lightly beaten**
- **1 teaspoon vanilla**
- **2 cups all-purpose flour**
- **½ cup chopped walnuts (optional)**
- **½ teaspoon salt**
- **3 cups powdered sugar**
- **¼ cup butter, softened**
- **2 tablespoons boiling water**
- **2 tablespoons coffee liqueur or 2 teaspoons instant espresso powder or instant coffee crystals**
- **½ teaspoon vanilla**
- **Coarsely chopped chocolate-covered coffee beans (optional)**
- **Instant espresso powder (optional)**

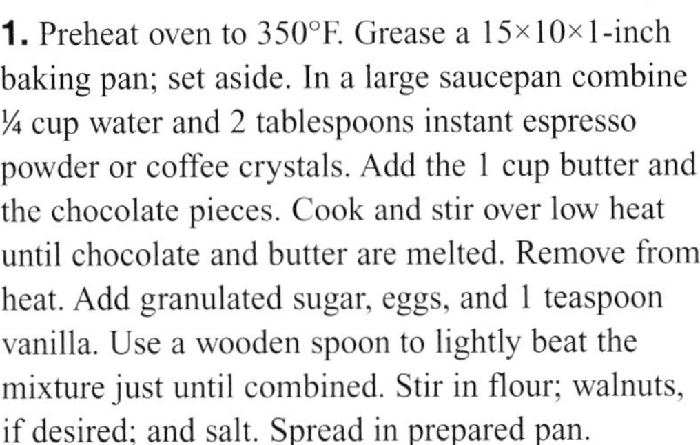

1. Preheat oven to 350°F. Grease a 15×10×1-inch baking pan; set aside. In a large saucepan combine ¼ cup water and 2 tablespoons instant espresso powder or coffee crystals. Add the 1 cup butter and the chocolate pieces. Cook and stir over low heat until chocolate and butter are melted. Remove from heat. Add granulated sugar, eggs, and 1 teaspoon vanilla. Use a wooden spoon to lightly beat the mixture just until combined. Stir in flour; walnuts, if desired; and salt. Spread in prepared pan.

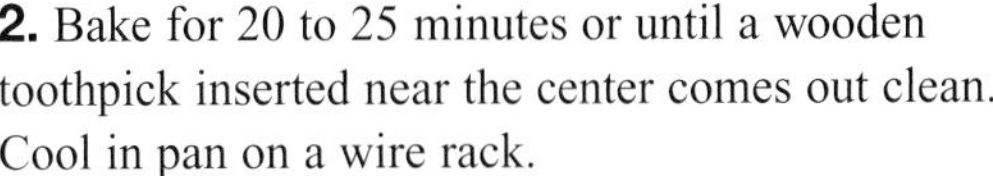

2. Bake for 20 to 25 minutes or until a wooden toothpick inserted near the center comes out clean. Cool in pan on a wire rack.

3. Meanwhile, for the frosting, place powdered sugar in a large mixing bowl. Add the ¼ cup butter, 2 tablespoons boiling water, the coffee liqueur or 2 teaspoons instant espresso powder or coffee crystals, and the ½ teaspoon vanilla. Beat with an electric mixer on low speed until combined. Beat for 1 minute on medium speed. Spread frosting evenly over cooled brownies. If desired, sprinkle with coarsely chopped chocolate-covered coffee beans and additional espresso powder. Cut into bars.

Advance Preparation: Prepare as directed. Place bars in a single layer in airtight container; cover. Store at room temperature up to 3 days. Or cover pan of uncut, unfrosted bars with heavy foil and freeze up to 3 months. Thaw brownies, then frost.

Per brownie: 145 cal., 7 g total fat (4 g sat. fat), 30 mg chol., 65 mg sodium, 20 g carbo., 0 g fiber, 1 g pro.

Chocolate-Hazelnut Marshmallow Bars

Lining the baking pan with foil makes removing the bars easy. Just grasp the extra foil at the edges and pull the uncut bars out of the pan.

Prep: 25 minutes **Chill:** 30 minutes **Makes:** 36 bars

- **1 10½-ounce package tiny marshmallows**
- **1 cup hazelnuts (filberts), toasted and coarsely chopped* or coarsely chopped peanuts**
- **2½ cups semisweet chocolate pieces**
- **½ cup chocolate-hazelnut spread**

Chocolate-Hazelnut Marshmallow Bars

- **½ cup whipping cream**
- **¼ cup butter, softened**
- **Powdered sugar (optional)**

1. Line a 13×9×2-inch baking pan with foil, extending foil over edges of pan; set aside. In an extra-large bowl stir together marshmallows and nuts; set aside. In a medium saucepan combine chocolate pieces, chocolate-hazelnut spread, whipping cream, and butter; cook and stir over medium-low heat until mixture is smooth.

2. Add chocolate mixture to marshmallow mixture; stir to coat well. Spoon mixture evenly into prepared pan or dish, pressing down lightly. Cover and chill for 30 minutes.

3. Use the edges of the foil to lift the uncut bars out of the pan or dish. Cut into 18 bars while cold. Cut each bar diagonally in half to make triangles. Store in the refrigerator (bars will soften at room temperature). If desired, sprinkle bars with powdered sugar.

***Test Kitchen Tip:** To toast hazelnuts, preheat oven to 350°F. Place the nuts in a single layer in a shallow baking pan. Bake about 10 minutes or until nuts are toasted, stirring once. Place the warm nuts on a clean kitchen towel. Rub nuts with the towel to remove loose skins.

Advance Preparation: Prepare as directed. Layer bars between waxed paper in airtight container; cover. Chill up to 3 days or freeze up to 3 months. Keep chilled until ready to serve (bars soften at room temperature).

Per bar: 151 cal., 9 g total fat (4 g sat. fat), 8 mg chol., 25 mg sodium, 17 g carbo., 1 g fiber, 1 g pro.

candy magic

Candy conjures up wonderful memories of barks, brittles, and fudge—just like Grandma used to make. Thanks to these easy-does-it microwave recipes, you can master several timeless classics in one afternoon.

Now that's sweet!

Candy Cane Bark, page 117

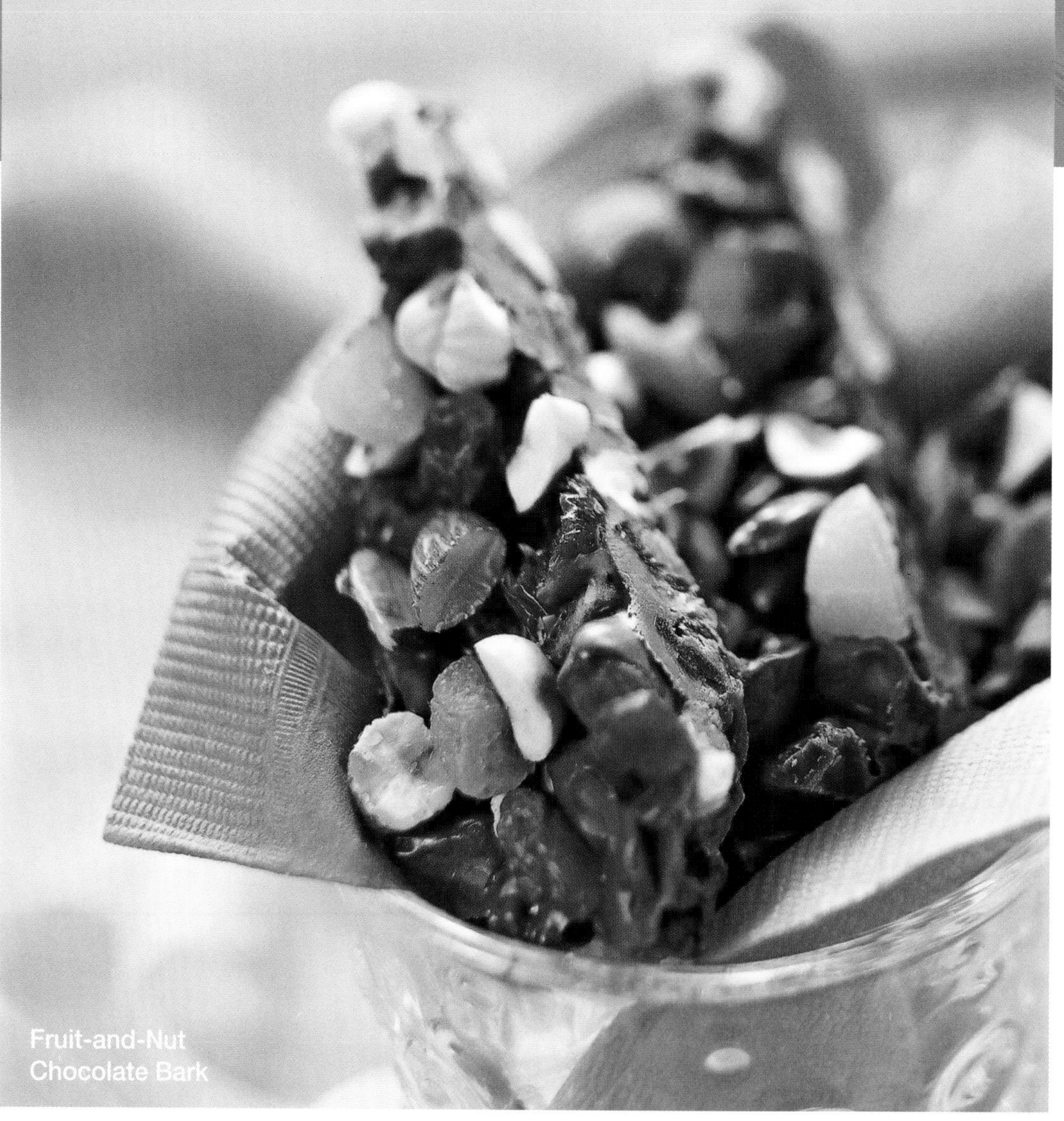

Fruit-and-Nut Chocolate Bark

A medley of dried fruit and toasted nuts enhances traditional chocolate bark. If using hazelnuts, remove the papery skins by rubbing the nuts with a clean dish towel.

Prep: 20 minutes **Chill:** 1 hour
Makes: 2¾ pounds (about 22 pieces)

- **2 cups almonds and/or hazelnuts (filberts), toasted and coarsely chopped**
- **⅔ cup golden raisins**
- **⅔ cup snipped dried apricots**
- **⅔ cup dried cranberries**
- **¼ cup diced candied orange peel**
- **12 ounces chocolate-flavor candy coating, cut up**
- **7 ounces milk chocolate, cut up**

1. Line a large baking sheet with waxed paper; set aside. In a large bowl combine nuts, raisins, apricots, cranberries, and orange peel. Reserve ¾ cup of fruit mixture for topping. Set both portions aside.

2. In a medium microwave-safe bowl combine candy coating and chocolate. Microwave, uncovered, on 100% power (high) for 2 to 3 minutes, stirring once halfway through cooking time. Stir until smooth. Stir in the larger portion of fruit mixture; mix well. Pour mixture onto prepared baking sheet. Spread about ⅜ inch thick. Sprinkle topping over mixture in pan, pressing pieces slightly with the back of a spoon.

3. Chill candy until firm, about 1 hour. Peel away the waxed paper. Carefully break candy into pieces.

Advance Preparation: Prepare as directed. Layer pieces between waxed paper in an airtight container; cover. Store in refrigerator up to 2 weeks. Serve at room temperature.

Per piece: 226 cal., 12 g total fat (7 g sat. fat), 2 mg chol., 11 mg sodium, 28 g carbo., 2 g fiber, 3 g pro.

Candy Cane Bark

Work quickly when making this candy-shop favorite or the white chocolate mixture will set before the milk chocolate is swirled in. Pictured on page 115.

Prep: 20 minutes **Chill:** 30 minutes
Makes: 1¼ pounds (about 20 pieces)

- **6 ounces vanilla-flavor candy coating, chopped**
- **3 ounces white chocolate baking squares, chopped**
- **6 ounces chocolate-flavor candy coating, chopped**
- **1 3-ounce bar milk chocolate, chopped**
- **¼ cup crushed peppermint candy canes**

1. Line a large baking sheet with foil; set aside. In a medium microwave-safe bowl combine vanilla-flavor candy coating and white chocolate baking squares. Microwave, uncovered, on 100% power (high) for 2 to 3 minutes, stirring once halfway through cooking time. Stir until smooth. Pour onto prepared baking sheet and spread into a 10×8-inch rectangle; set aside.

2. In another medium microwave-safe bowl combine chocolate-flavor candy coating and milk chocolate bar. Microwave, uncovered, on 100% power (high) for 2 to 3 minutes, stirring once halfway through cooking time. Stir until smooth.

3. Slowly pour chocolate mixture over white mixture on baking sheet. Use a thin spatula to swirl chocolate mixture into white mixture. Shake baking sheet gently for even thickness.

4. Sprinkle with crushed candy canes. Chill about 30 minutes or until firm. Use foil to lift candy from baking sheet; break candy into pieces.

Advance Preparation: Prepare as directed. Layer pieces between waxed paper in airtight container; cover. Store in refrigerator up to 10 days. Serve at room temperature.

Per piece: 151 cal., 8 g total fat (6 g sat. fat), 2 mg chol., 10 mg sodium, 18 g carbo., 0 g fiber, 1 g pro..

Two-Tone Pecan Bark

For even drizzling, place the melted candy coating in a heavy resealable plastic bag and snip one of the corners. The bittersweet-pistachio variation is pictured on page 94.

Prep: 10 minutes **Chill:** 15 minutes
Makes: about 1¼ pounds (about 30 pieces)

- **2 2-ounce squares vanilla-flavor candy coating, coarsely chopped**
- **1 12-ounce package (2 cups) semisweet chocolate pieces**
- **1 cup chopped pecans, toasted**

1. Line a baking sheet with waxed paper; set aside. Place vanilla-flavor candy coating in a medium microwave-safe bowl. Microwave, uncovered, on 50% power (medium) for 1 to 2 minutes or until melted, stirring once halfway through cooking time. Stir until smooth.

2. In another medium microwave-safe bowl microwave the chocolate pieces, uncovered, on 50% power (medium for 2 to 3 minutes or until melted, stirring once. Stir until smooth.

3. Spread melted semisweet chocolate to a 12×9-inch rectangle on prepared baking sheet. Sprinkle evenly with pecans; press lightly into chocolate. Drizzle melted candy coating evenly over pecan-chocolate mixture. Chill 15 minutes or until firm. Peel away the waxed paper. Break into pieces.

Advance Preparation: Prepare as directed. Layer pieces between waxed paper in an airtight container; cover. Store in refrigerator up to 1 week. Serve at room temperature.

Per piece: 101 cal., 7 g total fat (3 g sat. fat), 0 mg chol., 1 mg sodium, 10 g carbo., 1 g fiber, 1 g pro.

Bittersweet-Pistachio Bark: Prepare as directed, except use one 11.5-ounce package bittersweet chocolate pieces instead of the semisweet chocolate pieces and 1 cup chopped pistachios instead of the toasted pecans.

Fabulous Five-Minute Fudge

Toasting nuts enhances their flavor. Spread them in a shallow pan and bake in a 350°F oven for 5 to 10 minutes or until the nuts are golden and fragrant. Also pictured on the cover.

Prep: 5 minutes **Chill:** 30 minutes
Makes: 24 pieces

- **1 12-ounce package semisweet chocolate pieces (2 cups)**
- **⅔ cup sweetened condensed milk (half of a 14-ounce can)**
- **¾ cup chopped walnuts, toasted if desired**
- **1 teaspoon vanilla**

1. Line a cookie sheet with waxed paper; set aside. In a medium microwave-safe bowl combine chocolate pieces, sweetened condensed milk, and 1 tablespoon *water*.

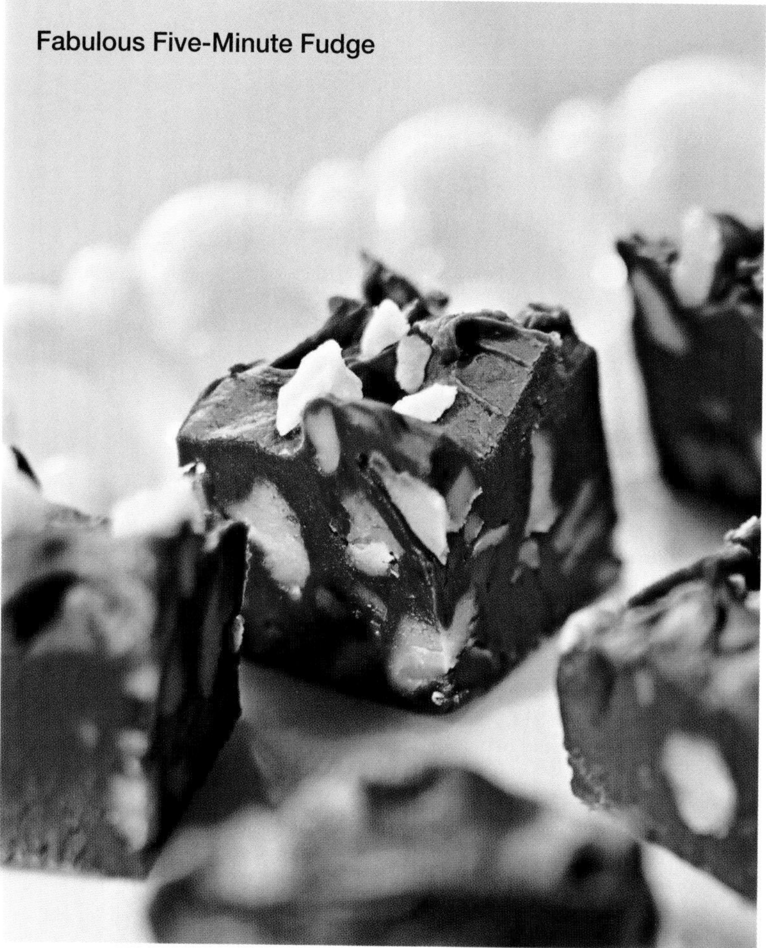
Fabulous Five-Minute Fudge

2. Microwave, uncovered, on 100% power (high) for 1 minute; stir. Microwave 1 minute more or until chocolate melts and mixture is smooth, stirring every 30 seconds. Stir in nuts and vanilla. Pour mixture onto the prepared cookie sheet and spread it into a 9×6-inch rectangle. (Or drop mixture by rounded teaspoons onto the prepared cookie sheet.) Chill about 30 minutes or until firm. Cut fudge into 1½-inch squares.

Advance preparation: Prepare as directed. Layer fudge between waxed paper in an airtight container; cover. Store at room temperature up to 1 week.

Per piece: 120 cal., 7 g total fat (2 g sat. fat), 3 mg chol., 13 mg sodium, 14 g carbo., 1 g fiber, 2 g pro.

Mock Toffee

Line a baking dish with parchment paper so you can remove the microwaved toffee easily from the dish.

Prep: 15 minutes **Cook:** 4½ minutes
Chill: 1 hour **Makes:** 12 to 16 pieces

- **10 graham cracker squares**
- **⅓ cup chopped almonds**
- **½ cup butter**
- **½ cup packed brown sugar**
- **⅓ cup miniature semisweet chocolate pieces**

1. Line a microwave-safe 2-quart rectangular baking dish with parchment paper, extending the paper over the edges of the dish. Line bottom of the prepared dish with a single layer of graham crackers, breaking crackers as necessary to completely cover the bottom of the dish. Sprinkle almonds over crackers. Set aside.

2. In a microwave-safe 4-cup glass measure or medium glass bowl place the butter and brown sugar. Microwave, uncovered, on 100% power (high) for 3 minutes, stirring every 30 seconds. Pour immediately over crackers and nuts in dish. (Work quickly because butter mixture separates.)

3. Place baking dish in microwave. Microwave, uncovered, on high for 1 minute 30 seconds. Sprinkle chocolate pieces over toffee mixture. Chill 1 to 2 hours or until chocolate is set.

Best-Ever Simple Nut Brittle

Use parchment paper to lift candy from dish. Break into irregular pieces.

Advance Preparation: Prepare as directed. Layer pieces between waxed paper in airtight container; cover. Store at room temperature up to 3 days or freeze up to 3 months. Serve at room temperature.

Per piece: 177 cal., 11 g total fat (6 g sat. fat), 20 mg chol., 92 mg sodium, 18 g carbo., 0 g fiber, 1 g pro.

Best-Ever Simple Nut Brittle

To use a microwave oven to caramelize sugar, or to cook it until brown, use a heavy-duty glass bowl that withstands high temperatures. The bowl must be free from cracks and chips or it may shatter.

Prep: 10 minutes **Makes:** 1 pound, 2 ounces (about 36 pieces)

- **1 cup sugar**
- **½ cup light-color corn syrup**
- **⅛ teaspoon salt**
- **⅛ teaspoon ground cardamom**
- **½ cup whole cashews**
- **½ cup pistachios**
- **½ cup pecan halves**
- **1 tablespoon butter**
- **1 teaspoon baking soda**
- **1 teaspoon vanilla**

1. Grease a large baking sheet; set aside. In a 2-quart microwave-safe bowl combine sugar, corn syrup, salt, and cardamom. Microwave, uncovered, on 100% power (high) for 6 minutes, stirring once halfway through cooking time.

2. Stir in cashews, pistachios, pecan halves, and butter. Microwave, uncovered, on high 2 minutes or just until mixture turns golden (mixture continues to cook and becomes more golden when removed from the microwave).

3. Quickly stir in baking soda and vanilla. Spread thinly and evenly on the prepared baking sheet. Let cool. Break into pieces.

Advance Preparation: Prepare as directed. Layer pieces between waxed paper in an airtight container; cover. Store at room temperature up to 1 week.

Per piece: 70 cal., 3 g total fat (1 g sat. fat), 1 mg chol., 69 mg sodium, 10 g carbo., 0 g fiber, 1 g pro.

Candy Cane Cookie Drops

Candy Cane Cookie Drops

Crush candy canes by placing them in a heavy resealable plastic bag. On a sturdy surface, use a meat mallet or rolling pin to crush the candies to the desired-size pieces. Also pictured on the cover.

Prep: 25 minutes **Stand:** 30 minutes
Makes: 40 cookie drops

- **6 ounces chocolate-flavor candy coating, chopped**
- **1 cup semisweet chocolate pieces**
- **1 tablespoon shortening**
- **1½ cups crushed chocolate wafer cookies**
- **½ cup finely crushed peppermint candy canes**
- **Additional crushed candy canes or whole striped round peppermint candies**

1. Line a baking sheet with 40 small foil or paper candy cups or with waxed paper; set aside.

2. In a medium microwave-safe bowl combine candy coating, chocolate pieces, and shortening. Microwave, uncovered, on 100% power (high) for 45 to 60 seconds or until softened. Stir until smooth. Gently stir in crushed wafers and the ½ cup crushed candy canes until all pieces are coated with chocolate.

3. Drop chocolate mixture by rounded teaspoons into candy cups or onto waxed paper. Sprinkle with additional crushed candy canes or top with whole candies. Let stand about 30 minutes or until firm.

Advance Preparation: Prepare as directed. Layer cookies between sheets of waxed paper in an airtight container; cover. Store at room temperature or in refrigerator up to 3 days, or freeze up to 3 months. Thaw frozen drops at room temperature for 30 minutes. Serve at room temperature.

Per cookie drop: 76 cal., 4 g total fat (2 g sat. fat), 0 mg chol., 25 mg sodium, 11 g carbo., 0 g fiber, 0 g pro.

Rocky Road Clusters

Prep: 15 minutes **Chill:** 1 hour
Makes: about 50 pieces

- **1 12-ounce package semisweet chocolate pieces (2 cups)**
- **1 cup creamy peanut butter**
- **1 10½-ounce package tiny marshmallows (5½ cups)**
- **1½ cups honey roasted or dry roasted peanuts**

1. Line two baking sheets with waxed paper or parchment paper; set aside. In a medium microwave-safe bowl combine chocolate pieces and peanut butter. Microwave, uncovered, on 100% power (high) for 1 to 2 minutes, stirring once, halfway through cooking time.

2. In a large bowl combine marshmallows and peanuts. Pour chocolate mixture over marshmallow mixture, stirring gently to coat. Working quickly, drop by heaping tablespoons onto prepared baking sheets. Chill 1 hour or until set.

Advance Preparation: Prepare as directed. Layer clusters between waxed paper in airtight container; cover. Store in refrigerator up to 2 weeks. Serve at room temperature.

Per piece: 98 cal., 6 g total fat (2 g sat. fat), 0 mg chol., 45 mg sodium, 11 g carbo., 1 g fiber, 3 g pro.

Marshmallow Pops

These minty lollipops are also pictured on the cover.

Start to Finish: 30 minutes **Makes:** 32 pops

32 wooden or short plastic skewers
32 large marshmallows
6 ounces vanilla- or chocolate-flavor candy coating
⅓ cup crushed peppermint candies and/or nonpareils

1. Line a baking sheet with waxed paper; set aside. Insert skewers into marshmallows; set aside. Place candy coating in a small microwave-safe bowl. Microwave, uncovered, on 100% power (high) for 1½ to 2 minutes, stirring once halfway through cooking time. Stir until smooth. Quickly dip each marshmallow halfway into melted candy coating, allowing excess to drip off. Sprinkle with crushed candies and/or nonpareils. Place pops on prepared baking sheet. Let stand until set.

Advance Preparation: Prepare as directed. Layer pops between waxed paper in airtight container; cover. Store in refrigerator up to 3 days. Serve at room temperature.

Per pop: 60 cal., 2 g total fat (2 g sat. fat), 0 mg chol., 6 mg sodium, 11 g carbo., 0 g fiber, 0 g pro.

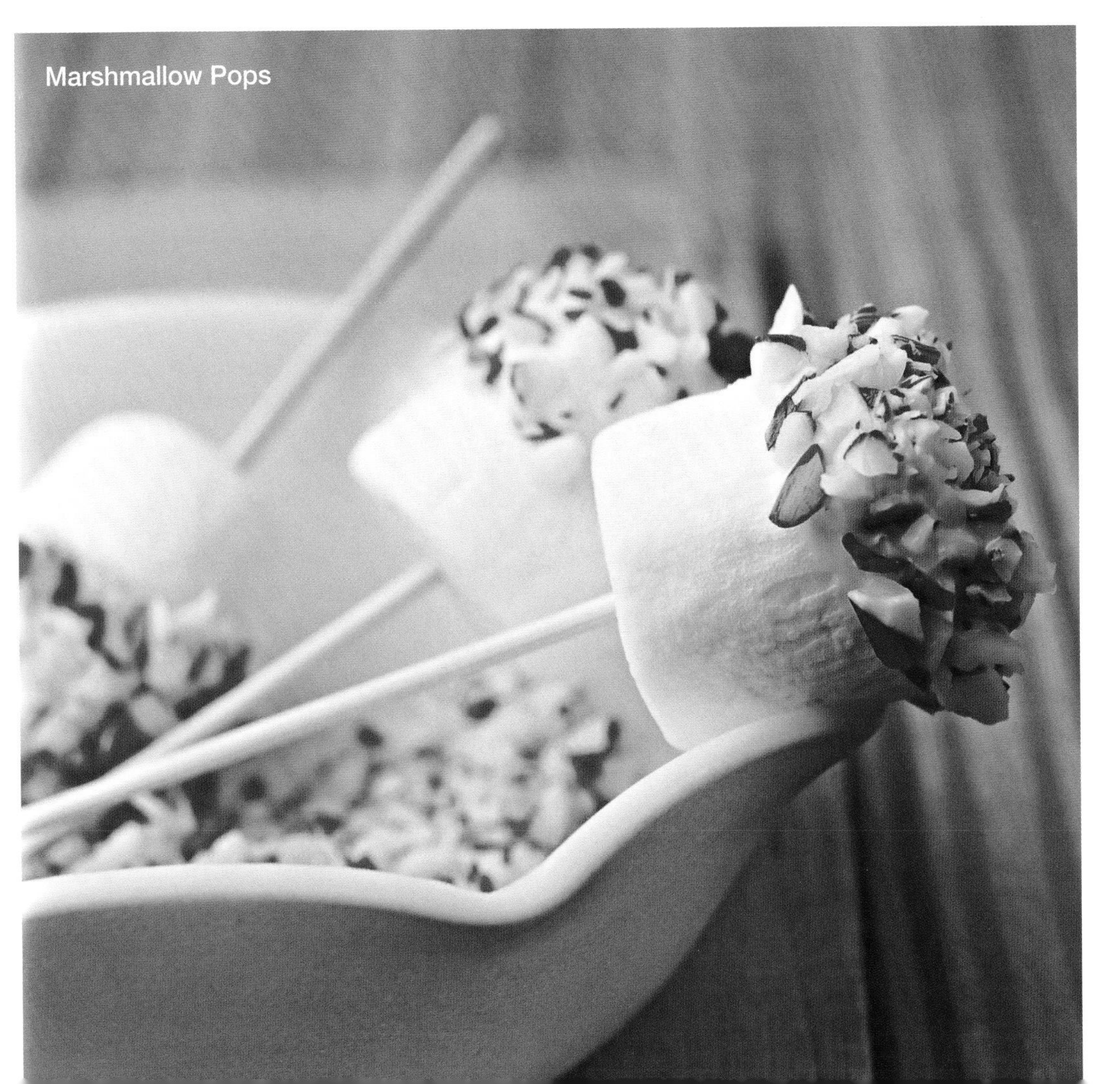
Marshmallow Pops

’tis a gift

Wrap up holiday gift giving with simple homemade foods that are sure to please and include the best gift of all—part of you. Use simple and readily available materials for packaging and see the joy it brings to you, your family, and friends.

Paprika Sesame
Breadsticks, page 124

Honey-Pecan Salad Dressing

Honey-Pecan Salad Dressing

Perfect for dressing a citrus or strawberry greens salad, this flavorful condiment shows nicely in a cork-sealed bottle. For a colorful addition, glue or tie on a shiny ornament.

Prep: 15 minutes **Makes:** about 2 cups

- **1 cup coarsely chopped pecans, toasted**
- **⅔ cup vegetable oil**
- **⅔ cup honey**
- **⅓ cup white wine vinegar or cider vinegar**
- **1 tablespoon snipped fresh dill or 1 teaspoon dried dill**
- **1½ teaspoons lemon juice**
- **3 cloves garlic, minced**
- **½ teaspoon salt**

1. In a blender or food processor combine pecans, oil, honey, vinegar, dill, lemon juice, garlic and salt. Cover and blend or process until mixture combines. Serve immediately or cover and store in refrigerator up to 1 week. Stir before serving.

If salad dressing is too thick or thickens upon standing, stir in 1 additional tablespoon vinegar and enough water to make drizzling consistency.

Advance Preparation: Prepare as directed. Cover and store in refrigerator up to 1 week.

Per 2 tablespoons: 172 cal., 14 g total fat (1 g sat. fat), 0 mg chol., 74 mg sodium, 12 g carbo., 1 g fiber, 1 g pro.

Paprika Sesame Breadsticks

Bundle a few of these breadsticks in parchment paper and secure with string. Embellish the package with a purchased or handmade gift label. For safe delivery, wrap the gift in cellophane. *Pictured on page 123.*

Prep: 20 minutes **Bake:** 15 minutes per batch
Oven: 400°F **Makes:** 18 breadsticks

- **1 egg, lightly beaten**
- **1 tablespoon water**
- **1 teaspoon toasted sesame oil**
- **1 17.3-ounce package frozen puff pastry sheets (2 sheets), thawed**
- **½ teaspoon smoked paprika or ¼ teaspoon ground chipotle chile pepper**
- **¼ teaspoon sea salt**
- **2 tablespoons white and/or black sesame seeds**

1. Preheat oven to 400°F. Line two large baking sheets with parchment paper or foil; grease foil, if using. Set sheets aside. In a small bowl combine egg, water, and sesame oil. Unfold one pastry sheet. Brush with some of the egg mixture. In another small bowl combine paprika and salt. Sprinkle half of the paprika mixture over the pastry. Fold pastry in half to form a rectangle, lining up edges and pressing to seal. Brush top of pastry with more of the egg mixture. Sprinkle top with half of the sesame seeds.

2. With a sharp knife cut pastry lengthwise into ½-inch strips. Twist each strip 5 to 6 times and place 1 inch apart on one of the prepared baking sheets, pressing ends down. Bake about 15 minutes or until golden. Repeat with remaining pastry sheet, egg mixture, paprika mixture, and seeds.

Advance Preparation: Prepare as directed. Layer breadsticks between waxed paper in an airtight container; cover. Store at room temperature up to 1 week.

Per breadstick: 162 cal., 11 g total fat (3 g sat. fat), 12 mg chol., 94 mg sodium, 13 g carbo., 1 g fiber, 3 g pro.

Fennel Seed Wine Crackers

Fennel Seed Wine Crackers

For the most tender crackers, use only the amount of liquid specified. Arrange a few of the crackers in a wine glass, tie ribbon around the stem and attach a label. Accompany the gift with a bottle of wine.

Prep: 20 minutes **Bake:** 18 minutes **Oven:** 325°F
Makes: 24 crackers

- **1 cup all-purpose flour**
- **2 teaspoons fennel seeds, crushed**
- **½ teaspoon salt**
- **⅛ teaspoon ground black pepper**
- **3 tablespoons dry white wine**
- **3 tablespoons olive oil**
- **Coarse kosher salt (optional)**

1. Preheat oven to 325°F. In a medium bowl combine flour, fennel seeds, salt, and pepper. In a small bowl combine wine and olive oil; gradually add to dry ingredients, tossing with a fork until combined. Form dough into a ball.

2. On a lightly floured surface, roll dough into a 12×9-inch rectangle, about 1⁄16 inch thick (trim uneven edges, if necessary). Use a fork to prick dough all over. Use a pastry wheel or knife to cut 3×1½-inch rectangles. Transfer rectangles to an ungreased baking sheet. If desired, sprinkle lightly with kosher salt.

3. Bake about 18 minutes or just until crackers start to brown and are firm to the touch. Cool completely on wire racks.

Food Processor Method: In a food processor combine flour, salt, fennel and pepper; cover and process just until combined. Add wine, and olive oil. Cover and process just until combined. Form dough into a ball. Roll as directed.

Advance Preparation: Prepare as directed. Layer crackers between sheets of waxed paper in airtight container; cover. Store at room temperature up to 1 week or freeze up to 3 months.

Per cracker: 36 cal., 2 g total fat (0 g sat. fat), 0 mg chol., 49 mg sodium, 4 g carbo., 0 g fiber, 1 g pro.

Popcorn Marshmallow Clusters

Take-out boxes, available at crafts stores, make fun, inexpensive containers for a snack mix that will appeal to many people. Use holiday stickers to decorate the outside of the containers.

Prep: 15 minutes **Bake:** 20 minutes
Oven: 275°F **Makes:** 14 (1-cup) servings

- **12 cups freshly popped popcorn**
- **½ cup roasted and salted shelled sunflower seeds**
- **½ cup butter**
- **4 ounces semisweet chocolate**
- **30 large marshmallows**
- **1 teaspoon vanilla**

1. Preheat oven to 275°F. Place popcorn and sunflower seeds in a large bowl; set aside.

2. In a large saucepan combine butter and chocolate. Heat and stir over medium-low heat until melted. Stir in marshmallows; heat and stir until melted and smooth. Remove from heat. Stir in vanilla.

3. Pour chocolate mixture over popcorn and sunflower seeds; stir to coat. Spread popcorn mixture in a greased large shallow roasting pan. Bake 20 minutes or until crisp, stirring once. Cool in pan on a wire rack. Break mixture into pieces.

Advance Preparation: Prepare as directed. Place popcorn clusters in an airtight container; cover. Store at room temperature up to 1 week.

Per serving: 230 cal., 16 g total fat (4 g sat. fat), 16 mg chol., 178 mg sodium, 22 g carbo., 2 g fiber, 2 g pro.

Popcorn Marshmallow Clusters

Lemony Glazed Shortbread Bars

A red, white, and green coffee mug and saucer add a splash of color as a container for petite lemon bars drizzled with white icing. Use these jumbo coffee mugs to hold the bars.

Prep: 40 minutes **Bake:** 40 minutes
Oven: 300°F **Makes:** 32 bars

- **3 cups all-purpose flour**
- **⅓ cup cornstarch**
- **1¼ cups powdered sugar**
- **¼ cup finely shredded lemon peel (6 to 7 lemons)**
- **1½ cups butter, softened**
- **1 tablespoon lemon juice**
- **½ teaspoon salt**
- **½ teaspoon vanilla**
- **1 recipe Lemony Glaze**
- **3 ounces white baking chocolate, chopped**

1. Preheat oven to 300°F. Line a 13×9×2-inch baking pan with heavy foil, extending foil 2 inches over ends of pan. Lightly grease foil; set aside.

2. In a medium bowl stir together flour and cornstarch. In a small bowl combine powdered sugar and lemon peel. Use your fingers to press against the sides of the bowl with a wooden spoon

Lemony Glazed Shortbread Bars

to work lemon peel into the powdered sugar until the sugar is yellow and very fragrant.* Set aside.

3. In a large mixing bowl combine butter, lemon juice, salt, and vanilla; beat with an electric mixer on medium speed until combined. Gradually beat in sugar mixture. Beat in as much of the flour mixture as possible with the mixer. Stir in any remaining flour mixture. Continue beating or stirring until dough comes together. Gather dough into a ball.

4. Press dough evenly into the prepared pan. Bake on center rack of the oven for 40 minutes.

5. Remove from oven. Immediately spoon glaze over top; gently spread to evenly distribute glaze. Let cool completely. In a small saucepan cook and stir white chocolate over low heat until melted. Drizzle over cooled bars. Let stand until chocolate is set. Use the edges of the foil to lift the uncut bars out of the pan. Cut into bars.

Lemony Glaze: In a medium bowl combine 2½ cups powdered sugar, 2 teaspoons finely shredded lemon peel, 3 tablespoons lemon juice, 1 tablespoon light-color corn syrup, and ½ teaspoon vanilla. Whisk until smooth.

***Test Kitchen Tip:** Rubbing the lemon peel with the sugar helps to release the lemon oils.

Advance Preparation: Prepare as directed. Layer bars between waxed paper in an airtight container; cover. Store in refrigerator up to 3 days or freeze up to 1 month.

Per bar: 181 cal., 9 g total fat (6 g sat. fat), 23 mg chol., 98 mg sodium, 25 g carbo., 0 g fiber, 0 g pro.

Per 1 tablespoon prepared Mediterranean dip: 31 cal., 3 g total fat (2 g sat. fat), 6 mg chol., 33 mg sodium, 1 g carbo., 0 g fiber, 0 g pro.

Per 1 tablespoon prepared pesto dip: 43 cal., 4 g total fat (2 g sat. fat), 6 mg chol., 33 mg sodium, 1 g carbo., 0 g fiber, 1 g pro.

Per 1 tablespoon prepared Bloody Mary dip: 23 cal., 2 g total fat (1 g sat. fat), 5 mg chol., 73 mg sodium, 1 g carbo., 0 g fiber, 0 g pro.

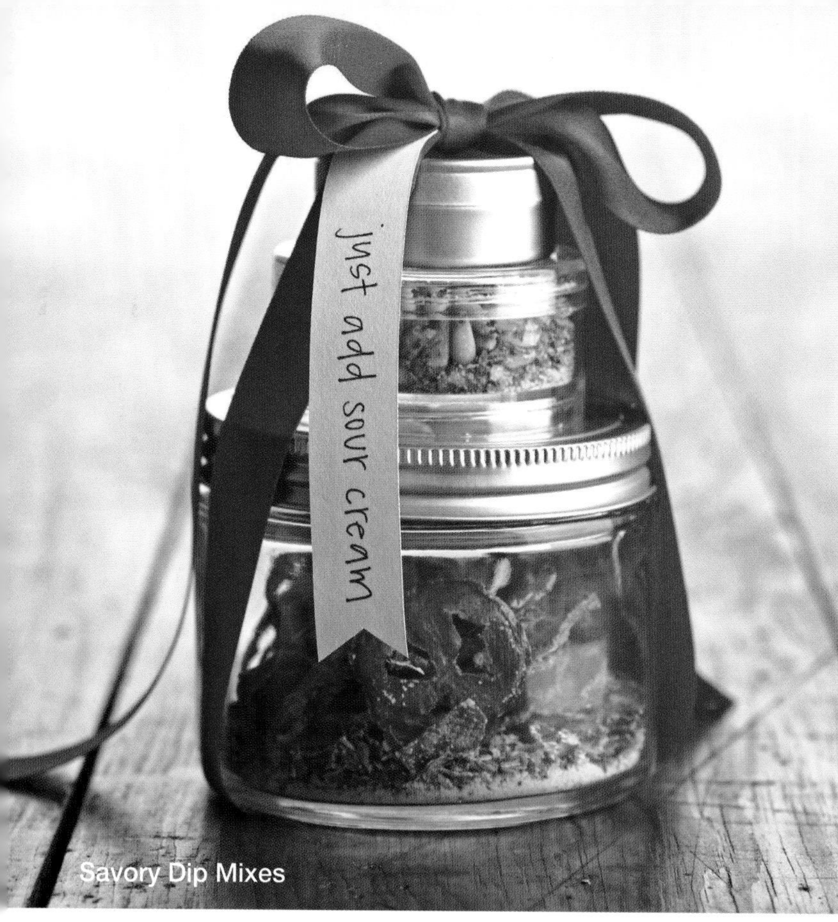

Savory Dip Mixes

Savory Dip Mixes

Give the gift of easy entertaining! Package this trio of dip mixes in simple jars or tin canisters. Add a festive ribbon and gift tag that includes the instructions below.

Prep: 5 minutes per dip mix

1. Mediterranean: Combine 1 tablespoon dried oregano, crushed; ½ teaspoon ground cumin; ¼ teaspoon dried lemon peel; and ¼ teaspoon sea salt.

2. Pesto: Combine ¼ cup toasted pine nuts, 1 tablespoon dried basil, ½ teaspoon garlic powder, and ¼ teaspoon sea salt.

3. Bloody Mary: Combine ⅔ cup (about ½ ounce) dried tomato slices or ⅓ cup chopped dried tomatoes, 2 teaspoons dried celery flakes, 1 teaspoon lemon-pepper seasoning, and ¼ teaspoon sea salt.

Gift Tag Instructions: Stir each savory blend into 1 cup dairy sour cream; cover and chill 4 to 24 hours before serving. For the Bloody Mary mix, chop dried tomato slices before combining with sour cream.

Advance Preparation: Prepare as directed. Store at room temperature up to 1 month.

Roasted Tomato Salsa

This peppy salsa looks festive and pretty when presented with holiday-themed plates tied with ribbon. Cover jars with lids before adding the plates.

Prep: 20 minutes **Roast:** 25 minutes
Cool: 20 minutes **Chill:** 4 hours **Oven:** 450°F
Makes: about 4 cups

- **2½ pounds roma tomatoes (about 15)**
- **3 fresh jalapeño peppers***
- **1 medium bulb garlic**
- **1 teaspoon salt**
- **2 medium red onions, finely chopped**
- **⅔ cup lightly packed cilantro leaves, snipped (¼ cup)**
- **1 tablespoon lime juice**

Roasted Tomato Salsa

1. Preheat oven to 450°F. Core the tomatoes. Place on one side of a 15×10×1-inch baking pan. Halve the jalapeño peppers. Remove stems and seeds. Place, cut sides down, on the other side of baking pan with tomatoes. Peel away outer skin from garlic. Cut off the pointed top portion with a knife, leaving the bulb intact but exposing the individual cloves. Add to pan. Roast, uncovered, for 25 minutes or until tomatoes are soft and pepper skins are charred. Cool.

2. Remove tomato and garlic skins. Place garlic, jalapeño peppers, and salt in a food processor or blender. Cover and process or blend with three or four on-off turns until finely chopped. Add half of the tomatoes; cover and process or blend with two or three on-off turns until coarsely chopped. Transfer to a large bowl. Add remaining tomatoes to food processor or blender cover and process or blend with two or three on-off turns until coarsely chopped. Stir into tomato mixture in bowl.

3. Stir onions, cilantro, and lime juice into tomato mixture until combined. Cover and chill several hours to blend flavors.

Advance Preparation: Prepare as directed. Transfer to jars; cover. Store in refrigerator up to 3 days.

Per ¼ cup: 23 cal., 0 g total fat (0 g sat. fat), 0 mg chol., 152 mg sodium, 5 g carbo., 1 g fiber, 3 g pro.

Caramel Graham Sandwiches

Fun to make, these caramel-filled treats are dipped in chocolate and coated with nuts. Arrange the treats in a parchment paper-lined box adorned with holiday gift wrap.

Prep: 40 minutes **Cool:** 30 minutes
Chill: 50 minutes **Makes:** 24 sandwiches

- **24 graham crackers**
- **1½ cups chopped milk chocolate or milk chocolate pieces (9 ounces)**
- **1 tablespoon shortening**
- **¾ cup chopped pecans**
- **20 vanilla caramels, unwrapped**
- **⅓ cup whipping cream**

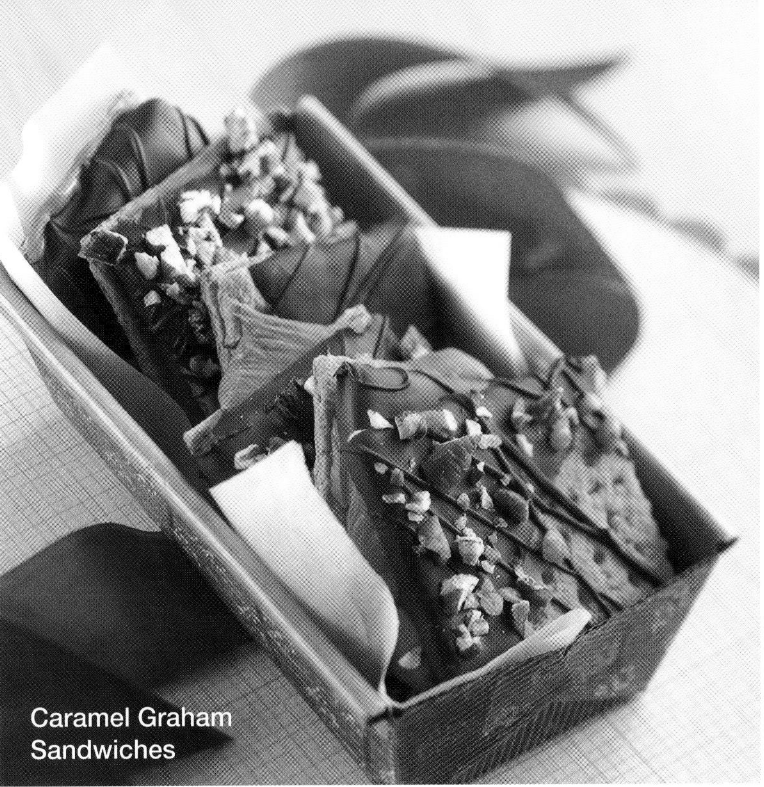
Caramel Graham Sandwiches

1. Line two baking sheets with waxed paper; set aside. Break each graham cracker crosswise along scored line into two equal sections; set aside. In a medium heavy saucepan combine chocolate and shortening; stir over medium-low heat until mixture melts and is smooth. Remove from heat. Dip half of the graham crackers into melted chocolate. Place on prepared baking sheet. Sprinkle nuts on top before chocolate cools. Drizzle with any remaining chocolate. Chill about 30 minutes or until chocolate sets.

2. Meanwhile, in a medium saucepan combine caramels and whipping cream; stir over low heat until mixture is smooth. Remove from heat; cool for 30 minutes or until mixture thickens slightly and spreads easily. Spread caramel on remaining half of the graham cracker sections. Top each frosted section with a chocolate dipped section to make a sandwich. Place on prepared baking sheets. Chill about 20 minutes or until set.

Advance Preparation: Prepare as directed. Place sandwiches in layers separated by waxed paper in an airtight container; cover. Store in refrigerator up to 3 days.

Per sandwich: 159 cal., 9 g total fat (3 g sat. fat), 7 mg chol., 71 mg sodium, 19 g carbo., 1 g fiber, 2 g pro.

Fruit and Nut Trail Mix

Present this wholesome snack in a sturdy plastic container decorated with your favorite ribbon.

Prep: 15 minutes **Bake:** 45 minutes
Cool: 30 minutes **Oven:** 325°F
Makes: about 9 (1-cup) servings

- **Nonstick cooking spray**
- **3 cups regular rolled oats**
- **1 cup unsalted sunflower kernels**
- **1 cup unsalted cashews, almonds and/or peanuts**
- **½ cup toasted wheat germ**
- **½ cup shredded coconut**
- **⅔ cup honey**
- **⅓ cup light-color corn syrup**
- **¼ cup orange or tangerine juice**
- **3 tablespoons vegetable oil**
- **1 teaspoon vanilla**
- **1 teaspoon ground cinnamon**
- **1 7-ounce package mixed tropical blend dried fruit bits**
- **½ cup raisins, dried cranberries or dried cherries**

1. Preheat oven to 325°F. Lightly coat a 15×10×1-inch baking pan with cooking spray; set aside. In a large bowl stir together oats, sunflower kernels, cashews, wheat germ, and coconut.

2. In a small bowl stir together honey, corn syrup, orange juice, vegetable oil, vanilla, and cinnamon. Pour honey mixture over oat mixture; toss to coat. Spread evenly in the prepared baking pan.

3. Bake for 45 to 50 minutes or until oats are lightly browned, stirring three times. Remove from oven. Stir in fruit bits and raisins. Immediately turn out onto a large piece of foil. Cool completely.

Fruit and Nut Trail Mix

Advance Preparation: Prepare as directed. Transfer to an airtight container; cover. Store at room temperature up to 1 week or freeze up to 2 months.

Per serving: 560 cal., 23 g total fat (5 g sat. fat), 0 mg chol., 42 mg sodium, 83 g carbo., 8 g fiber, 11 g pro.

Chocolate-Pistachio Trees

Package these cookies in a soup can, wrapped with decorative paper, and tied with a satiny ribbon.

Prep: 45 minutes **Bake:** 9 minutes per batch
Chill: 30 minutes **Oven:** 350°F
Makes: about 48 cookies

- **1 cup butter**
- **⅔ cup packed brown sugar**
- **1 teaspoon vanilla**
- **1 egg, beaten**
- **2¼ cups all-purpose flour**
- **¼ cup unsweetened cocoa powder**
- **¾ cup finely chopped pistachio nuts***
- **¾ cup semisweet chocolate pieces**
- **1 tablespoon shortening**
- **½ cup ground pistachio nuts**

1. In a medium saucepan combine butter and brown sugar; stir over low heat until butter melts. Remove saucepan from heat; stir in vanilla. Cool mixture for 15 minutes. Stir in egg, flour, and cocoa powder until mixture is combined. Stir in the ¾ cup pistachio nuts. Divide dough in half. Cover and chill about 30 minutes or until dough is easy to handle.

2. Preheat oven to 350°F. On a lightly floured surface, roll dough, half at a time, to a ¼-inch thickness. Use a tree-shaped cookie cutter to cut out cookies. Place cookies 1 inch apart on an ungreased cookie sheet.

3. Bake about 9 minutes or until edges are firm. Transfer to a wire rack; cool.

4. In a heavy small saucepan combine chocolate pieces and shortening; heat and stir over low heat until chocolate melts. Remove from heat. Dip one-third of each cookie into chocolate mixture; roll edges of cookie in ground pistachio nuts.

Chocolate-Pistachio Trees

*Test Kitchen Tip: To prepare the pistachios for this recipe, place 2 cups whole shelled pistachios into a food processor. Pulse several times until the nuts are finely chopped. Remove the ¾ cup to be used in the dough. Continue pulsing the remaining nuts until finely ground to use as the garnish.

Advance Preparation: Prepare as directed. Place cookies in layers separated by waxed paper in an airtight container; cover. Store (undecorated) at room temperature up to 3 days or in freezer up to 3 months. Thaw and decorate.

Per cookie: 105 cal., 7 g total fat (3 g sat. fat), 15 mg chol., 44 mg sodium, 10 g carbo., 1 g fiber, 2 g pro.

new year's favorites

The new year is all about starting fresh, and few foods are more refreshing than the bite-size appetizers, seasonal drinks, and special dinner choices here. Simple and scrumptious recipes help you celebrate in style!

Beef Tenderloin with
Blue Cheese-Shrimp Sauce,
page 139

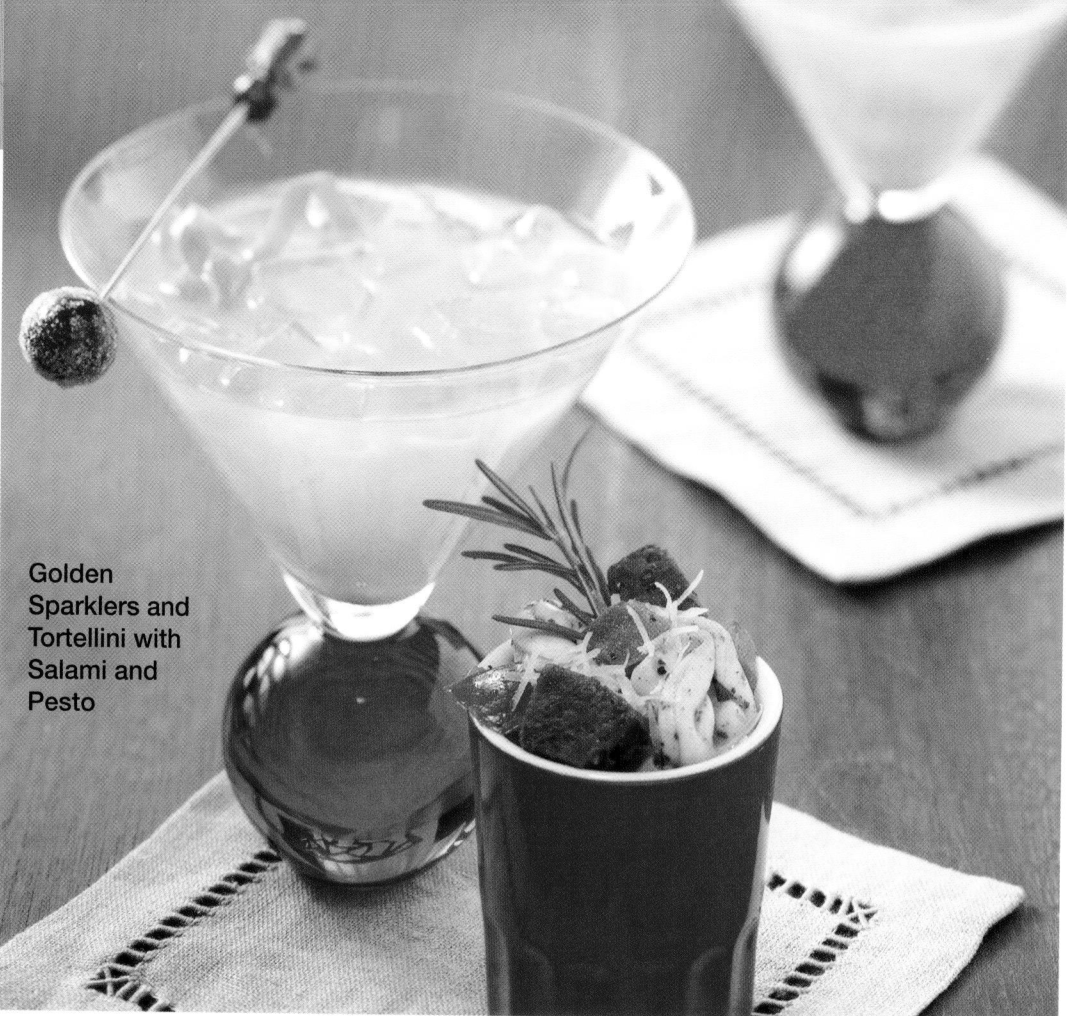

Golden Sparklers and Tortellini with Salami and Pesto

Tortellini with Salami and Pesto

Refrigerated tortellini and purchased pesto make this quick to fix. For an appetizer buffet, set out individual portions, which are easier to handle.

Start to Finish: 15 minutes **Makes:** 12 servings

- **1 9-ounce package refrigerated cheese-filled tortellini or ravioli**
- **1 medium tomato, chopped**
- **½ cup purchased basil pesto**
- **2 ounces salami, cut into ½-inch cubes**
- **Finely shredded Parmesan cheese (optional)**
- **Fresh rosemary sprigs (optional)**

1. Cook tortellini according to package directions. Place chopped tomato in a large colander; pour pasta over tomato to drain. Transfer pasta mixture to a medium bowl.

2. Add pesto and salami to pasta mixture; toss gently to coat. Sprinkle with Parmesan cheese. If desired, garnish with rosemary sprigs. Serve warm.

Per serving: 133 cal., 7 g total fat (2 g sat. fat), 21 mg chol., 276 mg sodium, 12 g carbo., 1 g fiber, 5 g pro.

Golden Sparklers

This festive drink contains orange juice, apricot nectar, and sparkling water. For an impressive party presentation, skewer sugared cranberries on cocktail picks to adorn the drinks.

Prep: 15 minutes
Makes: about 10 (4-ounce) servings

- **1 cup ice cubes**
- **1½ cups orange juice, chilled**
- **1½ cups apricot nectar, chilled**
- **1 375-milliliter bottle sparkling water, chilled**
- **Ice cubes**
- **Orange peel twists (optional)**

1. Place ice cubes in a large pitcher. Pour orange juice and apricot nectar over the ice cubes. Slowly add sparkling water, stirring gently. Serve immediately over additional ice cubes. If desired, garnish with orange peel twists.

Per serving: 38 cal., 0 g total fat, 0 mg chol., 9 mg sodium, 9 g carbo., 0 g fiber, 0 g pro.

Gorgonzola Coins

Slow-roasted garlic, sweet onions, and balsamic vinegar blend to make an irresistible jam topping for tangy blue cheese and walnut crackers.

Bake: 8 minutes **Chill:** 1 hour **Oven:** 425°F
Makes: 75 appetizers

- **1½ cups all-purpose flour**
- **¼ teaspoon ground black pepper**
- **½ cup butter, softened**
- **4 ounces gorgonzola cheese or blue cheese, crumbled (1 cup)**
- **¼ cup finely chopped walnuts, toasted**
- **2 teaspoons Dijon-style mustard**
- **1 recipe Sweet Onion Jam**

1. In a medium bowl combine flour and pepper. With an electric mixer beat in butter, cheese, walnuts, and mustard until the dough comes together. Divide the dough into thirds and roll each portion into an 8×1-inch log. Wrap logs in plastic wrap and chill at least 1 hour or freeze up to 2 months.

2. Preheat oven to 425°F. Line two baking sheets with parchment paper. Slice logs into ¼-inch slices. Place slices one inch apart on prepared baking sheets. Bake 8 to 10 minutes or until golden brown. Cool on wire racks. Top coins with Sweet Onion Jam and serve immediately.

Sweet Onion Jam: Preheat oven to 325°F. Cut off about ¼ inch of the pointed top of one whole garlic bulb to expose individual cloves. Place bulb, cut end up, in a custard cup. Drizzle with 1 teaspoon olive oil. Cover with foil and bake for 45 to 60 minutes or until garlic cloves feel soft when pressed. Cool. Gently squeeze garlic paste from individual cloves into a saucepan. Stir in 1 cup finely chopped sweet onion, ½ cup finely chopped Granny Smith apple, ½ cup balsamic vinegar, and ½ cup sugar. Bring to boiling over medium-high heat, stirring occasionally; reduce heat. Simmer, uncovered, about 30 minutes, stirring occasionally, until onion and apple soften, turn transparent, and mixture thickens. Cool. Transfer to a covered container and chill up to 1 week. Makes about ¾ cup.

Advance Preparation: Prepare coins as directed. Cool completely. Layer between sheets of waxed paper in an airtight container; cover. Freeze up to 3 months. To thaw, let stand at room temperature 15 minutes. Prepare Sweet Onion Jam; cover and chill up to 1 week.

Per appetizer: 38 cal., 2 g total fat (1 g sat. fat), 5 mg chol., 33 mg sodium, 4 g carbo., 0 g fiber, 1 g pro.

Gorgonzola Coins

Ham and Gruyère Pinwheels

Good quality baked ham is essential for this appetizer. Select the Black Forest variety for its marvelous smoky flavor.

Prep: 15 minutes **Bake:** 15 minutes
Chill: 30 minutes **Oven:** 400°F **Makes:** 32 appetizers

- **1 17.3-ounce package frozen puff pastry sheets (2 sheets)**
- **¼ cup honey Dijon-style mustard**
- **4 ounces very thinly sliced Black Forest ham or country ham**
- **4 ounces Gruyère cheese, shredded (1 cup)**
- **⅓ cup snipped dried apricots**
- **¼ teaspoon coarsely ground black pepper**
- **1 egg, lightly beaten**
- **1 tablespoon water**

1. Thaw puff pastry sheets according to package directions. Cut each sheet in half crosswise.

2. Spread each pastry sheet with mustard, leaving a ½-inch border along one long end. Divide ham between pastry sheets. Sprinkle with cheese, dried apricots, and pepper.

3. In a small bowl beat together egg and water. Brush unfilled border of pastry sheets with egg mixture. Starting from the opposite long end, roll pastry sheet, sealing edges. Repeat with remaining pastry sheet. Transfer, seam sides down, to a baking sheet. Cover and chill for 30 minutes.

4. Preheat oven to 400°F. Line baking sheet(s) with parchment paper; set aside. Use a serrated knife to gently slice each roll into ½-inch slices. Place on prepared baking sheet(s). Bake 15 minutes, or until golden brown. Serve warm.

Advance Preparation: Layer baked slices between sheets of waxed paper in an airtight container; cover. Freeze up to 3 months. Line a baking sheet with parchment paper. Place slices on prepared baking sheet. Let stand, uncovered, at room temperature for 15 minutes or until slices thaw. Meanwhile, preheat oven to 350°F. Bake for 5 minutes or until heated through.

Per appetizer: 98 cal., 6 g total fat (2 g sat. fat), 12 mg chol., 120 mg sodium, 7 g carbo., 0 g fiber, 3 g pro.

Pomegranate Fizzes

Grenadine, a pomegranate syrup, adds kick to many mixed drinks and cocktails. The fruit's juice is the star of this sprightly drink that combines carbonated water and mint.

Prep: 20 minutes **Chill:** 2 hours
Makes: about 20 (4-ounce) servings

- **¼ cup mint leaves**
- **4 cups pomegranate juice or cranberry juice**
- **¼ cup sugar**
- **2 1-liter bottles carbonated water**
- **Ice cubes**
- **Mint leaves (optional)**
- **Pomegranate seeds (optional)**

1. For syrup, place mint leaves in a pitcher. Use a wooden spoon to bruise leaves. Add pomegranate juice and sugar, stirring until sugar dissolves. Cover and chill for 2 to 4 hours. Use a slotted spoon to remove and discard mint leaves.

2. For each serving, in a small glass combine ¼ cup syrup and ½ cup carbonated water over ice cubes. If desired, garnish with mint leaves and pomegranate seeds. Serve immediately.

Advance Preparation. Prepare syrup, chill, and remove mint as directed. Cover and chill syrup up to 48 hours after removing mint.

Per serving: 40 cal., 0 g total fat, 0 mg chol., 21 mg sodium, 10 g carbo., 0 g fiber, 0 g pro.

Bourbon-Lime Spritzer

Keep a stock of ginger ale, limes, and bourbon or apple juice on hand to mix this fizzy drink whenever unexpected guests drop in.

Prep: 5 minutes **Makes:** 1 serving

- **1 tablespoon coarse sugar**
- **¼ teaspoon ground ginger**
- **1 lime wedge**
- **3 tablespoons bourbon or apple juice**
- **1 tablespoon lime juice**
- **½ cup ginger ale**

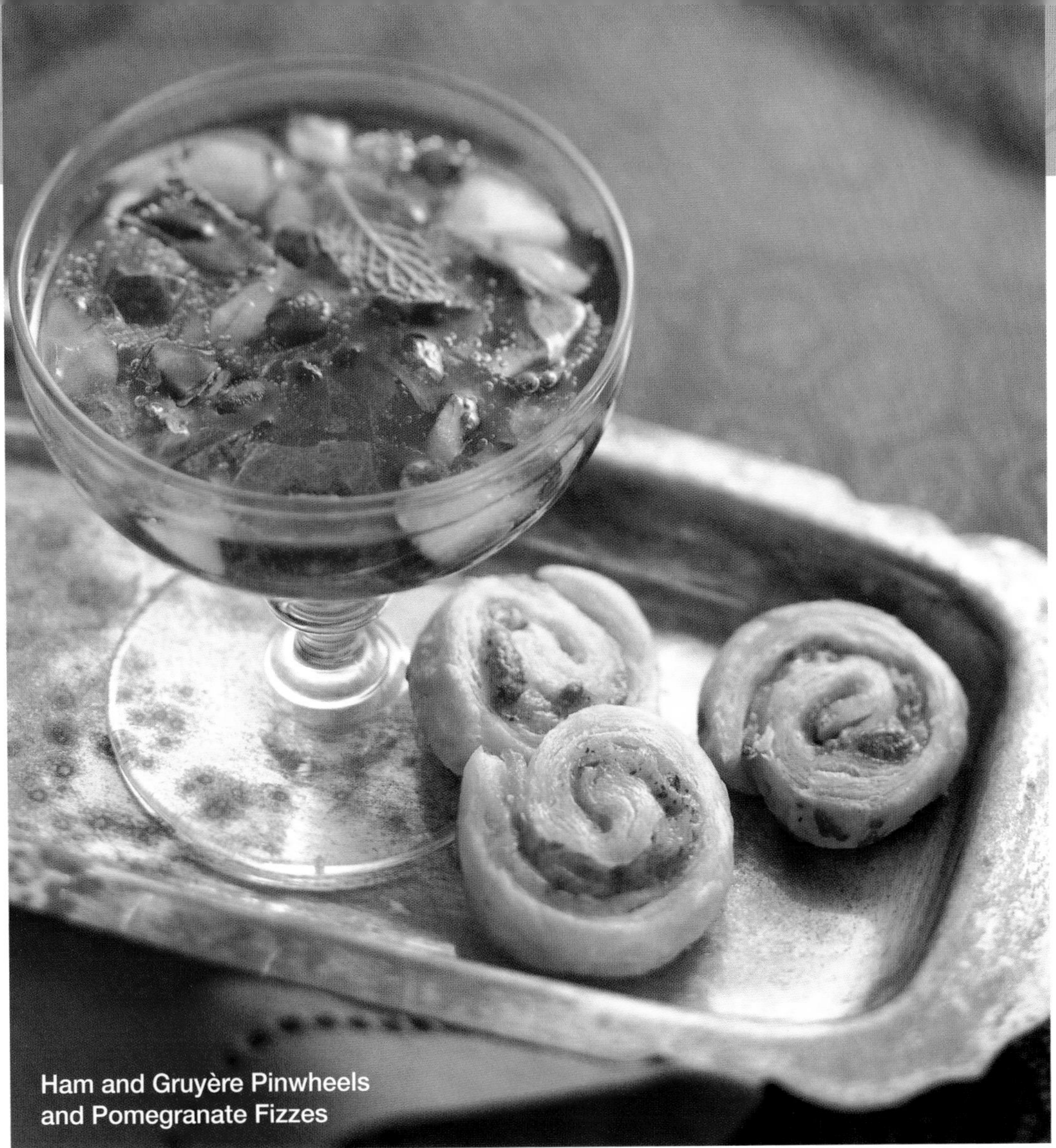

Ham and Gruyère Pinwheels and Pomegranate Fizzes

1. Combine sugar and ground ginger. For each drink, rub lime wedge around rim of cocktail glass. Dip rim in sugar mixture. Fill glass halfway with ice cubes. Add bourbon, lime juice, and ginger ale.

Per serving: 194 cal., 0 g total fat, 0 mg chol., 10 mg sodium, 26 g carbo., 0 g fiber, 0 g pro.

Baked Brie

Find tomato preserves next to other jams and preserves in large supermarkets or specialty stores.

Prep: 20 minutes **Bake:** 10 minutes
Oven: 325°F **Makes:** 8 servings

- 1 **small onion, cut into thin wedges**
- 2 **teaspoons butter or margarine**
- ⅓ **cup tomato preserves or mango chutney**
- ½ **teaspoon snipped fresh rosemary**
- ⅛ **teaspoon crushed red pepper**
- 1 **8-ounce round Brie cheese, with rind (about 4 inches in diameter)**
- **French bread slices and/or assorted crackers**

1. For caramelized onions, in a small covered saucepan cook onion in hot butter over low heat about 15 minutes or until tender and golden, stirring occasionally. Meanwhile, cut any large pieces of preserves. Stir together preserves, rosemary, and crushed red pepper.

2. Preheat oven to 325°F. Cut off and discard very thin slice from top of Brie cheese to remove rind. Place cheese in a 9-inch pie plate. Top with preserves mixture and caramelized onions.

3. Bake for 10 to 12 minutes or until cheese softens and is warm but not runny. Serve with crackers and/or bread slices.

Per serving: 143 cal., 9 g total fat (5 g sat. fat), 28 mg chol., 191 mg sodium, 10 g carbo., 0 g fiber, 6 g pro.

Chicken Wellington

Each flaky pastry packet encloses chicken breast on a bed of spinach and herbed cheese.

Prep: 25 minutes **Bake:** 25 minutes
Oven: 425°F **Makes:** 4 servings

- **½ of a 10-ounce package frozen chopped spinach, thawed and well drained**
- **1 5.2-ounce container semisoft cheese with garlic and herbs**
- **½ of a 17.3-ounce package frozen puff pastry sheets, thawed (1 sheet)**
- **4 skinless, boneless chicken breast halves (1¼ pounds total)**
- **¼ teaspoon salt**
- **2 tablespoons fine dry bread crumbs**
- **1 egg**
- **1 tablespoon water**

1. Preheat oven to 425°F. Lightly grease a baking sheet; set aside. In a small bowl stir together spinach and cheese; set aside.

2. On a lightly floured surface roll pastry sheet into a 15×13-inch rectangle. Trim to a 14×12-inch rectangle; reserve trimmings. Cut into four 7×6-inch rectangles.

3. Spread one-fourth of the spinach mixture over each pastry rectangle, leaving a ¾-inch border around the edge. Season both sides of each chicken breast half with salt. Top each pastry rectangle with a chicken breast, tucking under thin end of chicken, if present, to make an even thickness. Sprinkle with one-fourth of the bread crumbs. In a small bowl beat egg and water together. Brush egg mixture onto edges of rectangles. Gather the four corners of pastry at the top of the chicken and firmly pinch edges together to form a tight seal. Place packets on prepared baking sheet.

4. Cut small decorative shapes from remaining pastry. Brush egg mixture over pastry packets. Place decorations on top of packets; brush with additional egg mixture.

5. Bake for 25 minutes or until pastry is golden and an instant-read thermometer inserted into chicken registers 160°F.

Advance Preparation: Prepare packets as directed through Step 4. Cover and chill up

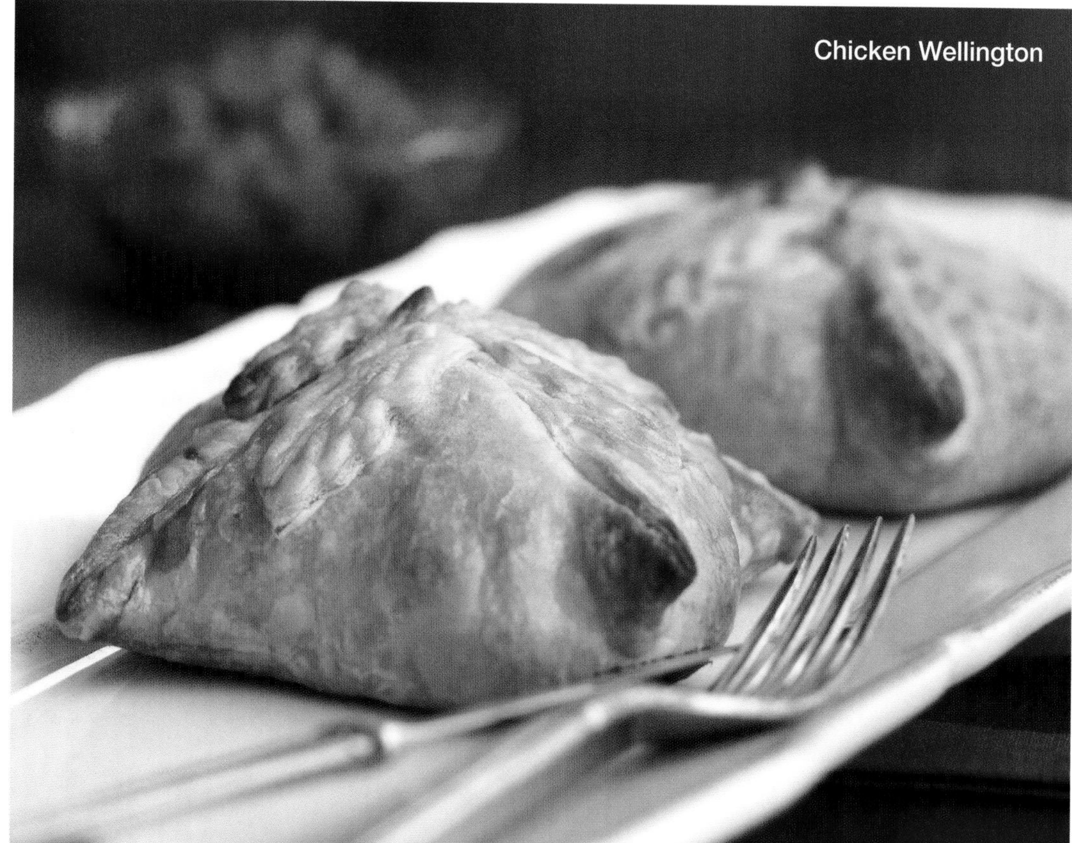
Chicken Wellington

to 24 hours. To serve, bake as directed. Or place packets in a freezer container; cover and freeze up to 1 week. Thaw packets overnight in refrigerator. Bake as directed.

Per serving: 681 cal., 42 g total fat (18 g sat. fat), 136 mg chol., 677 mg sodium, 33 g carbo., 2 g fiber, 43 g pro.

Filet Mignon with Cranberry-Red Wine Sauce

An elegant cut such as tenderloin deserves an equally upscale sauce. This fruity wine sauce is tasty over pork loin too.

Start to Finish: 25 minutes **Makes:** 4 servings

- **4 beef tenderloin steaks, cut ¾ inch thick (1 pound)**
- **¼ teaspoon salt**
- **¼ teaspoon freshly ground black pepper**
- **1 tablespoon butter**
- **¼ cup finely chopped shallots**
- **½ cup dry red wine**
- **½ cup beef broth**
- **½ cup dried cranberries or tart cherries**
- **1 tablespoon balsamic vinegar**
- **1 teaspoon dried thyme, crushed**
- **Salt and freshly ground black pepper**

1. Season both sides of steaks with salt and pepper. In a large skillet melt 1 tablespoon butter over medium-high heat. Add steaks; reduce heat to medium. Cook to desired doneness; turn once. Allow 7 to 9 minutes for medium-rare (145°F) to medium (160°F). Transfer steaks to a platter; cover and keep warm.

2. Add shallots to skillet; cook and stir for 2 minutes. Add wine and broth to skillet, stirring with a whisk to loosen any browned bits from the bottom of the pan. Add cranberries, vinegar, and thyme. Bring to boiling. Boil, uncovered, about 5 minutes or until the liquid reduces to about ¾ cup. Season sauce to taste with additional salt and pepper. Spoon sauce over steaks.

Per serving: 303 cal., 13 g total fat (6 g sat. fat), 78 mg chol., 488 mg sodium, 16 g carbo., 1 g fiber, 24 g pro.

Beef Tenderloin with Blue Cheese-Shrimp Sauce

Beef tenderloin is a special-occasion cut worth every penny when cooked to perfection and served with a rich seafood sauce. Let the meat rest before slicing to give the fibers time to absorb internal juices. *Pictured on page 133.*

Prep: 15 minutes **Cook:** 8 minutes
Roast: 45 minutes **Stand:** 10 minutes
Oven: 425°F **Makes:** 6 servings

- **6 cloves garlic, minced**
- **1 teaspoon salt**
- **1 teaspoon coarse ground black pepper**
- **1 3 to 4-pound beef tenderloin roast, trimmed**
- **2 tablespoon butter**
- **8 ounces medium shrimp, peeled and deveined**
- **¼ cup dry white wine or chicken broth**
- **½ cup whipping cream**
- **½ cup crumbled blue cheese (2 ounces)**
- **Snipped fresh chives**
- **Fresh tarragon sprigs and/or thyme sprigs**

1. Preheat oven to 425°F. In bowl combine 4 cloves of minced garlic, salt, and 1 teaspoon coarse ground pepper. Sprinkle over roast. Place in a shallow roasting pan. Roast for 45 to 50 minutes or until internal temperature registers 135°F for medium-rare (150°F for medium). Remove from oven and cover with foil. Let stand for 10 to 15 minutes. (Internal temperature will rise 5°F while standing.)

2. While roast stands, in a large skillet melt butter over medium heat. Add remaining 2 cloves minced garlic; cook and stir for 1 minute. Add shrimp; cook and stir for 2 minutes or until opaque. Remove skillet from heat. With a slotted spoon remove shrimp from skillet. Add wine. Return skillet to the heat. Cook for 2 to 3 minutes or until wine almost evaporates. Stir in cream and blue cheese. Cook and stir until cheese melts and cream thickens to desired consistency, about 3 minutes. Stir in shrimp and heat through. Keep sauce warm.

3. Slice roast and serve with shrimp sauce. Garnish with chives, tarragon and/or thyme. Sprinkle with additional coarsely *ground black pepper.*

Per serving: 539 cal., 29 g total fat (14 g sat. fat), 254 mg chol., 739 mg sodium, 3 g carbo., 0 g fiber, 61 g pro.

Walnut-Sage Potatoes au Gratin

Walnut-Sage Potatoes au Gratin

Thinly slice the potatoes in a food processor for this special company dish.

Prep: 30 minutes **Bake:** 70 minutes
Stand: 10 minutes **Oven:** 350°F
Makes: 10 to 12 servings

- **6 medium potatoes (2 pounds)**
- **1 medium onion, chopped**
- **1 teaspoon bottled minced garlic (2 cloves)**
- **3 tablespoons walnut oil or olive oil**
- **3 tablespoons all-purpose flour**
- **½ teaspoon salt**
- **¼ teaspoon ground black pepper**
- **2½ cups milk**
- **3 tablespoons snipped fresh sage**
- **1 cup shredded Gruyère cheese (4 ounces)**
- **⅓ cup broken walnuts**

1. If desired, peel potatoes; thinly slice potatoes to make about 6 cups. Rinse with cold water; drain.

2. Preheat oven to 350°F. For sauce, in a medium saucepan cook onion and garlic in hot oil over medium heat until tender. Stir in flour, salt, and pepper. Add milk all at once. Cook and stir until thickened and bubbly. Remove from heat; stir in fresh sage.

3. Layer half of the potatoes in greased 2-quart casserole. Top with half the sauce. Sprinkle with half of the cheese. Repeat layering with potatoes and sauce. (Cover and chill remaining cheese until needed.)

4. Bake, covered, for 40 minutes. Uncover and bake about 25 minutes or just until potatoes are tender. Sprinkle with remaining cheese; top with walnuts. Bake, uncovered, for 5 minutes. Let stand for 10 minutes before serving.

Per serving: 217 cal., 12 g total fat (3 g sat. fat), 17 mg chol., 187 mg sodium, 20 g carbo., 2 g fiber, 9 g pro.

Fresh Greens with Thyme-Dijon Vinaigrette

Mustard gives the dressing a bite that tastes good with both the greens and the apple.

Start to Finish: 25 minutes **Makes:** 4 servings

- **4 cups torn romaine lettuce**
- **1 cup torn arugula or radicchio**
- **1 small apple with green skin, such as Granny Smith or Newtown Pippin, cut into thin wedges**
- **½ cup thin red onion wedges**
- **¼ cup Thyme-Dijon Vinaigrette**

1. In a large bowl toss together romaine, arugula, apple, and onion. Drizzle with Thyme-Dijon Vinaigrette. Toss gently to coat.

Thyme-Dijon Vinaigrette: In a screw-top jar combine ¼ cup olive oil; ¼ cup white or regular balsamic vinegar; 2 teaspoons snipped fresh thyme or ½ teaspoon dried thyme, crushed; 1 teaspoon Dijon-style mustard; and ¼ teaspoon salt. Cover; shake well to mix. Makes ½ cup.

Advance Preparation: Prepare vinaigrette dressing as directed. Cover and chill up to 24 hours. Bring to room temperature and shake before serving.

Per serving: 93 cal., 6 g total fat (1 g sat. fat), 0 mg chol., 96 mg sodium, 11 g carbo., 2 g fiber, 1 g pro.

Fennel-Asiago Biscotti

These crunchy, twice-baked cookies are perfect to serve at a party or before a meal.

Prep: 30 minutes **Bake:** 39 minutes
Stand: 15 minutes **Cool:** 25 minutes
Oven: 350°F/325°F **Makes:** 80 biscotti

- **2 cups all-purpose flour**
- **¼ cup white cornmeal**
- **1 teaspoon baking powder**
- **1 teaspoon salt**
- **½ teaspoon coarsely ground black pepper**
- **⅛ teaspoon baking soda**
- **Dash cayenne pepper**
- **¾ cup freshly grated Asiago cheese**
- **½ cup pine nuts, toasted and chopped**
- **2 teaspoons fennel seeds**
- **2 eggs, lightly beaten**
- **½ cup buttermilk**
- **Parmigiano-Reggiano cheese (optional)**
- **Dried apricots and/or dried figs (optional)**
- **Pear slices (optional)**

1. Preheat oven to 350°F. Line a large cookie sheet with parchment paper or foil; set aside. In a medium bowl stir together flour, cornmeal, baking powder, salt, black pepper, baking soda, and cayenne pepper. Stir in Asiago cheese, pine nuts, and fennel seeds.

2. In a small bowl combine eggs and buttermilk. Add egg mixture to flour mixture; stir until dough clings together. Turn out onto a lightly floured surface. Gently knead just until dough is smooth (it may be slightly sticky). Shape dough into a ball. Wrap in plastic wrap and let stand at room temperature for 15 minutes to make dough easier to shape.

3. Divide dough into thirds. Shape into three 7-inch-long loaves. Place loaves 2 inches apart on the prepared cookie sheet.

4. Bake about 25 minutes or until golden brown. (The tops may split as the biscotti bake.) Cool on cookie sheet for 5 minutes. Carefully transfer loaves to a wire rack; cool 20 minutes more.

5. Reduce oven temperature to 325°F. Line another cookie sheet with parchment paper or foil. Use a serrated knife to cut loaves diagonally into ¼-inch-thick slices. Place slices on the prepared cookie sheet. Bake for 6 minutes. Turn slices over; bake about 8 minutes or until crisp and dry (do not overbake). Transfer slices to wire racks; cool.

6. If desired, serve biscotti with Parmigiano-Reggiano cheese, dried apricots and/or figs, and pear slices.

Advance Preparation: Prepare as directed. Layer biscotti between sheets of waxed paper in an airtight container; cover. Store in refrigerator up to 3 days or freeze up to 2 weeks.

Per biscotti: 25 cal., 1 g total fat (0 g sat. fat), 6 mg chol., 49 mg sodium, 3 g carbo., 0 g fiber, 1 g pro.

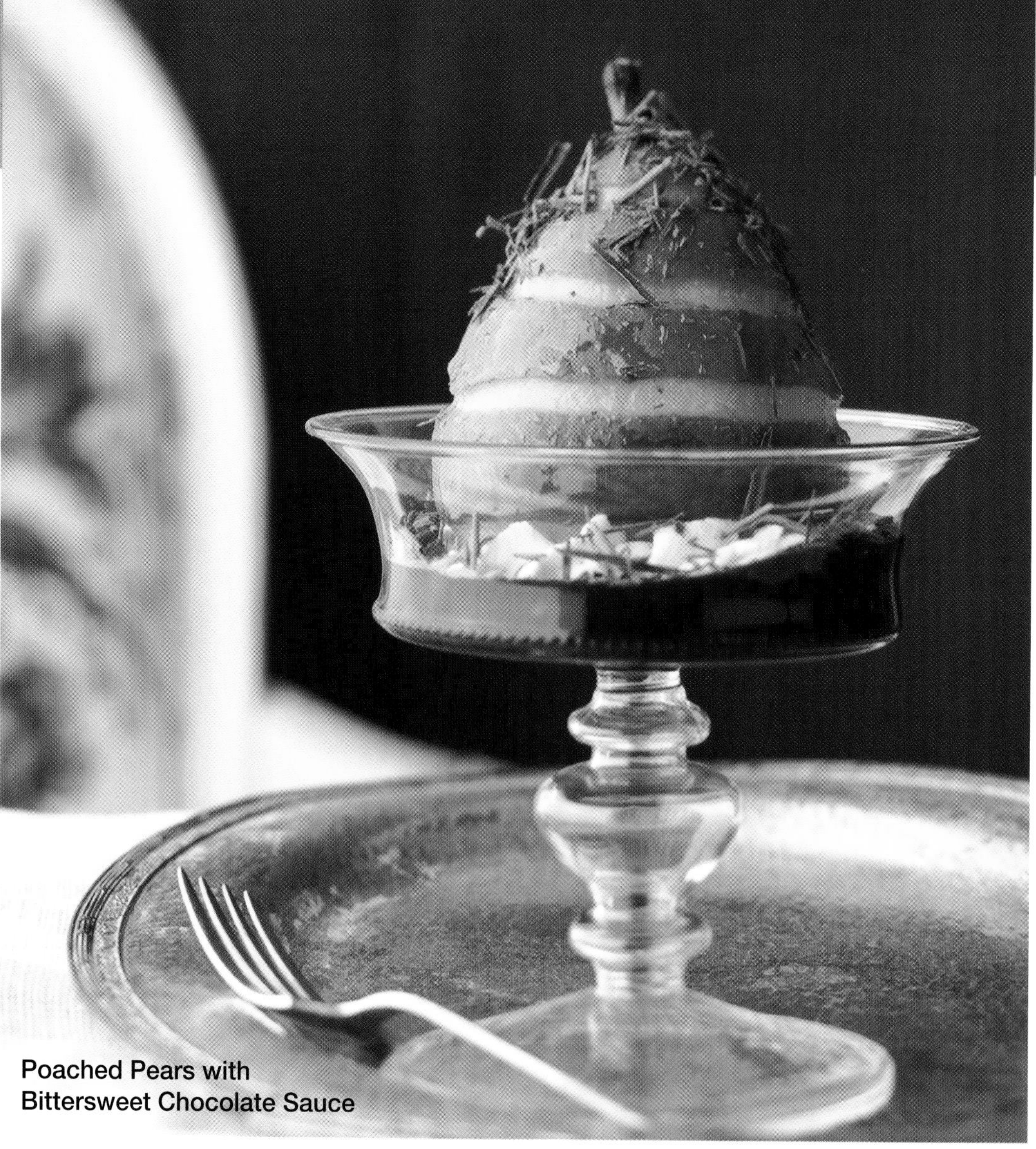

Poached Pears with
Bittersweet Chocolate Sauce

Poached Pears with Bittersweet Chocolate Sauce

The sweet fruitiness of wine-poached pears and the richness of chocolate are a sensational pairing for this simple, yet elegant dessert. Be sure to leave the pear stems attached for the full visual effect.

Prep: 45 minutes **Cook:** 30 minutes
Chill: 2 hours **Makes:** 8 servings

- **8 medium Anjou or Bartlett pears (about 4 pounds)**
- **1 750-milliliter bottle Riesling wine**
- **1 11.3- to 12-ounce can pear nectar**
- **⅓ cup honey**
- **1½ teaspoons vanilla**
- **6 ounces bittersweet chocolate, chopped**
- **1 teaspoon instant espresso coffee powder (optional)**
- **1 cup whipping cream**
- **¼ cup crème fraîche or sour cream**
- **Bittersweet chocolate shavings**

1. Peel pears, leaving stems intact. Or if desired, use a zester to remove a thin strip of peel in a spiral design from each pear. Cut a thin slice from the bottom of each pear so the pears stand up. Use a melon baller to remove the core through the bottom of each pear.

2. In a 4-quart kettle combine wine, pear nectar, and honey. Cook, uncovered, over medium heat until gently boiling, stirring occasionally to dissolve honey. Add pears. Return liquid just to boiling; reduce heat. Simmer, covered, 15 to 20 minutes or just until pears are tender. Remove from heat and stir in 1 teaspoon of the vanilla; cool pears slightly in syrup. Transfer pears and syrup to an extra-large bowl. Cover and chill for 2 to 24 hours. Drain pears to serve, reserving syrup.

3. To serve, in a medium saucepan bring 2 cups of the cooking liquid to boiling. Reduce heat and boil gently, uncovered, for about 15 minutes until reduced by half (about 1 cup). In a medium bowl combine 6 ounces chocolate and instant espresso coffee powder, if using. Pour reduced liquid over the chocolate mixture. Let stand for 5 minutes. Whisk until smooth.

4. In a chilled mixing bowl combine whipping cream, crème fraîche, and remaining ½ teaspoon vanilla. Beat with an electric mixer on high speed for 4 minutes or until soft peaks form.

5. To serve, spoon some of the chocolate mixture onto each dessert dish. Spoon some of the whipped cream over top. Stand a pear in the center of the whipped cream. Sprinkle with chocolate shavings. Serve immediately.

Advance Preparation: Cook pears as directed. Transfer to bowl; cover. Chill for 2 to 24 hours.

Per serving: 494 cal., 24 g total fat (14 g sat. fat), 52 mg chol., 18 mg sodium, 61 g carbo., 7 g fiber, 3 g pro.

Chocolate-Dipped Amaretti Sundaes

Amaretti are crisp almond-flavored Italian cookies that are delicious dipped in chocolate and served in a simple dessert like this.

Prep: 25 minutes **Makes:** 6 servings

- **2 ounces semisweet chocolate, chopped**
- **24 purchased amaretti**
- **1 tablespoon finely chopped almonds, toasted**
- **3 cups butter brickle ice cream**

1. In a small heavy saucepan melt chocolate over low heat, stirring occasionally. Dip tops of amaretti into melted chocolate and sprinkle with almonds. Let stand until chocolate is set.

2. In each of six martini glasses, place 1 of the amaretti. Top with scoops of ice cream. Top ice cream with 3 amaretti. Serve immediately or freeze sundaes until ready to serve.

Advance Preparation: Prepare sundaes as directed. Loosely cover and freeze up to 24 hours. Let stand for 10 minutes before serving.

Per serving: 257 cal., 14 g total fat (6 g sat. fat), 20 mg chol., 116 mg sodium, 29 g carbo., 1 g fiber, 4 g pro.

Chocolate-Dipped Amaretti Sundaes

houseguest specials

The challenge of hosting guests in your home over the holidays demands that you pull off great meals in a streamlined fashion. Whether it's something quick or something to prep ahead, here are eight easy recipes to help you enjoy your meals and your company.

Smoky Salmon Casserole,
page 147

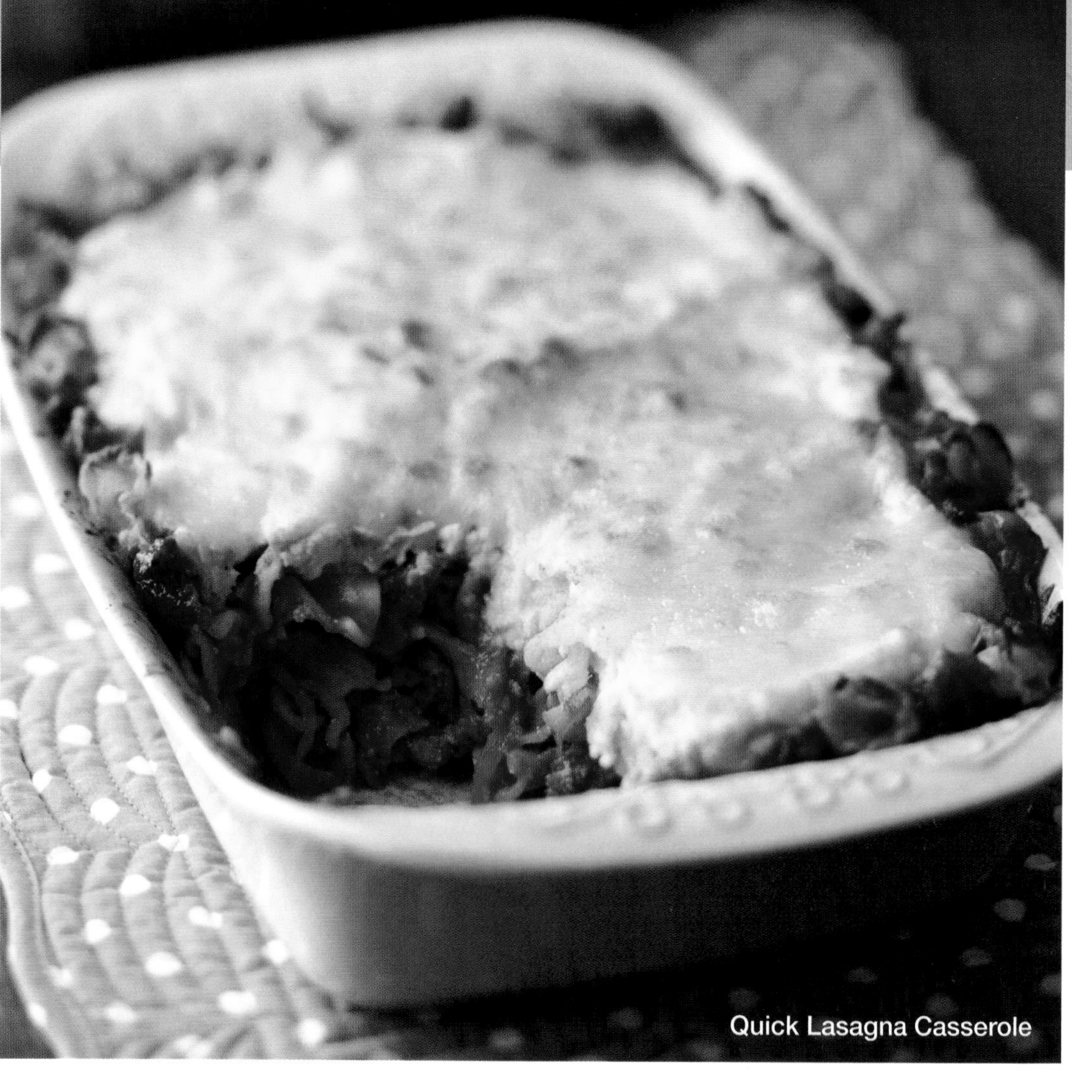
Quick Lasagna Casserole

Quick Lasagna Casserole

The traditional way to assemble lasagna is to layer the ingredients. Tossing together the pasta and sauce and adding one cheesy topping cuts prep time.

Prep: 25 minutes **Bake:** 35 minutes
Stand: 10 minutes **Oven:** 375°F
Makes: 8 to 10 servings

- **12 ounces dried campanelle or cellantani pasta**
- **1 pound bulk Italian sausage**
- **1 large onion, cut in thin wedges**
- **1 medium yellow sweet pepper, cut in bite-size strips**
- **3 cloves garlic, minced**
- **1 24- to 28-ounce jar marinara sauce**
- **1 teaspoon fennel seeds, crushed**
- **1 15-ounce carton ricotta cheese**
- **1 egg, lightly beaten**
- **1 8-ounce packaged shredded Italian blend cheeses (2 cups)**

1. Preheat oven to 375°F. Cook pasta according to package directions; drain.

2. In a large skillet cook sausage, onion, sweet pepper, and garlic until sausage is no longer pink; drain fat. Transfer sausage mixture to a very large bowl. Stir in marinara sauce, fennel seeds, and cooked pasta.

3. Transfer the pasta mixture to a 3-quart rectangular baking pan. In a medium bowl stir together ricotta cheese, egg, and 1 cup of the Italian blend cheeses. Spoon the ricotta cheese over the pasta mixture in large spoonfuls. Sprinkle the remaining shredded Italian blend cheeses over the top. Bake, uncovered, for 35 to 40 minutes or until heated through. Let stand for 10 minutes before serving.

Advance Preparation: Transfer pasta mixture to a 3-quart rectangular baking dish. Cover with plastic wrap. Chill 2 to 24 hours. Remove plastic wrap. Bake in a 350°F oven for 50 to 60 minutes or until heated through. Let stand as directed.

Per serving: 636 cal., 35 g total fat (17 g sat. fat), 112 mg chol., 1,133 mg sodium, 47 g carbo., 5 g fiber, 34 g pro.

Smoky Salmon Casserole

If you love smoked salmon, you'll love this exceptional pasta dish where the salmon is flaky in texture and fragrant with smoke. Pictured on page 145.

Prep: 30 minutes **Bake:** 25 minutes **Oven:** 350°F
Makes: 6 servings

- **8 ounces dried bow tie pasta or penne (3½ cups)**
- **1 cup chopped red sweet pepper**
- **½ cup chopped green onions**
- **2 tablespoons butter**
- **2 tablespoons all-purpose flour**
- **¼ teaspoon ground black pepper**
- **2½ cups milk**
- **6 ounces smoked gouda cheese, shredded**
- **½ teaspoon finely shredded lemon peel**
- **1 tablespoon lemon juice**
- **1 4.5-ounce package smoked salmon, flaked with skin and bones removed**
- **1 14-ounce can artichoke hearts, drained and quartered**
- **1 cup soft bread crumbs or panko (Japanese-style bread crumbs)**
- **¼ cup pine nuts**
- **Freshly ground black pepper**

1. Preheat oven to 350°F. Cook pasta according to package directions. Drain and set aside.

2. In a large skillet cook red sweet pepper and green onions in hot butter for 3 minutes or until tender. Stir in flour and ¼ teaspoon black pepper. Add milk all at once. Cook and stir until slightly thickened and bubbly. Stir in cheese until melted. Stir in lemon peel and lemon juice (mixture may appear curdled).

3. In a large bowl combine pasta, cheese sauce, smoked salmon, and artichoke hearts. Transfer to a 2-quart square or rectangular baking dish. Sprinkle with bread crumbs, pine nuts, and black pepper. Bake, uncovered, for 25 to 30 minutes or until heated through and topping is golden. Let stand for 10 minutes before serving.

Advance Preparation: Prepare as directed except do not top with bread crumbs and nuts; cover. Chill up to 24 hours. Top with bread crumbs and pine nuts. Bake, uncovered, in a 350°F oven for 45 to 50 minutes or until heated through and topping is golden.

Per serving: 470 cal., 19 g total fat (10 g sat. fat), 74 mg chol., 780 mg sodium, 45 g carbo., 4 g fiber, 30 g pro.

Garlic Cheese Bread

For soft bread, wrap the loaf in foil and bake as directed. For crisp toasted bread, place slices on a broiler pan and broil for a few minutes, watching closely.

Prep: 15 minutes **Bake:** 20 minutes **Oven:** 350°F
Makes: about 18 slices (6 to 8 servings)

- **¼ cup butter, softened**
- **1 tablespoon snipped fresh Italian (flat-leaf) parsley or fresh basil**
- **3 cloves garlic, minced**
- **¼ teaspoon ground black pepper**
- **1 1-pound loaf crusty Italian bread**
- **¼ cup shredded Italian blend cheeses**

1. Preheat oven to 350°F. In a small bowl stir together butter, parsley, garlic, and pepper.

2. Cut the Italian bread crosswise into ¾-inch slices, cutting to, but not through, the bottom crust. Spread butter mixture lightly on one side of each bread slice. Sprinkle cheese between the slices. Wrap the loaf tightly in foil.

3. Place the wrapped loaf on an oven rack in oven. Bake about 20 minutes or until cheese melts and loaf is hot. For easier serving, unwrap loaf and transfer to a cutting board; carefully cut bread slices apart.

Advance Preparation: Prepare as directed through Step 2. Place foil-wrapped loaf in refrigerator and chill up to 24 hours. To serve, continue as directed in Step 3.

Per serving: 290 cal., 12 g total fat (6 g sat. fat), 24 mg chol., 530 mg sodium, 39 g carbo., 2 g fiber, 8 g pro.

Next-Day Turkey Panini

Next-Day Turkey Panini

Any parsley or sage leaves left over from preparing stuffing make a flavorful addition to this grilled sandwich.

Prep: 20 minutes **Cook:** 6 minutes
Makes: 8 servings

- **8 soft French or sourdough rolls**
- **Olive oil**
- **½ to 1 cup cranberry relish or chutney**
- **Fresh baby spinach leaves**
- **1 pound cooked sliced (leftover) turkey**
- **4 ounces thinly sliced country ham or prosciutto**
- **1 pound sliced smoked cheese, such as mozzarella, Provolone, or cheddar**

1. Preheat covered indoor grill.* Split rolls horizontally. Lightly brush cut sides of rolls with oil. Spread 1 to 2 tablespoons cranberry relish on bottom halves of rolls. Layer greens, turkey, ham, and cheese on rolls. Place tops of rolls on filling.

2. Place four of the sandwiches in grill. Cover and cook for 6 minutes or until cheese melts and rolls are crisp. Repeat with remaining sandwiches.

***Test Kitchen Tip:** If you don't have a tabletop grill, heat a large heavy nonstick skillet over medium heat. Place sandwiches in skillet; weigh down sandwiches with another large heavy skillet. Cook for 3 to 4 minutes on each side or until cheese melts and rolls are crisp.

Per serving: 532 cal., 20 g total fat (9 g sat. fat), 95 mg chol., 1,056 mg sodium, 48 g carbo., 3 g fiber, 38 g pro.

Italian Egg Drop Soup with Spinach

A thin stream of egg drizzled into the broth develops a wonderful silken texture while Parmesan adds distinctive Italian flavor.

Prep: 10 minutes **Cook:** 8 minutes
Stand: 1 minute **Makes:** 4 to 6 main-dish or 8 to 10 side-dish servings

- **2 32-ounce boxes chicken broth**
- **1 cup dried miniature bow tie pasta (3 ounces)**
- **3 tablespoons semolina flour**
- **1 tablespoon chopped fresh Italian (flat-leaf) parsley**
- **¼ teaspoon freshly grated nutmeg**
- **4 eggs**
- **1½ cups shredded fresh spinach**
- **3 tablespoons finely shredded Parmesan cheese**

1. In a 4-quart Dutch oven bring broth to boiling. Add pasta and cook, uncovered, 5 minutes. Stir in semolina, parsley, and nutmeg. Cook, uncovered, 3 minutes more.

2. In a medium bowl whisk eggs together. Pour beaten eggs into hot soup mixture in a thin, steady stream while stirring two or three times to create shreds. Remove from heat. Cover and let stand for 1 minute.

3. Stir in spinach until it just wilts. Serve immediately. Sprinkle each serving with Parmesan cheese.

Per serving: 226 cal., 7 g total fat (2 g sat. fat), 219 mg chol., 1,959 mg sodium, 25 g carbo., 1 g fiber, 14 g pro.

Southwestern Potato Sausage Chowder

It's easy to feed a famished houseful with this simple slow-cooker soup. Vary the spiciness by choosing sweet or hot sausage and serrano or jalapeño pepper.

Prep: 25 minutes **Cook:** 8 to 10 hours low-heat setting; 4 to 5 hours high-heat setting
Makes: 6 servings

1 pound bulk pork sausage
1 pound round red potatoes, chopped
1 large onion, chopped
1 medium red sweet pepper, chopped
1 medium green sweet pepper, chopped
1 serrano or jalapeño pepper, seeded and chopped*
2 cloves garlic, minced
2 teaspoons ground cumin
¼ teaspoon ground black pepper
2 14-ounce cans chicken broth
Shredded Monterey Jack cheese with jalapeño peppers (optional)
1 recipe Fried Potato Sticks (optional)

1. In a large skillet cook sausage until no longer pink; drain fat.

2. In a 3½- or 4-quart slow cooker combine cooked sausage, potatoes, onion, sweet peppers, serrano pepper, garlic, cumin, and ground black pepper. Stir in chicken broth.

3. Cover and cook on low-heat setting for 8 to 10 hours or on high-heat setting for 4 to 5 hours. Top each serving with cheese or potato sticks, if desired.

***Test Kitchen Tip:** Because hot chile peppers, such as serranos and jalapeños, contain volatile oils that can burn your skin and eyes, avoid direct contact with chiles as much as possible. When working with chile peppers, wear plastic or rubber gloves. If your bare hands do touch the chile peppers, wash your hands with soap and water.

Per serving: 377 cal., 25 g total fat (10 g sat. fat), 71 mg chol., 1,114 mg sodium, 19 g carbo., 3 g fiber, 18 g pro.

Fried Potato Sticks: In a medium skillet cook 1 cup of julienned red potatoes in 2 tablespoons hot oil over medium heat for 5 to 7 minutes or until golden brown and crisp. Sprinkle with ½ teaspoon salt. Remove with a slotted spoon and drain on paper towel.

Southwestern Potato Sausage Chowder

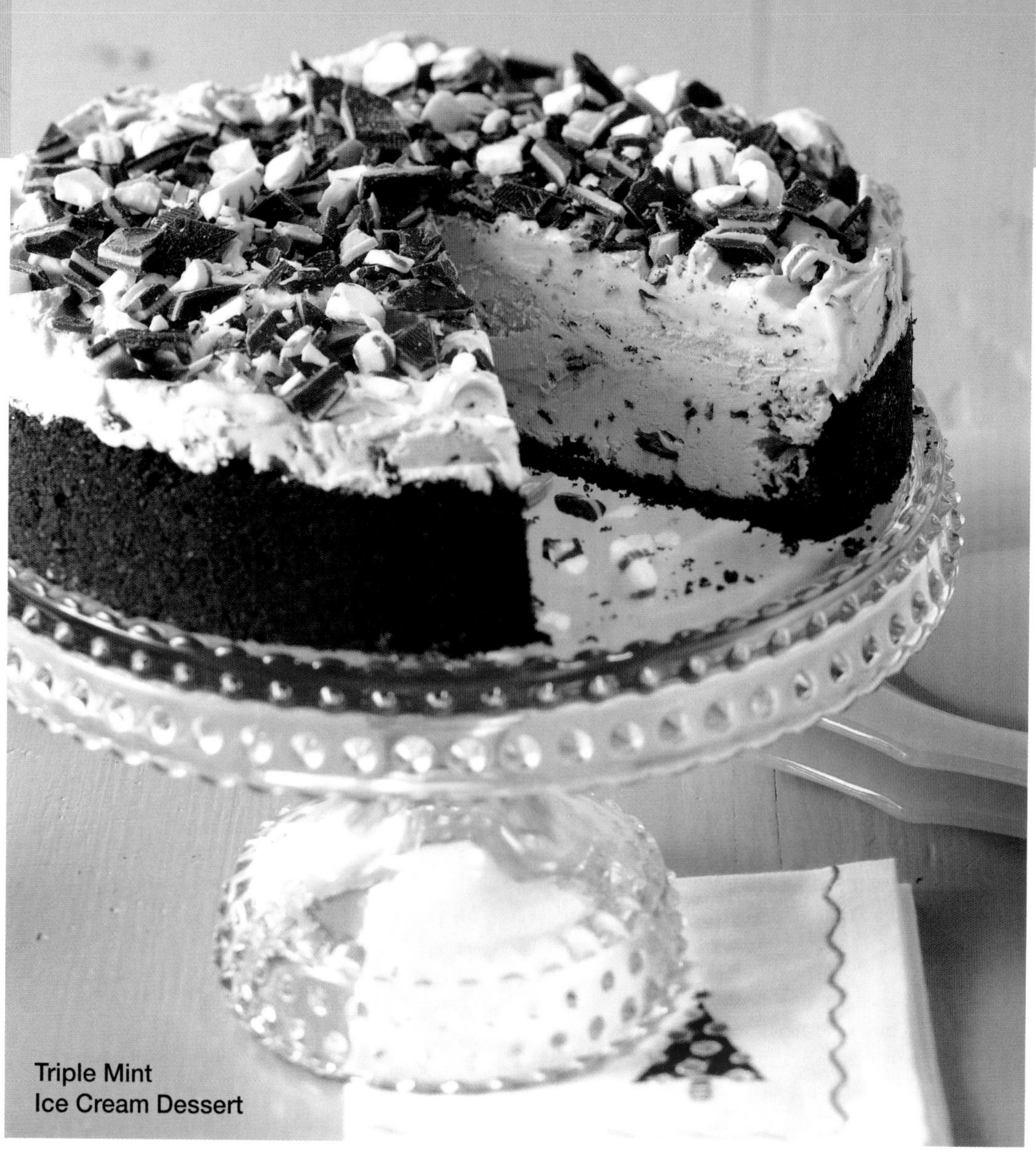
Triple Mint Ice Cream Dessert

Triple Mint Ice Cream Dessert

No time to bake? This refreshing holiday dessert features chocolate mint ice cream in a cookie crust. It is remarkably easy and will be a hit anytime.

Prep: 30 minutes **Stand:** 10 minutes **Chill:** 1 hour **Freeze:** 8 hours **Makes:** 10 servings

- **⅓ cup butter, melted**
- **¼ cup sugar**
- **1½ cups finely crushed chocolate wafer cookies (about 25)**
- **1 quart mint chocolate chip ice cream**
- **1 cup coarsely crushed peppermint sticks or candy canes (about 5 ounces)**
- **1 cup chopped layered chocolate-mint candies (about 28)**

1. Combine melted butter and sugar. Stir in crushed wafers; mix well. Press mixture evenly on the bottom and 1 inch up the sides of an 8-inch springform pan. Or spread evenly onto bottom and sides of a 9-inch pie plate. Chill for 1 hour.

2. In a large chilled bowl soften ice cream by using a wooden spoon to stir and press ice cream against the side of the bowl. Stir until soft but not melted. Stir in ½ cup of the peppermint sticks and ½ cup of the chocolate mint candies. Quickly spoon softened ice cream into the pan or pie plate. Cover and freeze for 1 hour or more.

3. Sprinkle top with remaining peppermint sticks and mint candies. Cover; freeze for several hours or overnight until firm. To serve, remove dessert from freezer. Let stand 10 to 15 minutes before serving.

Advance Preparation: Prepare as directed. Transfer to an airtight container; cover. Freeze up to 1 week.

Per serving: 393 cal., 19 g total fat (13 g sat. fat), 33 mg chol., 175 mg sodium, 51 g carbo., 1 g fiber, 4 g pro.

Black Bottom Cheesecake

Add chopped toasted pecans and a chocolate garnish to popular cheesecake when impressing holiday guests.

Prep: 30 minutes **Bake:** 30 minutes **Cool:** 2 hours
Chill: 4 hours **Oven:** 350°F **Makes:** 12 servings

⅓ cup butter, melted
¼ cup sugar
1¼ cups finely crushed graham crackers
⅔ cup whipping cream
1 cup semisweet chocolate pieces
1 cup chopped pecans, toasted (optional)*
2 8-ounce packages cream cheese, softened
½ cup sugar
2 eggs
½ cup caramel-flavor ice cream topping
Chopped pecans, toasted (optional)*
1 recipe Chocolate Drizzle Garnish (optional)

1. Preheat the oven to 350°F. For crust, in a medium bowl combine melted butter and the ¼ cup sugar. Add crushed crackers; toss to mix well. Press mixture onto the bottom and about 1½ inches up the side of a 9-inch springform pan. Bake for 10 minutes. Cool on a wire rack.

2. In a small saucepan bring whipping cream just to boiling over medium-high heat. Remove from heat; add chocolate (do not stir). Let stand 5 minutes. Stir until smooth. Pour chocolate mixture evenly over the crust. Sprinkle with 1 cup pecans, if desired.

3. For filling, in a medium mixing bowl beat cream cheese and the ½ cup sugar with an electric mixer on medium speed until combined. Add eggs, beating on low speed just until combined (do not overbeat). Pour over chocolate pecan layer in pan.

4. Bake for 30 to 35 minutes or until center appears nearly set when gently shaken. Cool cheesecake in pan on a wire rack for 15 minutes. Loosen and remove from side of springform pan; cool completely on wire rack. Cover and chill for at least 4 hours.

5. Let cheesecake stand at room temperature for 20 minutes before serving. Garnish each serving with a drizzle of caramel ice cream topping and, if desired, additional toasted pecans and Chocolate Drizzle Garnish.

***Test Kitchen Tip:** To toast pecans, spread in a single layer in a shallow baking pan. Bake in a 350°F oven for 5 to 10 minutes or until light golden brown, watching carefully and stirring once or twice so the pecans don't burn.

Advance Preparation: Prepare recipe as directed. Transfer to an airtight container; cover. Freeze up to 1 month. Before serving, thaw frozen cheesecake in refrigerator for 24 hours. Garnish as directed.

Per serving: 431 cal., 30 g total fat (18 g sat. fat), 109 mg chol., 298 mg sodium, 39 g carbo., 1 g fiber, 6 g pro.

Chocolate Drizzle Garnish: Line a baking sheet with foil; set aside. In a small saucepan heat 1 ounce of chopped semisweet baking chocolate over low heat until melted. Drizzle chocolate over the prepared baking sheet in a crisscross pattern. Chill, uncovered, until firm. Carefully break chocolate mixture into 2-inch pieces.

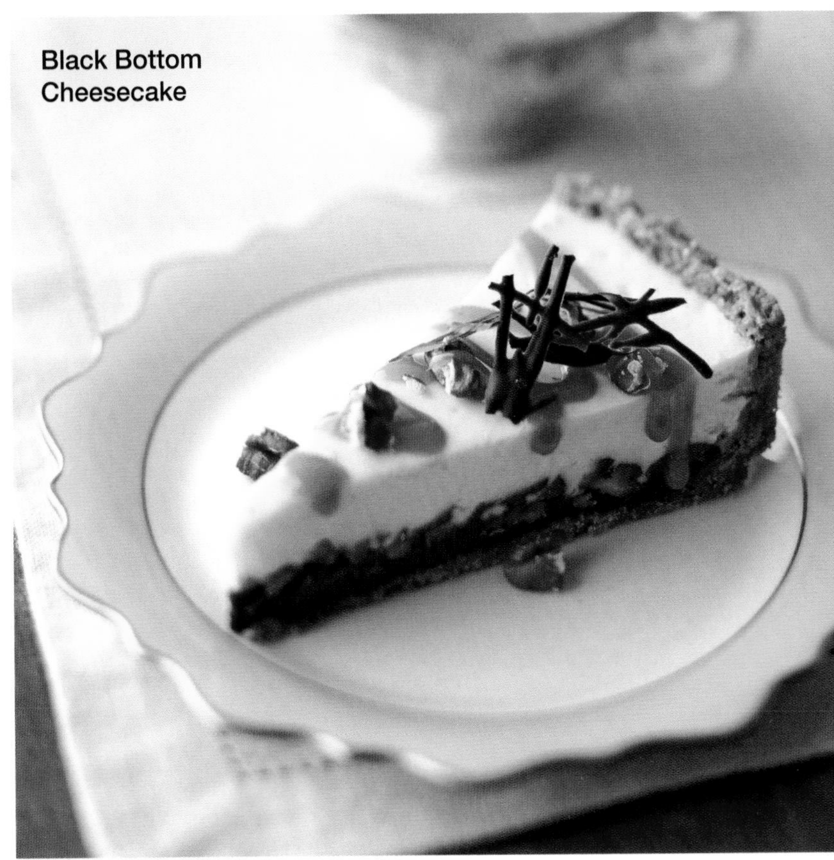
Black Bottom Cheesecake

holiday menus

Create delightful feasts that family and friends will love, starting with the six sample menus that follow. Each one features delicious, easy-to-fix recipes that work well together. You also can create your own menu by choosing recipes to supplement your family's must-have dishes.

menu 1

Bring-A-Dish Gathering

Share the cooking with others, using this potluck menu, so everyone can contribute to the fun.

Orange-Glazed Ham, page 11
Checkerboard Rolls, page 77
Green Beans with Almonds, page 24
Maple-Glazed Sweet Potatoes and Apples, page 22
Strawberry Pretzel Salad, page 33
Walnut-Sage Potatoes au Gratin, page 140

menu 2

Cookie and Candy Exchange

Invite the guests, set out the sweets, and provide holiday tins so each person or family can select an assortment of holiday goodies.

White Chocolate Chunk and Cherry Cookies, page 100
Toffee Fingers, page 101
Spiced Gumdrop Snowballs, page 98
Caramel-Cashew Cookies, page 98
Cranberry-Date Bars, page 110
Fabulous Five-Minute Fudge, page 118

menu 3

Deck-the-Halls Decorating Party

Set up a buffet in the kitchen where everyone can gather to nibble on finger foods and sip festive drinks.

Buffalo-Style Chicken Fingers, page 42

Ripe Olive Cheese Balls, page 40

Crunchy Nut Snack Mix, page 41

Two-Tone Pecan Bark, page 117

Orange-Kissed Egg Nog, page 47

Warming Wassail, page 45

menu 4

Holiday Open House

Invite friends for the afternoon to enjoy cookies, candies, and bite-size desserts.

Double Chocolate Diamonds, page 102

Swirls of Peppermint Cheesecake Bars, page 112

Mock Toffee, page 118

Cherry Chip and Coconut Tartlets, page 83

Holiday Seven-Layer Bars, page 110

menu 5

Christmas Eve Soup Supper

Celebrate the occasion with a traditional sit-down meal with family.

Wild Rice Mushroom Bisque, page 16
Southwestern Potato Sausage Chowder, page 149
Paprika Sesame Breadsticks, page 124
Bacon-Onion Biscuits, page 77
Cashew Crunch Salad, page 32
Apple Cranberry Crostada, page 86

menu 6

Heirloom Thanksgiving

Easy recipes and make-ahead options ensure a relaxed feast.

Marmalade-Glazed Turkey, page 14
Sausage-Corn Bread Stuffing, page 19
Mashed Potatoes with Caramelized Onions, page 20
Vegetable-Puree Gravy, page 27
Rosemary-Chive Parker House Rolls, page 76
Pumpkin Walnut Praline Pie, page 91

N–O

P

R